ook is to be returned or be
the !   date st

D1621273

LIVERPOOL POLYTECHNIC LIBRARY

3 1111 00416 1962

Dijk, T.A. van
Handbook of discourse analysis
H M 415 DIJ Vol.2 1985

ARTS, MEDIA & DESIGN LIBRARY

HANDBOOK OF DISCOURSE ANALYSIS

VOLUME 2
Dimensions of Discourse

HANDBOOK of DISCOURSE ANALYSIS

HANDBOOK
of DISCOURSE ANALYSIS

VOLUME 2
Dimensions of Discourse

Edited by

TEUN A. VAN DIJK

Department of General Literary Studies
Section of Discourse Studies
University of Amsterdam
Amsterdam, The Netherlands

ACADEMIC PRESS
Harcourt Brace Jovanovich, Publishers

London   San Diego   New York   Berkeley
Boston   Sydney   Tokyo   Toronto

"yes is a pleasant country" from *Complete Poems* 1913–1962 by E. E.
Cummings, copyright 1981, with permission of Granada Publishing Limited.

COPYRIGHT © 1985, BY ACADEMIC PRESS, INC. (LONDON) LTD.
ALL RIGHTS RESERVED.
NO PART OF THIS PUBLICATION MAY BE REPRODUCED OR
TRANSMITTED IN ANY FORM OR BY ANY MEANS, ELECTRONIC
OR MECHANICAL, INCLUDING PHOTOCOPY, RECORDING, OR
ANY INFORMATION STORAGE AND RETRIEVAL SYSTEM, WITHOUT
PERMISSION IN WRITING FROM THE PUBLISHER.

ACADEMIC PRESS LIMITED
24/28 Oval Road
LONDON NW1 7DX

Second printing 1987
Third printing 1989

United States Edition published by
ACADEMIC PRESS INC.
San Diego, CA 92101

LIBRARY OF CONGRESS CATALOGING IN PUBLICATION DATA
Main entry under title:

Handbook of discourse analysis.

 Includes indexes.
 Contents: v. 1. Disciplines of discourse — v. 2.
Dimensions of discourse — v. 3. Discourse and dialogue —
[etc.]
 1. Discourse analysis. I. Dijk, Teun Adrianus van,
Date   . II. Title.
P302.H343   1985   001.51   84-6482
ISBN 0-12-712002-5 (v. 2 : alk. paper)

Printed in Great Britain by St Edmundsbury Press Ltd
Bury St Edmunds, Suffolk

Contents

1
Introduction: Levels and Dimensions of Discourse Analysis
Teun A. van Dijk

2
On the Integration of Linguistic Description
J. McH. Sinclair

3
Dimensions of Discourse Analysis: Grammar
M. A. K. Halliday

4
Phonology: Intonation in Discourse
David Brazil

5
Morphology
Wolfgang U. Dressler

6
Lexicon
János S. Petöfi

7
Semantic Discourse Analysis
Teun A. van Dijk

8
Pragmatics
Alessandro Ferrara

9
An Analysis of Argumentation
Josef Kopperschmidt

10
Narrative Analysis
Elisabeth Gülich and Uta M. Quasthoff

11
Analysis of Nonverbal Behavior
Klaus R. Scherer and Harald G. Wallbott

Contributors

Numbers in parentheses indicate the pages on which the authors' contributions begin.

DAVID BRAZIL (57), Department of English Language and Literature, University of Birmingham, Birmingham B15 2TT

WOLFGANG U. DRESSLER (77), Institut für Sprachwissenschaft, Universität Wien, A-1090 Vienna, Austria

K. ANDERS ERICSSON (259), Department of Psychology, University of Colorado at Boulder, Boulder, Colorado 80309

ALESSANDRO FERRARA (137), Departimento di Sociologia, Università di Roma, via V. E. Orlando 75, Roma, Italy

ELISABETH GÜLICH (169), Universität Bielefeld, Fakultät für Linguistik und Literaturwissenschaft, D-4800 Bielefeld 1, Federal Republic of Germany

M. A. K. HALLIDAY (29), Department of Linguistics, University of Sydney, Sydney, New South Wales 2006, Australia

NANCY S. JOHNSON[1] (245), Department of Psychology, State University of New York at Buffalo, Amherst, New York 14226

WALTER KINTSCH (231), Department of Psychology, University of Colorado at Boulder, Boulder, Colorado 80309

JOSEF KOPPERSCHMIDT (159), Department of Linguistics, Fachhochschule Niederrhein Krefeld, Federal Republic of Germany

JÁNOS S. PETÖFI (87), Fakultat für Linguistik und Literaturwissenschaft, Universität Bielefeld, D-4800 Bielefeld 1, Federal Republic of Germany

UTA QUASTHOFF (169), Fakultat für Linguistik und Literaturwissenschaft, Universität Bielefeld, D-4800 Bielefeld 1, Federal Republic of Germany

KLAUS R. SCHERER (199), Fachbereich Psychologie, Justus Liebig-Universitat Giessen, D-6300 Giessen, Federal Republic of Germany

---

[1] Present Address: Department of Psychology, Bowdoin College, Brunswick, Maine 04011.

HERBERT A. SIMON (259), Department of Computer Science and Psychology, Carnegie-Mellon University, Pittsburgh, Pennsylvania 15213

J. McH. SINCLAIR (13), Department of English, University of Birmingham, Birmingham B15 2TT, England

TEUN A. VAN DIJK (1, 103), Department of General Literary Studies, Section of Discourse Studies, University of Amsterdam, Amsterdam, The Netherlands

HARALD G. WALLBOTT (199), Fachbereich Psychologie, Universitat Giessen, D-6300 Giessen, Federal Republic of Germany

Preface to the Four Volumes

One of the most conspicuous and interesting developments in the humanities and the social sciences in the past decade has undoubtedly been the widespread, multidisciplinary attention paid to the study of discourse. This development began to take shape in the early 1970s, after some scattered attempts in the late 1960s, in such disciplines as anthropology, linguistics, semiotics, poetics, psychology, sociology, and mass communication research. This shared interest for various phenomena of language use, texts, conversational interaction, or communicative events soon became more integrated, under the common label of discourse analysis (or, e.g., *Textwissenschaft* in German).

The variety of theoretical and descriptive approaches in this new interdisciplinary field is impressive: for example, the study of narrative in nearly all disciplines mentioned above, the attention paid to natural forms of language use in the social context in sociolinguistics, the experimental or computer-simulated study of text processing in psychology and artificial intelligence, the construction of text grammars in linguistics, the ethnography of speaking in anthropology, as well as the continued attention to the analysis of style, rhetoric, argumentation, and persuasive communication in several branches of the humanities and the social sciences.

To document the development and the current state of this new field of discourse analysis, it became imperative to unite these various directions of research in one multidisciplinary publication. The present *Handbook of Discourse Analysis*, in four volumes, is the result of this enterprise. This *Handbook* provides surveys of and introductions to the respective approaches in discourse analysis. In concrete sample analyses, its chapters show how discourse analysis acutally works at several levels of description. It summarizes our insights into the structures and functions of various discourse types or genres. And it demonstrates for a number of important social domains and problems how discourse analysis can be usefully and critically applied. The four volumes deal, respectively, with these major aims: presentation of the various disciplines of discourse analysis, introduction to descriptive methods, study of important genres of (dialogical) discourse, and application in critical social analysis.

For each topic we have invited leading scholars to contribute essays in their area of specialization. Most of these scholars are widely known, in and beyond their own fields. Young researchers have also been invited to write about the topic in which they have become specialists. To make the *Handbook* not only interdisciplinary but also international, care has been taken to include scholars from several countries.

The *Handbook* has been set up according to a few basic leading principles. First, as an introductory state of the art, its chapters satisfy a number of didactic criteria so that it is accessible at least to advanced and interested students in all disciplines of the humanities and the social sciences, and not only to specialists in some area of research. Second, the *Handbook* has a descriptive and analytic bias, to allow more direct application in concrete discourse research. Detailed attention to theoretical issues, as well as excessive formalization, have been avoided. Third, in line with the important interest in spontaneous uses of language, illustrations are given predominantly of natural discourse forms. Fourth, within the constraints of the thematic setup of the *Handbook*, authors are free to present their own perspectives and to summarize their own research findings. The variety of approaches, however, guarantees that the major directions, theories, or methods of research are represented.

Despite its multidisciplinary and wide-ranging scope, even a four-volume handbook must have self-imposed limitations. There are, of course, more disciplines involved in discourse analysis than could be represented here. Thus, space limitations forced us to exclude, for example, the study of mass communication and literary scholarship. Similarly, of the hundreds of discourse genres, only some of the most important could be treated here. The same holds for various details of discourse structures. And, finally, not all directions of research or schools of thought could be covered (such as discourse analysis in France). Yet the selection we made should result in a coherent, representative, and up-to-date state of the (new) art of discourse analysis.

The preparation and editing of this *Handbook* have been a considerable task that would have been impossible to perform without the help, the advice, and the assistance of many people—too many to mention here. I hereby thank them all for their cooperation.

University of Amsterdam   TEUN A. VAN DIJK
Autumn, 1984

Preface to Volume 2: Dimensions of Discourse

In this second volume of the *Handbook of Discourse Analysis*, a systematic introduction to the various descriptive methods of discourse analysis is given. First, these methods are articulated along the usual levels of grammatical description in linguistics, such as phonology, morphology, lexicon, syntax, and semantics. Second, dimensions of analysis at the boundary of linguistics and other disciplines, such as pragmatics and analyses of argumentation, narrative, and nonverbal communication, are introduced. Other disciplines such as psychology have developed their own descriptive techniques. Thus, in this last case we find structural descriptions not only of discourse structures, but also of the processes of interpretation of resulting textual representations in memory, or of techniques for the analysis of experimental or problem-solving protocols. In other words, description is no longer the exclusive specialization of linguistics. Discourse analysis, as an independent discipline, has also borrowed descriptive framework and methods or techniques of analysis from other disciplines. Although grammar continues to exert its powerful influence as the most sophisticated analytic tool for the characterization of verbal structures, other important structures of discourse and their concomitant theoretical approaches need attention: Style, rhetorical structures, argumentative patterns, or narrative schemata require their own descriptive tools. Whereas Volume 1 of this *Handbook* provides disciplinary and theoretical backgrounds, the level-specific methods presented in the chapters of this volume have a more analytic bias. Through sample analyses, it is shown how each relevant level or dimension of discourse can be systematically and explicitly described.

Part of this job, however, must be performed by a separate next volume, which is exclusively dedicated to the description of dialogical discourse genres and forms of social interaction. Whereas the descriptive orientation in this next volume is inspired by the methods of conversational analysis and its background theories from sociology and ethnography, the present volume is mainly inspired by linguistics and psychology. Space limitations do not allow us to include the more familiar methods of stylistic and rhetorical analysis of discourse, about which, however, there are sufficient introductory studies available elsewhere. Also, these receive further attention in the subsequent volumes of the *Handbook*.

The separation of different levels or dimensions of analysis is of course a theoretical artifact. Adequate description requires integration, not only of the various structural dimensions but also of the relations between text and context. In the chapters of this volume it will become clear that the various methods and aproaches are integral parts of a coherent and complete description of discourse phenomena. The history of discourse analysis in the past 20 years has shown, however, that in the future even more relevant dimensions of analysis may be discovered.

Contents of Volumes 1, 3, and 4

Volume 4: Discourse Analysis in Society

CHAPTER 1

Introduction: Levels and Dimensions of Discourse Analysis

Teun A. van Dijk

VARIETIES OF DESCRIPTIVE APPROACHES

The variety of descriptive methods in discourse analysis is impressive. Whether inspired by intuitive or by more theoretical considerations about the nature of discourse, many of the disciplines in the humanities and the social sciences have developed their own approaches. Clearly, these methods are biased by the specific structures or functions, or by the kinds of discourses relevant in these disciplines. In this Introduction, we cannot do more than sketch the outlines of a unified descriptive framework, integrating the apparently rather disparate analytical tools at our disposal. In the chapters of this volume, some of these approaches are introduced and explained in detail.

Since discourse is first of all a form of language use, it goes without saying that linguistic methods of analysis have played a predominant role in the study of text and talk. Many types of structural, generative, or functional grammars have been developed to describe the properties of verbal utterances. Thus, phonology, morphology, and syntax have emerged as increasingly explicit subcomponents of such grammars in order to characterize sound structures, word formation, and the formal structures of sentences. Similarly, semantics was developed to provide an account of the meaning of such expressions, for example, by means of rules of interpretation. Pragmatics soon followed in order to describe the role of utterances in the context, namely, as speech acts. Much of this earlier work in various grammars was restricted to single, isolated sentences. It was not until the late 1960s that pleas were made to extend this framework to the real forms of language use, that is, discourse.

HANDBOOK OF DISCOURSE ANALYSIS, Vol. 2
Dimensions of Discourse

Copyright © 1985 by Academic Press London.
All rights of reproduction in any form reserved.
ISBN 0-12-712002-5

Attempts were made to apply the theoretical machinery of grammar to the description of discourse structures beyond the sentence. In this volume it will be shown that this grammatical approach not only yielded the necessary explicitness and sophistication but also imposed a number of serious limitations.

Yet, linguistics is not equivalent with grammar, although the practice of many linguists would often suggest such an identification. Verbal utterances, that is sentences and discourses, also may have style, for instance. However, the phenomenon of style was studied more often in poetics, sociolinguistics, or ethnography. Whereas grammars would often be constrained to the possible, grammatical forms of given language system, style had to do with the context-dependent variations of language use. Thus sociolinguistics paid attention to the choice of a specific style as a function of social situation, class or ethnic membership, or of social factors such as gender, age, status, or power. And literary scholarship was more interested in the characteristic, personal style of some unique work of art, or of an author or a period, or in the esthetic functions of specific stylistic choices. Common to these approaches, however, was the account of variable grammatical expression, such as specific sound realizations, intonation, lexical items, or syntactic structure, given the same underlying meaning or reference, as a function of different personal or social properties of the context of communication. In this sense, style is, so to speak, a major "indexical" property of discourse: It indicates at the surface the adequacy of the discourse within its social situation.

Classical rhetoric, however, had already suggested more than two thousand years ago that discourse involves more than just grammar, that is, rules for correct speaking of a language. Within a communicative framework, discourses also have specific functions, and rhetoric spelled out in great detail the conditions on the effectiveness of discourse within persuasive communicative functions. Adequate style is only one necessary dimension of such conditions of effectivess. Additionally, we may find optional operations (figurae) at each level of grammatical description: figures of sounds, words, syntactic structure or meaning. Such figures would consist, for example, of specific transformations of such structures, for instance in the form of additions, repetitions, deletions, permutations, or substitutions. In other words, besides the grammar, and related to a stylistic account, we here find another structural approach to the description of discourse. Specific, however, is the functional dimension, namely effectiveness in bringing about acceptance or attitude change by the recipient in some social setting. That is, in addition to the structural aspects, cognitive and social psychological dimensions of discourse are involved. Discourse in that perspective is not just a verbal object but essentially a form of social interaction. The full consequences of this fact have been drawn only in research since the mid 1970s, as we will see shortly.

Even in the framework of the structural characterization of language use, therefore, another dimension is lacking. Utterances are not just static verbal objects but ongoing dynamic accomplishments, that is, forms of action. In spoken discourse, we find not only discursive expressions of grammatical forms but also a complex array of nonverbal or paraverbal activities, such as intonation, gestures, facial expression, body position, and so on. Much of the interpretation and hence the functions of discourse depends on the interpretation of these activities and their relations with the verbal dimension of discourse. Although the more specific discourse implications of research on nonverbal communication are being drawn only recently, it is obvious that we here find another crucial approach to the description of discourse as a form of action.

Whereas most of the approaches mentioned above yield descriptions both for sentences and for discourse structures, we finally find another class of descriptive methods that deal more specifically with the overall organization of discourse and discursive interaction. Thus, stories not only consist of grammatical forms, meanings, style, or rhetorical operations; they also exhibit more specific schematic organizational patterns, that is, some kind of superstructures. These narrative structures can be characterized in terms of their own conventional categories and formation rules, so that even notions such as 'narrative grammars' have been used in order to explicitly account for such story structures. Similar remarks can be made for the overall organization of other discourse forms, such as argumentations or news discourse. Classical syllogisms, thus, are not only a form of (logical or natural) reasoning but are at the same time patterns for reasoning in discourse, that is, of argumentation. Future work must systematically explore what other schematic patterns of this sort can be made explicit for different discourse types.

In fact, such schematic patterns can be found also in other domains of discourse analysis, for example, in metrics and the study of prosody. Familiar examples from literary scholarship are the distribution and organization of sounds and syntactic or morphological structures, in poetry and drama.

While many of these specific patterns and units apply to written or fixed discourse types, it goes without saying that other forms of organization can be found in discourse when it is taken as a form of interaction. Speaker turns and strategic moves on the microlevel and, on the macrolevel, overall organization of conversations and other dialogues such as openings and closings have been proposed as new elements of discourse analysis.

At this point we have come far from the structural characterizations of verbal utterances as they were proposed by structural grammars. Speech acts, style, figures of speech, nonverbal interaction, metrical patterns, narrative schemata or dialogical units of interaction have been added, some two millenia ago, others two decades ago. Obviously, such different properties of discourse may each require its own subtheory, but ultimately such descriptions should of course be integrated. For instance, the precise relations between pragmatics and grammar remain subject to much confusion. Similarly, it remains to be made explicit in detail how narrative schemata relate to the linguistic properties, such as the global meanings, of discourse. Other notions, such as strategic moves in interaction, as yet hardly have an explicit theoretical foundation. The same holds for the interrelations with nonverbal interaction or other semiotic codes, such as pictures, film, or symbols, for example, in mixed discourse such as comic strips, movies, dramatic performances, or TV programs. In this respect, even the rather sophisticated developments of structural discourse analysis have still little to offer. We find here some of the many suggestions for work in the future.

FROM STRUCTURAL DESCRIPTIONS
TO FUNCTIONAL ANALYSIS

Structural descriptions characterize discourse at several levels or dimensions of analysis and in terms of many different units, categories, schematic patterns, or relations. They do so both for monological texts, as well as for dialogical forms of interaction, that is, talk. The definition of discourse as a form of social interaction, however, still leaves us with an isolated unit of analysis. That is, structural analysis disregards the functional relations with the contexts of which discourse is a part. This holds for grammar, metrics, narrative theory, and conversational analysis alike. And even stylistics and rhetoric, of which the functional nature is constitutive (if we want to define the context-dependent notions of 'variable adequacy' or 'persuasive effectiveness'), have often paid only lip service to their contextual foundations. In other words, a complete characterization of discourse as a complex event requires further analysis in terms of the relations with the cognitive, social, and cultural contexts.

To illustrate this inherent interdependence of text and context, we may consider the role of discourse in a cognitive model. Scholars in the fields of psychology and artificial intelligence are not only interested in the various structures of discourse as abstractly characterized by the many subdisciplines of discourse analysis enumerated above. They also want to provide an account of the actual processes involved in the use of discourse, that is in the production and comprehension of discourse by speakers and hearers (writers and readers). They are interested in the cognitive representations of discourse in memory as well as in other information, such as knowledge and beliefs, necessary during discourse understanding. If we want an adequate picture of what people are actually doing when engaged in discourse, this more empirical analysis is of course crucial. Grammatical structures, style or narrative structures, and the organizational patterns of dialogue are in this respect merely theoretical abstractions of the kinds of structures, units, representations, schemata, and rules or strategies used in verbal interaction. This abstraction may be theoretically and methodologically useful for a while and will certainly advance our thinking about such context-free structures. Yet the roles, functions, effects, and conditions of discourse in processes of under-standing, information processing, and communication in the sociocultural context depend on these cognitive representations of discourse and not on the abstract reconstruction of discourse structures in grammars or theories of style, rhetoric, or narrative schemata. Speakers in conversation plan their next turn in talk on the basis of their understanding of what has been said by the previous speaker and on the basis of their cognitive representation of the whole social situation. A full account of what takes place in conversation and other discourse forms, therefore, should not take such cognitive processes for granted or reconstruct them in abstract or intuitive terms; it requires an integration with a cognitive model of conversational understanding, monitoring, planning, and strategic interaction.

The conclusion from this argument is that an interdisciplinary approach to discourse cannot be limited to structural analysis of its various levels or dimensions but also needs to pay attention to cognitive processes and to memory representations of discourse. Storage, retrieval, cognitive strategies, memory limitations, and effective organization procedures for information processing become relevant in such an account. For instance, the possible effects or functions of discourse in the social context crucially depend on what information about the text, dialogue, or communicative situation can be retrieved from memory (when, by whom, and under what conditions). Any model of learning, persuasion, attitude change, or the acquisition of social knowledge and beliefs through verbal com-munication presupposes such an account.

The approaches taken to describe what goes on cognitively have been strikingly and often uncomfortably close to the more abstract structural models sketched above: grammar, logic, and narrative grammars. It has been realized, however, that cognitive models need their own independent units, categories, and levels of analysis. These may not be organized along the precise delimitation of the levels and dimensions of the structural theories. They may involve complex cognitive strategies of processing information, online procedures, handling simultaneous levels and parallel information and so on. Other notions such as goals, plans, scripts, or cognitive schemata are involved to account for the understanding and representation of stories. And finally, the complex interactions between textual representations of this type with other forms of personal and social knowledge, or beliefs and attitudes, in memory need to be spelled out. This complex framework, then, counts as an empirical description of the interpretation of a discourse by language users. It is obvious that formal semantics can only be a distant abstraction of this kind of meaning assignment. We see that the notion 'meaning of a discourse' requires analysis within several frameworks, and one of the tasks of an integrated discourse analysis is to link these frameworks into one theory.

Similar remarks may be made for the relations with the social context. Sociolinguistics—or the sociology of language—has performed part of the task of relating discourse to the social context. Yet an integrated analysis of discourse in social situations is theoretically still primitive. Even the social-psychological and sociological analysis of situations and interactions has a tradition that is hardly older than that of discourse analysis itself. Speech act theory, which should function as one of the bridges between utterances as verbal objects and utterances as social acts, has been largely a philosophical and linguistic enterprise. Appropriateness conditions for speech acts are, much like the rules of grammar, fairly abstract representations of the actual cognitive and social preconditions for the successful performance of discourse as social action. A full social analysis of threats, promises, congratulations, or accusations of course involves more than required propositional content or the knowledge and wants of speakers with respect to the actions of hearers. Threats, for instance, would require a complex analysis of the social situation in terms of dominance relations, power, control, roles, norms, and their dynamic interpretation and enactment. Besides the ideal conditions for threatening, we need to know how people actually go about threatening each other, both in terms of detailed conversational strategies and in terms of the other properties of interaction in the situation. Besides the illocutionary meanings of threats, such an account would of course also involve the perlocutionary effects of threatening acts, such as acceptance or rejection, the execution of action, and the changes in the social situation. We have suggested above that such an account cannot be independent of a cognitive approach. Interpretative sociology has emphasized the importance of the commonsense strategies people use when dealing with social reality. Communication and interaction are real, therefore, only according to these (cognitive) categories and maneuvers of making sense, and these reconstructive interpretations are the input for further interaction. Abstractions and intuitions about such processes may of course carry us far in the account of commonsense procedures of social members, but it has become obvious that such an approach can be explicit and empirically warranted only when we devise a cognitive interface among discourse, interaction, and the social situation.

Next, the features of the social situation that are relevant for language users as social members should be systematically worked out. This would require, for instance, a typology of communicative social situations. Some of the elements of such a typology have been studied in more detail, such as informal conversations, doctor's visits, classroom dialogues, job interviews, and police practices. Many others, for example, parliamentary debates, decision-making procedures in corporations and the production and understanding of TV programs, have received much less attention from a (social) discourse analytical point of view. Also, the relevant categories in such situations need further attention. Gender, age, class, and ethnic group are conventional sociological abstractions of which the relevance for grammatical variation, style, narrative structures, and rhetoric have been demonstrated in rather global terms. Exactly how such features of discourse depend on them remains unclear.

One example in point is the description of interethnic communication. The characterization of discourse and nonverbal activities and their social functions and implications in interaction between members of different ethnic groups has often been made from the point of view of the (white) majority members. The consequences for a sociology of discourse of such a perspective are far-reaching. First, the explication of the commonsense categories used by social members in the interpretation and execution of ongoing encounters with ethnic minority members may well be in conflict with an explication in terms of the interpretations of minority members. What is a normal reproach for one group may be a racist remark for the other group. Second, the relevant categories, principles, and rules of discourse and interaction, and hence also our analysis, may have a cultural bias.

Such biases in description are of course well known in the anthropological and ethnographic literature and also apply to the description of discourse in other societies and cultures. Especially for those discourse structures that are closely linked with social structure, such as style, rhetorical features, narrative categories, and the schematic organization of communicative events, ethnocentrism in the categories of description and the norms or principles of evaluation is a highly relevant danger. For our discussion it is therefore important to stress that the methods of description in discourse analysis as they have been outlined in this Introduction are necessarily heavily influenced by a long historical and cultural tradition and are therefore ethnically context bound and certainly not universal.

OTHER APPROACHES

In the previous sections we have surveyed a considerable number of descriptive approaches to discourse. We have tried to indicate how these various methods of analysis and their underlying theories can or should be connected. Yet, it is obvious that none of these orientations can claim to be the only method for discourse analysis. To stress this diversity and the need for integration, a brief selection of additional approaches in the humanities and social sciences follows.

The understanding and explanation of the Bible and other sacred texts led in the Middle Ages to what was called a "hermeneutic" approach. One feature of hermeneutics was that the analysis of texts should take place at several levels. Beyond the level of literal expressions and meanings, a nonliteral or metaphorical level was distinguished, for example, for the description of biblical parables. And even beyond such a level, some kind of transcendent meaning, a metaphysical meaning or function of the text, needed to be assessed. In the twentieth century, hermeneutics has been especially applied in the realm of literary, historical, and legal discourse and was extended to a more general theory of interpretation. Unlike the formal and more objective rules of interpretation of grammar or logic, this approach stressed the role of subjective interpretation procedures, involving, for example, empathy with interpreted objects and the relevance of personal experiences of the interpreter. One line of this approach later characterized the phenomenological underpinnings of current interpretative sociology.

A quite different line of research can be summarized under the label of "ideological analysis" of discourse. Inspired mainly by Marxist views about the relations between socioeconomic infrastructures and cultural superstructures, such an analysis primarily views discourse as an expression of class conflicts, false consciousness, exploitation, or power relations in society. That is, discourse features are interpreted as social indicators of interests of the speakers or writers. In this respect, ideological analysis shares with hermeneutics the subjective nature of discourse analysis, while on the other hand it stresses the objective nature of the social determination of discourse production itself. Ideological analysis will often have a critical dimension in the sense that it intends to reveal underlying class conflicts, power relations, and ideologies through discourse analysis. It is therefore often applied in the analysis of public discourse such as political discourse, news, or the texts of governments or big organizations.

Most of the analytical methods introduced above have a qualitative nature. They characterize structures or representations, or specify rules or strategies of interpretation. We find, however, a quantitative emphasis in the various methods known under the label of "content analysis." In fact, these methods presuppose the categories of qualitative analysis, such as words, sentences, and stylistic features. Yet, they may also involve more ad hoc units of analysis, such as news headlines or column centimeters in the content analysis of news in the press. Especially for large amounts of discourse data, and in order to establish frequencies and to apply statistical methods, such forms of discourse analysis have become an important practical tool in the social sciences. It may be expected that explication of qualitative analyses, and especially the automatic, computerized description of texts, may lead to an integration of quantitative and qualitative approaches.

Similar remarks may be made for the vast array of experimental methods in psychology. We have seen above that cognitive models are being designed in psychology and artificial intelligence that involve qualitative methods for the analysis of representations of discourse or beliefs in memory. However, not only representations, but especially also processes such as strategies, are crucial in discourse understanding. The usual units, categories, and rules of grammars, stylistics, rhetoric, and narrative theories are not developed for such dynamic features of discourse. Other approaches such as production systems, transition networks, procedural semantics, and processes of spreading activation and their simulation in computer programs are examples of different approaches to the cognitive reality of discourse processing. Special experimental techniques such as the measurement of reaction times, interpretation times, recall or recognition ratios, and priming methods may be relevant in the assessment of such underlying discourse processes. Protocol analysis, similarly, is an important method for reconstructing cognitive processes of understanding and problem solving through the self-reports (think-aloud reports) of subjects. One important result of these experimental methods and techniques is that it may be shown that many structural properties of discourse such as syntactic sentence organization, pronominalization, topic-comment articulation, and story structures may have a cognitive basis. In this way, structural and cognitive models of discourse may be integrated.

Although the methods briefly mentioned above are very different in style, theoretical foundation, and aims, they share some common properties.

First, they very often show a primary interest for the explicit (and sometimes implicit or absent) content of discourse. In that respect they are sometimes intuitive forms of semantic analysis. Second, this analysis is carried out not for its own sake but in order to get at underlying cognitive or social facts. Hermeneutics, thus, focuses on the expression of subjective, personal world views or values. The emphasis in ideological analysis is the underlying ideology of speakers or writers and hence class-dependent interests and their socioeconomical basis. Content analysis, as its name suggests, analyzes content mainly as an expression of social or institutional features of production and communication in general. And the various methods of psychology and artificial intelligence are geared toward the assessment of underlying (or determining) cognitive representations or processes. In other words, many of the methods of discourse analysis in the social sciences have an instrumental nature. Now, it is realized that social discourse also deserves attention in its own right, that is, not only as an expression or indication of something else but as an autonomous form of social action and interaction.

Finally, it should be added that the goal in all methods and directions of research discussed above has been more explicit, more systematic, and more formal analyses. This obvious scientific requirement has led to a widespread use of logical, mathematic or other formal systems. Predicate logic, set theory, modal logics, graph theory or network analysis, and various theories of probability and decision making have been called on for help, for instance in the various branches of a theory of language and discourse interpretation (semantics). Besides their usual role in formalization, such approaches might yield the level of abstraction necessary for the integration of the rather disparate qualitative analyses in the many branches of discourse analysis. As yet, however, such a formal integration is still premature. It has been indicated repeatedly above that a large amount of elementary substantial descriptions are still necessary at all levels and dimensions of text and context. Nontrivial formalization presupposes systematic theory formation and the precise defition of units, categories, rules, strategies, and other processes in these various domains.

CONCLUSIONS

It may have become clear from the previous sections that discourse analysis is not a simple enterprise. In its full richness it involves all the levels and methods of analysis of language, cognition, interaction, society, and culture. This is of course not surprising, since discourse itself is a manifestation of all these dimensions of society. This means that integral discourse analysis is necessarily an interdisciplinary task and also that its complexity forces us to make specific choices among the many available methods, depending on the goals and functions of our analysis.

Another conclusion we have reached is that the classical theories and descriptive methods of linguistics and grammar yield only a partial account of discourse structures. Other properties of discourse such as style, rhetoric, schematic organization, overall patterns, and interactive aspects need to be described in their own right. Also, the various structural theories need to be integrated, so as to specify the interrelations between the various levels or dimensions.

Next, it has been stressed that discourse cannot fully be characterized in terms of an isolated, abstract verbal object but also requires analysis in terms of its relations with various contexts. Cognitive processes of production, understanding, and representation are crucial in this respect and are essential for an account of the interpretations and uses of discourse by participants in social situations. Similarly, the details of the links between discourse structures and the structures and processes of social interaction and situations must be made explicit. It hardly needs to be emphasized that such an account should be aware of ethnic or cultural differences and hence realize its own possible biases.

Finally, there are more specific methods of discourse analysis, aiming at the revelation of underlying personal or social patterns as they are expressed or indicated by text and talk, as in the ideological analysis of discourse, the methods of psychology, or the simulation programs of artificial intelligence.

Without pretending to be complete, we have stressed this large variety of descriptive, analytic, and explanatory approaches, often across several disciplines, in order to place the chapters in this volume in a wider framework. It has been stressed in the Preface to this volume that all descriptive approaches cannot possibly be accommodated in a single book. We therefore have selected a number of well-known, explicit theoretical approaches that have become familiar in linguistics and psychology. The methods of the analysis of talk and interaction and ideological approaches to discourse, are exemplified in the next two volumes of this *Handbook*, respectively. This Introduction has gone beyond the presentation of the various structural methods as they are treated in more detail in the following chapters in order to show the interdependence with other functional and social accounts of discourse. It will be one major task of discourse analysis in the future to integrate these different descriptions and partial theories.

CHAPTER 2

On the Integration of Linguistic Description

J. McH. Sinclair

INTRODUCTION

This chapter outlines a descriptive system that is designed to bring out the underlying similarities of structure in all text and discourse. At present, despite theoretical frameworks that are general enough, descriptions are too dependent on the text or discourse type.

There is no attempt to trace the origins of the concepts and categories used, many of which will be familiar enough. To do so would overbalance the chapter and obscure the argument. For similar reasons, there is not a full bibliography; instead I have listed work that is not all easily accessed but that is relevant to the articulation of a fully integrated descriptive system.

The student of conversation is struck by the immediacy of speech events. Real time—the actual passing of seconds and minutes—is often the most influential feature of the context as participants play their parts in the complex fabric of verbal interaction. Timing is all important in turn taking and turn giving and turn holding; time is a major factor in the construction and delivery of a turn, and time is to be reckoned with in the business of keeping a check on how the conversation is going.

Each individual contribution to spoken discourse shows a curious tension between personal and social pressures. It is simultaneously cooperative and face threatening; it is a step toward the achievement of some personal goal, but it is put together in the knowledge that the goal can only be achieved through the construction of discourse, which by definition requires two participants. Because of this fundamental tension, it is easy to see discourse as essentially manipulative, and indeed it is often difficult to find morally reputable terminology for what seems to be going on.

HANDBOOK OF DISCOURSE ANALYSIS, Vol. 2
Dimensions of Discourse

Copyright © 1985 by Academic Press London.
All rights of reproduction in any form reserved.
ISBN 0-12-712002-5

The student of written language, in contrast to the student of conversation, is probably most impressed by the orderly nature of the events he is describing. Printed material is presented in accordance with thousands of conventions and is measured to thousandths of an inch. The text is read during preparation many times by different people, and in most cases time is not a structural influence. Where printed material has to be prepared against strict deadlines, as in newspaper production, every effort is made to neutralize the effect of time, and there is very little impromptu material in newspapers.

The responsibility for coherence lies with the utterer, which in the case of printed material is a composite entity including everyone who participated in the production of the text. The text appears to be quite static and nonnegotiable; it is there, and it cannot be altered. It seems quite different from the ever-changing, hardly predictable movement of conversation. It can be described, and is normally described, as a complex contraption, and linguistic terms like 'structure' betray the underlying metaphor. Written language is not primarily seen as activity. Its relation to time is that of an unchanging record.

But in apparent contrast to the rigidity of written text, we are assured that each reading of it, even two readings by the same reader, is a unique communicative event. So the text has an interactive role that is related to time in a different way, since a reading of a text is an event in time. We can relate the fixed nature of a written text to the unique experience of any reading of it by making a reasonable assumption: Since the main purpose of a text is to be read, its destined role in a series of interactions has a backwash effect upon its composition.

One further assumption is that a writer who is composing a text that is to be efficient interactively has an obvious model in conversation. From this a line of inquiry emerges that can lead to an integrated framework of description. If the same basic model is used in both documents and conversation, then, at least at an abstract level, the same categories of description are applicable. The influence of the particular medium, however, becomes stronger as we proceed toward realization, and we must guard against imposing categories appropriate to one medium on data from another.

A DYNAMIC MODEL OF DISCOURSE

An integrated description, deriving from a model of verbal interaction, describes language in use, as written or spoken discourse. The model is dynamic rather than static, and we must consider this contrast in order to relate discourse description to traditional descriptions of language.

The main differences between a dynamic and a static model of discourse are (1) the dynamic model must show how the discourse proceeds from one point to another, and (2) the dynamic model must show how the components of the discourse play their part in the achievement of some purpose. In both cases, the differences take the form of additional requirements on the dynamic model. In the first case, the discourse is seen as a continuous movement from one state of affairs or *posture* to another. Our habits of studying language tend to obscure this movement, because we tend to study language with hindsight; when we are considering one stretch of language, we already know what happens next. In such circumstances, the importance of prospection, prediction, and the like is not as obvious as it should be.

In a dynamic model the elements of structure are described with reference to the state of the discourse at their point of occurrence. Hence the unfolding or existential quality of discourse description. Only language that has already occurred can be taken as given; the description of subsequent items of language is conditioned by the state of the discourse at *their* point of occurrence.

Once the directionality of discourse has been fully appreciated, it follows that there is a marked difference in the way we describe previous and subsequent language. Each element of structure is considered both retrospectively and prospectively, but in different terms. Looking backward, the following issues are relevant to each element: (1) If the state of the discourse includes any firm predictions, does this element offer partial or total fulfillment of the predictions? (2) If the state of the discourse includes any prospections (less-than-firm predictions), does this element offer partial or total fulfillment of them? Looking ahead, the main issue can be stated as follows: (3) What framework of choice for the next element is created by the selection of this element?

Any utterance can follow any utterance—we are free agents. Although we tend to follow conventions in social behavior, there are no absolute rules, because people make mistakes or make use of the conventions for more subtle tactics, irony, and so forth. However, each utterance sets the scene for the next. No matter what it is, the way it will be interpreted is determined by the previous utterances and in particular the immediately previous one. This is fairly obvious in question–answer pairs, but is a general feature of discourse. There are some complexities introduced by the hierarchic nature of discourse structure, because, for example, boundary utterances have a more far-reaching role than medial ones, but the main point is sound, and the prospective function of all utterances is of first importance.

The second requirement of a dynamic model balances the first by introducing purposefulness into the description. The dynamic view sees discourse as directional, a succession of changing postures; but it must be heading somewhere. We already have in the static models some notions of complete encounters and of finished artifacts in writing. Units of this kind link language and the physical world. With the addition of purposes that are recognized within the discourse, they are valuable units in a dynamic model. They provide a special kind of boundary.

The problem of purposes in language description is not that people believe human behavior to be largely without purpose. Plans, goals, and aims, for example, are readily admitted. The problem is mainly where to stop. Language activity is but one component of our general activity, which itself is largely purposeful. The separation of purposes that are recognized as being carried out through discourse from those that are not so circumscribed requires units that perform a linking role and relate complete patterns of linguistic activity to aspects of our general social behavior. Hence the importance of identifying a unit at this interface.

Linguists are so accustomed to describing small-scale stretches of language that the contribution of each particular to the overall effect of an artifact may well be missed. In a dynamic model it is necessary to continue the directional description until a point is reached where the verbal activity performs in its totality some action that lies outside language. Each successive component has an effect that may be perceptible in passing but is certainly provisional until the artifact is completed and the overall action has been performed and is no longer negotiable except in terms of a subsequent artifact. An example from conversation is the polite refusal of an invitation that is eventually replaced by acceptance; often this kind of behavior is within the normal social courtesies and recognized by participants. In writing it is commonplace for a writer to state a position that is contrary to the position he wishes the reader to adopt; the eventual effect can only be described when the artifact has unfolded in full.

The provisional interpretations of purpose are therefore subject to a backwash effect from the artifact as a whole; the analyst can make final assignments in review. But in most cases the provisional interpretations are confirmed, and only in manipulative discourse of conversations between naive and sophisticated participants is there likely to be substantial reassignment.

It is normal, in fact, for speakers and writers to keep a running check on what they are doing, and much of this becomes part of the discourse. There is a whole vocabulary and syntax of language about language (point, question, object, etc.), so that the focus of the discourse can shift to the discourse itself. Less explicitly, many of the apparently meaningless words and phrases (*uhum, actually, well,* etc.) and devices (e.g., repeating a word or two of a previous speaker) in conversation are signals of how one speaker is interpreting the discourse. Unless challenged, these are taken by the participant as signals of the provisional categorization of the discourse.

Despite the different circumstances of spoken and written language and the different realizations of linguistic categories, the view of a dynamic model is to see them as essentially similar. Both are interactive, both are directional, and both are purposeful. The description of formal written language is transformed by the application of a dynamic model, because much of its interactive quality is covert.

The fundamental categories of a description that integrates such disparate behavior are more abstract than the normal categories of linguistics. But the job of integration must encompass further distinctions as well as those between speech and writing.

Literary discourse is treated as a special case even by linguists who claim that it is subject to the normal conventions of language description. The creation of the subject area of stylistics serves to insulate literature from the more mundane texts of everyday life. Patterns of language that are not remarked upon in nonliterary text are invested with meaning in stylistics.

Despite these concessions, the literary critics have remained largely aloof, maintaining that there is a difference in kind between descriptive and evaluative study. However sensitive and painstaking a description may be, it does not engage with the central issues of criticism. There are other problems, too, about stylistics that can only be mentioned here, such as the lack of principle in selecting a focus of description, the uneasy status of interpretations from stylistic evidence, and the difficulty of description of long texts. There is little or no theory in stylistics; the value of its observations is related strictly to the results of individual studies.

If we view literary text as discourse, we must begin the description in the same way as with any other text, establishing first of all its location in the world around us. Who is addressing whom, on what occasion, and with what end in view? The analysis of the utterer shows that we must postulate at least two entities—an author in the real world and a narrator in a world of fiction. Such a distinction has been recognized in literary analysis for many years.

The relation between the author and the narrator is that the author reports the narrator but does not attest the truth of what the narrator says. Frequently this relationship is implicit, and the reader deduces from external evidence that sentences like *I love you,* or *It is the year*

2002 are not being averred by the author to the reader. In the absence of any such deduction, our normal assumption is that anything said to us or written to us is averred by the author or speaker to be true at the moment of utterance.

The purpose of a literary text is to secure from its readers a complex, evaluative interpretation; both globally (asking readers to answer questions like "What does this mean to me?") and analytically (how the components of the artifact have their several effects). Such evaluations occur after an encounter with an artifact and do not need to be articulated.

So from a discourse point of view, literary text falls well within the categories that are already available for nonliterary text. The dynamic model requires an elaborate evaluation network for the description of any text; the oddity about literary text is that it has no function except to be evaluated. It is argued later in this chapter that stylistic evidence is no different from any other linguistic evidence.

An integrated approach to description should in fact be flexible enough to cover all distinctive varieties of a language, not just literary text. In the many studies of varieties that have accumulated over the years, the emphasis has been on distinctiveness and the descriptions fairly ad hoc. If an overall framework can be developed in detail, the varieties can be compared with each other on reliable criteria.

A dynamic model makes available the level of discourse necessary to mediate between form and purpose. Any particular pattern of syntax or lexis, or a combination of both, may have different functions in different types of text; thus allowing the small central organization of the language to be adapted to a wide variety of purposes.

Work is not yet very far advanced in this area; there are notes on characteristic features of a language variety, like the passive voice in formal prose; there are informal explanations of many of the features. But we do not have as yet any substantial research on, for example, the complementary distribution of features in different varieties. Research is needed on the levels of delicacy of classification of varieties that accords best with differentiating features. A serious deficiency is the lack of a framework of interpretation, through which the characteristics of a variety can be related to the generalized purposes of the variety.

For the present, we assume only a few major received categories such as narrative and expository writing and their spoken counterparts. Narratives are organized largely by time expressions and verb tenses, so if a reader or listener has prior knowledge that he will encounter a narrative, his expectations are attuned accordingly. He assumes that the time expressions are likely to be organizational rather than incidental. On the other hand, if he knows or quickly deduces that he is encountering expository language, he is alert to the sentence connectors, modal verbs, and the other realizations of textual organizations in expository writing. These tend to be in prominent positions.

There are probably not many texts that do not quickly indicate their primary classification, because the different organizations are frequently incompatible. It would be bizarre for example, for a narrative to report alternatives such as *Mr Smith went out for lunch, or else he had sandwiches in the office.* Such a sentence can be worked into narrative under protective coverings such as:

(1)   *Throughout his working life*
(2)   *I suppose that . . .*

But without such an insulation, an author, whether as factual or fictional narrator, could hardly report alternative events.

A primary classification of discourse types is also valuable because no text is fully explicit about its organization as it goes along, and many are very covert. It is necessary to accept a default hypothesis, which states that in the absence of contra-indications, a linguistic item has the same function as its predecessor. When this is applied in description, the signals of maintenance or change of function must be accurately identifiable, and knowledge of the discourse type helps in the identification. Reference to chronology, for example, is prima facie taken as a signal of a change in posture in a narrative text; absence of such reference by default suggests a maintenance of posture. But in an expository text the presence or absence of chronological reference is unlikely to be structurally relevant.

We can now bring together the elements of an integrated descriptive system and apply them to some text examples. At the present stage of development, the descriptions are indicative only, and more varied application is necessary before they can be claimed to be comprehensive and reliable. But they illustrate the direction of current research.

APPLICATIONS OF THE MODEL

Basic Structure

The minimum free element of structure in a discourse is the sentence or move (s/m), and these are considered equivalent. An integrating definition is attempted in due course, but in the meantime we can list what must

be known about each s/m: (1) indications of interaction, (2) the position
of the author with reference to the text, (3) attribution to narrator(s),
(4) indications of argument, (5) indications of self-reference, and (6) the
dominant verb form. These are not in any particular order, nor is it yet
clear whether an order of priority will be established among them, particularly with reference to the primary classification of discourse.

Indications of Interaction

For each s/m, there has to be an identification of utterer and receiver,
that is, those who would be referred to by the pronouns *I* and *you* if
present. This requirement can be represented as:

I VB YOU

It must be understood that the above is a formula in the metalanguage
of description. It does not imply that sentences can be paraphrased or
generated in terms of the formula or that English happens to have a
reliable class of performative verbs to realize the element VB. Although
the conceptual origin of this kind of notation is speech act theory, it
would be misleading to assume anything beyond the basic notion of
illocutionary force.

In the analyses that follow, the descriptive apparatus is represented
as very close to English, but only for clarity. Capital letters are used to
identify the apparatus. To avoid ambiguity, the pronoun ''I'' is rendered
as *I* if it is part of the text or discourse and ɪ if it is part of the metalanguage.

	Interactive			**Autonomous**
I	VB	YOU		
I	*must compliment*	*you*		*on your hat*
I	*promise*	YOU	THAT	*I'll come tomorrow at six*
I	AVER	TO YOU	THAT	*it's getting late*

The Position of the Author with Reference to the Text

There is only one author of any s/m. He is the leftmost I in the analytic
display. The minimum he can do is aver and that verb is used here as
the signal of the default condition. The interactive segment of an s/m is
placed first in the analytic display and is followed by a transition (usually
expressible by THAT) to the remainder of the s/m, which is in the nature
of a report in a broad meaning of the term. The analysis of s/ms by
division into interactive and autonomous segments corresponds to the

same distinction in planes of discourse and is a central feature of a dynamic model. Roughly speaking, the interactive segment depicts what is going on in the real world at the time of utterance, while the autonomous segment is a report about something that may include the current state of the real world but is certainly not restricted to it.

Any recurrence of *I* in the autonomous segment is thus in a report. An s/m does not normally return to the interactive plane after leaving it, and then only for running repairs like *obviously,* or *I understand,* which show in analysis as separate from the main structure of the s/m and are shown in parenthesis in the Interactive column.

Interactive			Autonomous
I	VB	YOU	
I	*say*	TO YOU THAT	*you do look happy*
I	AVER	TO YOU THAT	*the book is*
[*I*	*understand*]		*being reprinted*

Attribution to Narrator(s)

An author can attribute parts of his s/m to one or more narrators (a narrator is any subject that is not the leftmost I of the structure, nor the subject of the rightmost main clause). He can say, or write

(3)   *Many people say that King Arthur actually lived.*

We do not know if the author concurs with this belief or not; he merely avers that others believe it. Similarly,

(4)   *It is generally supposed that glass is fragile.*

An author can also report or quote by attribution to a named character in his discourse (including himself):

(5)   *Peter said he was coming.*

(6)   *And then I said "Look here!"*

If, for whatever reason, a receiver decides that the autonomous segment is fictional, then the analysis introduces a fictional narrator F; a nonfictional but unidentified narrator is represented by N.

This possible layering of narrators is recursive and so has to be worked out separately for each text. It is entirely in the autonomous segment. In this analysis, at each transitional point there is a choice between report (THAT) and quotation (QUOTE). Note that the original author cannot quote himself.

Interactive	Autonomous	
I AVER TO YOU THAT	*many people say*	*that King Arthur actually lived*
I AVER TO YOU THAT	*it is generally supposed* BY N	*that glass is fragile*
I AVER TO YOU THAT	*Peter said*	THAT *he was coming*
I AVER TO YOU THAT	*I said*	QUOTE *look here*
I AVER TO YOU THAT	F SAID	QUOTE *Once upon a time*

Indications of Argument

The words and phrases of argument, logical connection, and so on, are important indicators of changes in posture. *But, however, or,* and sometimes *and,* are examples, as are the lexical paraphrases *in addition, as an alternative, on the other hand.*

Each time an author or narrator takes up a noticeably different attitude to his subject matter, there is a prima facie case for a change in posture. In the sentence,

(7)   *I'd like to come but it's very expensive.*

the second clause is interpreted as implying *I wouldn't like to come,* for the reason given.

Each prima facie change of posture is shown in the analysis by a new line.

Interactive	Autonomous	
I AVER TO YOU THAT		*I'd like to come*
	but	*it's very expensive*
I AVER TO YOU THAT	*either*	*you've made a mistake*
	or	*we've won a prize*

A wide range of words and phrases contribute evidence of change of posture in addition to those that are associated with the construction of argument. *Actually, well, anyway, of course, in fact, for example* are common examples.

Indications of Self-Reference

A change in posture is achieved whenever an s/m is explicitly referred to in the discourse. At any s/m boundary, there is an option open to speaker or writer.

1. He relates the next s/m to the preceding one by attending to its assumptions and prospections. For example, if asked a question he answers it.
2. He refers to the preceding s/m by a pronoun or a discourse vocabulary word, thus canceling the requirement of dealing with its prospections. For example, if asked a question he says *That's a very interesting question.*

The Dominant Verb Form

In most s/ms the verb of the main clause is taken as the dominant one. Sometimes there is more than one main clause and a change of verb form; in such cases it may be necessary to identify two s/ms.

Writers on narrative (e.g., Grimes, 1975; Labov & Waletzky, 1967) point out the importance of verb choices in the structure. Genette (1980) studies relative chronology in detail. Pearce (1977) uses verb choices as the cornerstone of his analysis of Joyce. In other types of writing and speaking, verb choices and related indications of timing are often signals of a change in posture. In practical analysis, usually the most revealing clue to structure is the disposition of the verb forms.

Any change between present and past, simple and continuous, modal and nonmodal, perfect and nonperfect allows a change in posture.

This observation is just the tip of a grammatical iceberg, which requires much further research into the relations between grammar and discourse. Theme, voice, and subject-referent, for example, are themselves interrelated and can create the kind of reorientation associated with a change in posture. 'Posture' is offered as the linking concept between internal and external patterning in s/ms. Certain configurations of syntax, compared with the previous s/m, provide evidence for an optional or obligatory change in posture. This evidence is then related to the current state of the discourse, and a decision is made about the place of the s/m in discourse structure.

In addition to the syntactic role of sentence elements, their lexical role and their physical disposition provide further evidence for discourse description. Patterns of lexical cohesion and stylistic devices such as parallelism cannot be easily integrated in a sentence-based description but are important features of discourse; the limitations of this chapter prevent full treatment of them.

Examples

The examples that follow show prospective structuring only. That is only a half, or less, of the recoverable linguistic patterning. The retrospective links are not shown because a reliable description of them has not yet been achieved. But it is already reasonable to state how stylistic patterns, which are largely retrospective, can be integrated into a dynamic description of discourse. The principle is that any variation from the minimal, straightforward verbal expression of propositions can be interpreted as evidence for a change in posture or as evidence for maintenance of posture. From this very general position, the experience of analysis is gradually revealing the conventions of interpretations.

Three examples follow, one from written technical material, one transcribed from conversation, and one from literature. The analysis is in column layout, and changes in posture are shown horizontally. Since many of the structural features are recursive, each text prescribes for itself the number of columns and the classification of each. The examples are text fragments and so do not show the full hierarchy of patterning up to the artifact.

Example 1: Written Technical Material

Cromemco's CDOS is claimed to be compatible with CP/M version 1.3. In other words, CP/M version 1.3 commands are embedded into CDOS. However, the reverse is not true: programs relying on CDOS' facilities might not run under CP/M. In addition, CDOS provides a number of additional facilities when compared to CP/M. CDOS uses a file system that is identical to CP/M so any diskette which may be read by CP/M may also be read by CDOS. There are minor differences: the system prompt used by CDOS is a period instead of a > sign. Also, the special CONPROC (Console Processor) program must be present on all system diskettes as a file. In CDOS, another version of the PIP program is provided under the name XFER. It operates essentially like PIP with a few enhancements. However, PIP can also be executed under CDOS. (From ZAKS *The CP/M handbook with MP/M*, Sybex, 1980.)

(tabular analysis facing)

Interactive			Autonomous	
Interaction	Argument	Narrator	Self-reference	
1 I AVER TO YOU THAT		N claims THAT		Cromemco's CDOS is compatible with CP/M version 1.3
2	In other words			CP/M version 1.3 commands are embedded into CDOS
3	However		the reverse is not true	
4				programs relying on CDOS' facilities might not run under CP/M
5	In addition			CDOS provides a number of additional facilities when compared to CP/M
6				CDOS uses . . . read by CDOS
7				There are minor differences
8	Also			The system prompt . . . a > sign
9				The special . . . as a file
10				In CDOS . . . the name XFER
11				It operates . . . with a few enhancements
12	However			PIP can also be executed under CDOS

Notes to Example 1: Most of the activities are indications of argument. There are a few interpretive problems: 4, the verb *might* casts some doubt on whether this is the reverse of 2. 6, from the previous line one anticipates a statement of additional facilities, while this seems to be about compatibility. 9, Is this a difference? In that case, it is a requirement of CDOS but not CP/M. 11, Although in fact a difference, this is not presented as one.

Example 2: Conversation

1 A: Do you like Leicester George
2 D: It's nice . . . yeah
3 A: Do you find it grows on you
4 D: Grows—like a limpet
5 A: Well yes
6 C: Yes or a wart
7 A: mm
8 D: No—it's O.K It's um . . .'s like any big town in the Midlands

Interactive		Autonomous
	Self-reference	
1 A: I ASK YOU George	IF	(do) you like Leicester
2 B: yeah		
I AVER TO YOU	THAT	It's nice
3 A: I ASK YOU	IF	(do) you find THAT it grows on you
4 B: I CHALLENGE YOU	ON	grows
I ASK YOU	IF	IT IS like a limpet
5 A: Well Yes		
6 C: Yes		
I AVER TO YOU	THAT	IT IS like a wart
7 A: mm		
8 B: no		It's O.K.
I AVER TO YOU	THAT	It's um like any big town in the Midlands.

Notes on Example 2: Most of the activity is in the interactive segment, and utterance 4 shows a type of self-reference, where a word of the preceding utterance is picked out and talked about. The next three utterances maintain the concern with this word. *No* in utterance 8 indicates a shift of topic, and we understand the pronoun reference of *it* to be *Leicester* in utterance 1. Utterances 5 and 7 are entered only in the interactive segment because they do not express a proposition.

Example 3: Literature

To be, or not to be—that is the question;
Whether 'tis nobler in the mind to suffer
The slings and arrows of outrageous fortune,
Or to take arms against a sea of troubles,
And by opposing end them? To die, to sleep—
No more; and by a sleep to say we end
The heart-ache and the thousand natural shocks

That flesh is heir to. 'Tis a consummation
Devoutly to be wish'd. To die, to sleep;
To sleep, perchance to dream. (*Hamlet,* William Shakespeare, Collins' Text)

In this example, the elaborate recursion of attribution cannot be set out horizontally. The following is an alternative layout with notes.

I AVER TO YOU THAT, (Interactive)
⟍F SAYS QUOTE, (Fictional Narrator)
⟍I AVER TO YOU THAT, (see notes)
⟍*Hamlet* SAYS QUOTE, (Narrator)
⟍I AVER TO YOU THAT, (see notes)

	Narrator	Self-reference	Argument	
1	X SAYS QUOTE			*To be*
			or	
2	X SAYS QUOTE			*not to be*
3		*that is the question*		
4	X SAYS QUOTE		*Whether*	*'tis nobler in the mind*
5				*to suffer the slings and arrows of out-rageous fortune*
			or	
6	X SAYS QUOTE			*to take arms against a sea of troubles and by opposing end them*
7	X SAYS QUOTE			*To die, to sleep*
8	X SAYS QUOTE			*No more*
9	X SAYS QUOTE			*and by a sleep to say we end the heart-ache and the thou-sand natural shocks that flesh is heir to*
10	X SAYS QUOTE			*'Tis a consummation devoutly to be wished*
11	X SAYS QUOTE			*To die, to sleep*
12	X SAYS QUOTE			*perchance to dream*

Notes on Example 3: Only the first line (I AVER TO YOU THAT) is genuinely interactive; the other instances of this element, following the narrator F and the internal posture change X, are pseudointeractive, since there is no real world situation in which they occur.

Each occurrence of X SAYS QUOTE is potentially a different X. A further stage in interpretation would be to decide if the X persona of 1 is the same as that of 4, and maybe 8 or even 12. Similarly, the X of 2 may be associated with 6, 7, 9, 10, 11, or only some of these. The framework of the analysis raises these questions.

The division into postures may well be challenged; also I have put *'tis nobler in the mind* as lying outside the following alternative, but a case could be made for *in the mind* being a part of 5 only.

BIBLIOGRAPHY

Bolivar, A. (in preparation). *A linguistic description of newspaper editorials*. Unpublished doctoral dissertation, University of Birmingham.

Cooper, M. (1983). *Textbook discourse structure: An investigation into the notion of predictable structuring in the discourse of scientific textbooks*. Unpublished doctoral dissertation, University of Birmingham.

Coulthard, R. M., & Montgomery, M. M. (Eds.). (1981). *Studies in discourse analysis*. London: Routledge & Kegan Paul.

de Mello, C., (in preparation). *Interaction in narrative text*. Unpublished master's thesis, University of Birmingham.

Genette, G. (1980). *Narrative discourse*. Oxford: Blackwell.

Grimes, J. (1975). *The thread of discourse*. The Hague: Mouton.

Hoey, M. (1979). *Signalling in discourse* (ELR Monograph No. 6). University of Birmingham.

Hunston, S. (1982). *Text and sub-text: An investigation into the viability of sub-text creation as a means of revealing the complexity of written texts*. Unpublished master's thesis, University of Birmingham.

Labov, W., & Waletzky, J. (1967). Narrative analysis, oral versions of personal experience. In J. Holm, (Ed.), *Essays on the verbal and visual arts* (pp. 12–44). Seattle: University of Washington Press.

Pearce, R. D. (1977). *The analysis and interpretation of literary texts, with particular reference to James Joyce's "A Portrait of the Artist as a Young Man."* Unpublished doctoral dissertation, University of Birmingham.

Phillips, M. (1983). *Lexical macrostructure in science text*. Unpublished doctoral dissertation, University of Birmingham.

Tadros, A. (1981). *Linguistic prediction in economics text*. Unpublished doctoral dissertation, University of Birmingham.

CHAPTER 3

Dimensions of Discourse Analysis: Grammar

M. A. K. Halliday

INTRODUCTION

This chapter presents a brief sketch of a lexicogrammatical text interpreter for Modern English, in terms of systemic–functional grammar. The grammar is in general neutral between spoken and written English, but the text used for illustration is taken from spoken language; it is a discussion among an adult and three nine-year-old schoolgirls. Here is the text in standard orthography and punctuation:

(1) (Hasan, 1965, p.65)

Adult: Do you—when you have a small baby in the house, do you call it 'it', or do you call it 'she' or 'he'?

Elsie: Well if it's just—if you don't know what it is I think you ought to call it 'it', because you don't know whether you're calling it a boy or a girl, and if it gets on and if you start calling it 'she' then you find out that it's a boy you can't stop yourself 'cause you've got so used to calling it 'she'.

Lacey: Em—Mrs. Siddons says that if—if some neighbour has a new baby next door and you don't know whether it's a he or a she, if you refer to it as 'it' well then the neighbour will be very offended.

Tilly: Well if it's in your family I think you should call it either 'he' or 'she' or else the poor thing when it grows up won't know what it is.

Adult: Well what did Mrs. Siddons suggest you should do if

HANDBOOK OF DISCOURSE ANALYSIS, Vol. 2
Dimensions of Discourse

Copyright © 1985 by Academic Press London.
All rights of reproduction in any form reserved.
ISBN 0-12-712002-5

> . . . your neighbour has a baby and you don't know whether it's a boy or a girl?
>
> Tilly: She didn't. I don't suppose she knew.
>
> Elsie: Call it 'the'.
>
> Lacey: Hello, The!
>
> Elsie: Oh, I know. Call it 'baby'.

Systemic grammar is an analysis–synthesis grammar based on the paradigmatic notion of choice. It is built on the work of Saussure, Malinowski and Firth, Hjelmslev, the Prague school, and the American anthropological linguists Boas, Sapir, and Whorf; the main inspiration being J. R. Firth. It is a tristratal construct of semantics (meaning), lexicogrammar (wording), and phonology (sound). The organizing concept at each stratum is the paradigmatic 'system': A system is a set of options with an entry condition, such that exactly one option must be chosen if the entry condition is satisfied. Options are realized as syntagmatic constructs or structures; a structure is a configuration of functional elements— functions or function bundles. The functions are motivated (nonarbitrary) with respect to the options they realize; the grammar as a whole is motivated with respect to the semantics. The only line of (relative) arbitrariness is that between content and expression (between the lexicogrammar and the phonology).

A text in systemic–functional grammar is an instantiation of the system (in the Hjelmslevian sense of 'the linguistic system'). (Note that 'instantiation' is not the same thing as 'realization'; the two concepts seem to be confused in Saussure.) Text may be studied as process or as product; in either case, interpreting a text means showing how it derives from the system and therefore why it means what it does. It is not possible here to present the networks of systems from which the text is derived, since that would involve representing large portions of the grammar. Instead we employ structural notations, with brief discussion of some of the options from which the structural functions are derived.

The analysis is given in 10 steps, with a short commentary on each. The 10 steps are as follows:

1. transcription and analysis of intonation and rhythm
2. analysis into clauses and clause complexes, showing interdependencies and logical–semantic relations
3. analysis of clauses, and clause complexes, for thematic (Theme–Rheme) structure
4. comparison of clauses and information units, and analysis of the latter for information (Given–New) structure
5. analysis of finite clauses for mood, showing Subject and Finite

6. analysis of all clauses for transitivity, showing process type and participant and circumstantial functions
7. analysis of groups and phrases (verbal group, nominal group, adverbial group, prepositional phrase)
8. analysis of grammatical and lexical cohesion
9. identification, rewording and reanalysis of grammatical metaphors
10. description of context of situation, and correlation with features of the text

TRANSCRIPTION AND ANALYSIS OF INTONATION AND RHYTHM

The text is transcribed orthographically with notation for intonation and rhythm:

Adult: // do you . . . //4. when you have a / small / **baby** in the / house //.2. do you call it / **it** or //.1. do you call it / she or / **he** //

Elsie: //4. ˰ well / if it's just . . . / if you / don't know / what it / **is** I //.1 + think you / ought to / call it / **it** because you //.1. don't know / whether you're / calling it a / boy or a / **girl** and //4 if it / gets / **on** and //4 if you / start / calling it / **she** then you //4 find / out that it's a / **boy** you //.1 + can't / **stop** yourself / ˰ / 'cause you've got //.1. so / used to / calling it / **she** //

Lacey: //4. ˰ em / Mrs / **Siddons** / says that //4. if . . . / if some / **neighbour** has a //4. new / baby next / **door** and you //4. don't know / whether it's a / he or a / **she** //4. if you re/fer to it as / **it** well //.1. then the / neighbour will be / very of/**fended**//

Tilly: //4. ˰ well / if it's / in your / **family** I //.1. think you should / call it either / he or / **she** //4 ˰ or else the / poor thing / when it grows / **up** //.1. won't know / what it / **is** //

Adult: //.1. ˰ well / what did / Mrs / Siddons sug/gest you should / **do** if . . . //.1. ˰ your / neighbour / has a / **baby** and you //.1. don't know / whether it's a / boy or a / **girl** //

Tilly: //5. she / **didn't** //5. ˰ I / don't sup/pose she / **knew** //
Elsie: //.1. call it / **the** //
Lacey: //1.3 **hello** / the //
Elsie: //1. **oh** //5.3 I / **know** //.1. call it / **baby** //

Systems and Notation for Intonation and Rhythm.

A. Boundary Markers in Text:
    double slash // tone group, realizing an information unit
    single slash / foot (rhythm group)
B. Tone Symbols

1	tone one: falling	'polarity known': statement, WH- question, command
1+	wide tonic	strong key
1.	medium tonic	neutral key
1−	narrow tonic	weak key
.1	steady pretonic	neutral
...1	listing pretonic	listing (enumerating)
−1	broken pretonic	forceful
2	tone two: rising	'polarity unknown': yes/no question
2.	rise (only) tonic	neutral question
2	fall-rise	query-point question
.2	high pretonic	neutral (British)
−2	low pretonic	'surely' question; neutral (U.S.)
3	tone three: level (low rising)	'non-committal': secondary, incomplete, tentative
.3	neutral pretonic	neutral
−3	low pretonic	casual
4	tone four: falling-rising	'known ⟶ unknown': reservation, contrast, hypothesis
4.	high tonic, steady pretonic	neutral key
4	low tonic broken pretonic	strong key
5	tone five: rising–falling	'unknown ⟶ known': override, assertion, exclamation
5.	high tonic	neutral key
5	low tonic (breathy)	exclamatory key
13	tone one three: falling + level	statement plus secondary information
53	tone five three: rising–falling + level	override plus secondary information

C. Other Symbols

caret (below line)	^	silent beat
suspension marks	. . .	pause (sufficient to disrupt rhythm)
bold type	**baby**	tonic accent (nucleus), realizing information focus (culmination of New)

CLAUSES AND CLAUSE COMPLEXES

The text is analyzed into clause complexes, showing the interdependencies and logical–semantic relations among their constituent (ranking, nonembedded) clauses.

Clause complex 1	$\times\beta \; ^\frown \; \alpha \, (\, 1 \; ^\frown \; +2 \,)$
1.1	$\times\beta$ ‖‖ *when you have a small baby in the house* ‖
1.2	$\alpha 1$ ‖ *do you call it it* ‖
1.3	$\alpha + 2$ ‖ *or do you call it she or he* ‖‖

Clause complex 2 α ($\times\beta$ (α ^ 'β) ^ α) ^ $\times\beta$ (1 (α ^ 'β) ^ +2 ($\times\beta$
                          (1 ^ +2 (1 ^ $\times$2 (α ^ 'β))) ^ α (α ^ $\times\beta$)))

2.1	α $\times\beta$ α	|||	*well if you don't know* ||
2.2	α β 'β	||	*what it is* ||
2.3	α α	||	*I think you ought to call it it* ||
2.4	$\times\beta$ 1 α	||	*because you don't know* ||
2.5	β 1 'β	||	*whether you're calling it a boy or a girl* ||
2.6	β +2 $\times\beta$ 1	||	*and if it gets on* ||
2.7	β 2 β +2 1	||	*and if you start calling it she* ||
2.8	β 2 β 2 $\times$2 α	||	*then you find out* ||
2.9	β 2 β 2 2 'β	||	*that it's a boy* ||
2.10	β 2 α α	||	*you can't stop yourself* ||
2.11	β 2 α $\times\beta$	||	*'cause you've got so used to calling it she* |||

Clause complex 3 α ^ "β ($\times\beta$ (1 ^ +2 (α ^ 'β)) ^ α ($\times\beta$ ^ α))

3.1	α	|||	*Mrs. Siddons says* ||
3.2	"β $\times\beta$ 1	||	*that if some neighbour has a new baby next door* ||
3.3	β β +2 α	||	*and you don't know* ||
3.4	β β 2 'β	||	*whether it's a he or a she* ||
3.5	β α $\times\beta$	||	*if you refer to it as it* ||
3.6	β α α	||	*well then the neighbour will be very offended* |||

Clause complex 4   1 ($\times\beta$ ^ α) ^ $\times$2 (α (α ⟨⟨ $\times\beta$) ⟩⟩ ^ 'β)

4.1	1 $\times\beta$	|||	*well if it's in your family* ||
4.2	1 α	||	*I think you should call it either he or she* ||
4.3	$\times$ 2 α α	||	*or else the poor thing* ⟨⟨ ⟩⟩ *won't know* ||
4.4	2 $\times\beta$	⟨⟨	*when it grows up* ⟩⟩
4.5	2 α 'β	||	*what it is* |||

Clause complex 5   "β (α ⟨⟨ ⟩ α (⟩⟩ ^ $\times\beta$ (1 ^ +2 (α ^ 'β)))

5.1	"β α	|||	*well what* ⟨⟨ ⟩⟩ *you should do* ||
5.2	α	⟨⟨	*did Mrs. Siddons suggest* ⟩⟩
5.3	β $\times\beta$ 1	||	*if your neighbour has a baby* ||
5.4	β β +2 α	||	*and you don't know* ||
5.5	β β 2 'β	||	*whether it's a boy or a girl* |||

Clause complex 6

6.1		|||	*she didn't* |||

Clause complex 7

7.1		|||	*I don't suppose she knew* |||

Clause complex 8

8.1		|||	*call it the* |||

Clause complex 9

9.1		|||	*hello the* |||

Clause complex 10

10.1		|||	*oh I know* |||

Clause complex 11

11.1		|||	*call it baby* |||

Systems and Notation for Clause Complex

Boundary Markers in Text

|||		clause complex boundary
|| ||		clause boundary
⟨⟨ ⟩⟩		clause boundary, inclosed clause
[[ ]]		clause boundary, embedded clause
| |		group or phrase boundary
⟨ ⟩		group or phrase boundary, inclosed
[ ]		group or phrase boundary, embedded

Type of Interdependency

1 2 3 . . .	paratactic
α β γ . . .	hypotactic

Internal Bracketing (nesting)

11 12 13	or 1 (1 2 3)
αα αβ	or α (α β)
α β1 β2α β2β	or α β (1 2 (α β))

Sequence

⌢	'followed by', e.g., β ⌢ α
⟨⟨ ⟩⟩	'encloses', e.g., α ⟨⟨ β ⟩⟩

Logical–Semantic Relation

=	expansion: elaboration (restating)
+	expansion: extension (adding)
×	expansion: enhancement (qualifying)
"	projection: locution (wording)
'	projection: idea (meaning)

Speech Function

.	statement
?	question
!	command
%	offer

Finiteness

[no symbol]	finite
ŋ	nonfinite: imperfective (-ing form)
t	nonfinite: perfective (infinitive)

The major portion of the text consists of five turns, each made up grammatically of one clause complex. These contain, respectively, 3, 11, 6, 5, and 5 clauses. They show a preference for hypotactic (17) over paratactic (7) interdependencies; the predominant logical–semantic relation is that of enhancement, typically hypothetical (11 instances)—the discussion centers around what to do if and when a certain situation arises. Of the 15 other instances, 5 are extension, 'and/or'; the remainder (8) are projection, of which 2 are saying (the teacher as Sayer) and 6 are knowing, mainly negative and with a generalized Senser '(if) you don't know'— this being an aspect of the problem under discussion. (The two instances of *I think* are metaphorical modalities, not projections, as can be shown by adding a tag: The tagged form of *I think you should call it he or she* is *shouldn't you?* not *don't I?*)

All these clause complexes are not only complex but also impeccably well formed, as is typical of casual spontaneous speech (including that of children!).

So much for the "reasoning" component of the discussion. The remainder consists of "suggesting," partly humorous and partly serious, and here the turns are short, one or two clauses each. The clause complexes are even shorter, since each consists of just one clause. There is no parataxis or hypotaxis. (6.1 and 7.1, *She didn't. I don't suppose she knew,* could be considered to form a paratactic elaboration, given the tone concord; but the latter, though necessary, is probably not a sufficient condition.)

As far as the organization of the information is concerned, a comparison of the two transcriptions shows that in the majority of instances one clause is one information unit, this being the unmarked (default) situation in English. This holds throughout, with the following systematic exceptions: (1) seven out of the eight projections have both projecting and projected clause on one tone group, for example, // *if you* / *don't know* / *what it* / *is* //—this is the locally unmarked form; and (2) one clause consists of two information units, one for the Theme and one for the Rheme: // *if some* / **neighbour** *has a* // *new* / *baby next* / **door** //—this is the predominant pattern when two information units are mapped on to one clause. For the analysis of theme and information structure see the next two sections.

THEME

Each clause, and each clause complex characterized by rising dependency ($\beta \char94 \alpha$), is analyzed for thematic structure:

Clause Theme

Clause	Textual	Interpersonal	Topical	Markedness of topical theme
1.1	*when*		*you*	unmarked
1.2		*do*	*you*	unmarked
1.3	*or*	*do*	*you*	unmarked
2.1	*well if*		*you*	unmarked
2.2		[*what*]	*what*	unmarked
2.3		*I think*	*you*	unmarked
2.4	*because*		*you*	unmarked
2.5	*whether*		*you*	unmarked
2.6	*and if*		*it*	unmarked
2.7	*and if*		*you*	unmarked
2.8	*then*		*you*	unmarked

Clause	Textual	Interpersonal	Topical	Markedness of topical theme
2.9	that		it	unmarked
2.10			you	unmarked
2.11	'cause		you	unmarked
3.1			Mrs. Siddons	unmarked
3.2	that if		some neighbour	unmarked
3.3	and		you	unmarked
3.4	whether		it	unmarked
3.5	if		you	unmarked
3.6	well then		the neighbour	unmarked
4.1	well if		it	unmarked
4.2		I think	you	unmarked
4.3	or else		the poor thing	unmarked
4.4	when		it	unmarked
4.5		[what]	what	unmarked
5.1	well	[what]	what	unmarked
5.2		did	Mrs. Siddons	unmarked
5.3	if		your neighbour	unmarked
5.4	and		you	unmarked
5.5	whether		it	unmarked
6.1			she	unmarked
7.1		I don't suppose	she	unmarked
8.1			[imperative]	unmarked
9.1			[minor]	—
10.1	oh		I	unmarked
11.1			[imperative]	unmarked

Rising Dependency Sequences (marked thematic)

Sequence	Theme (marked)	Rheme
1.1–1.3	when you have a small baby in the house	do you call it 'it' or do you call it 'she' or 'he'?
2.1–2.3	well if you don't know what it is	I think you ought to call it 'it'
2.6–2.10	if it gets on, and if . . . you find out that it's a boy	you can't stop yourself
3.2–3.6	if some neighbour has a new baby next door . . . if you refer to it as 'it'	well then the neighbour will be very offended
4.1–4.2	well if it's in your family	I think you should call it either 'he' or 'she'
4.3–4.5	or else the poor thing when it grows up	won't know what it is

The Theme is the (speaker's) point of departure for the clause. It is realized in English by position in the sequence: Thematic elements are put first. Hence the thematic structure of the clause is Theme ^ Rheme.

Each of the three metafunctional components of the content plane—ideational, interpersonal, textual—may contribute thematic material. The textual Theme is some combination of continuative (e.g., *oh, well*), conjunctive (e.g., *then, if*) or relative (e.g., *that, which*). The interpersonal Theme is modality (e.g., *perhaps*), interrogative mood marker (WH-element or Finite verbal auxiliary), or Vocative. The topical Theme is any element functioning in the transitivity structure of the clause. The typical sequence is textual ^ interpersonal ^ topical, and the Theme in any case ends with the topical element: In other words, the Theme of a clause extends up to the first element that has a function in transitivity.

The unmarked Theme for any clause is determined by the choice of mood: Subject in declarative, WH- or Finite element in interrogative, [zero] in imperative and minor clauses. Semantically, the unmarked Theme is the natural starting point for the particular speech function: in a question, 'this is what I want to know'—the information-seeking (WH-) or polarity-carrying (Finite) element; in a statement, 'this is the entity on which the argument rests' (Subject).

The ongoing choice of clause Themes reveals the method of development of the text. In the example, every clause has an unmarked topical Theme. At first, the impersonal *you* predominates, followed later by specific third person participants: the teacher (Mrs. Siddons), the neighbour, and the baby. Many are preceded by textual Themes, continuative and/or conjunctive. Thus the text develops as a discussion of a general topic with particular personalities brought in to carry it forward, the whole being linked together both dialogically and logically. At the higher rank of the clause complex, on the other hand, the logical structure of the argument becomes the dominant motif: Here there are a number of marked Themes, in the form of hypotactic (dependent) clauses introduced by *if*. The picture is that of a shared discourse being developed as a logical generalization with hypothetical cases, without much concern for attitudinal rhetoric (the only interpersonal Themes are questions and uncertainties), and with some concretization towards the end.

INFORMATION STRUCTURE

Each information unit is analyzed for infomation structure (numbers refer to clause complexes, letters to information units):

	Focus	New	Markedness
1a	baby	*a small baby*	marked
1b	it	*[do you call (it)] it*	unmarked
1c	he	*she or he*	unmarked
2a	is	*[if you don't know what (it)] is*	unmarked
2b	it	*[you ought to (call it)] it*	unmarked
2c	girl	*a boy or a girl*	unmarked
2d	on	*gets on*	unmarked
2e	she	*[start (calling it)] she*	unmarked
2f	boy	*[find out that (it's)] a boy*	unmarked
2g	stop	*can't stop yourself*	unmarked
2h	she	*[so used to (calling it)] she*	unmarked
3a	Siddons	*Mrs. Siddons*	marked
3b	neighbour	*some neighbour*	unmarked
3c	door	*[a new baby] next door*	unmarked
3d	she	*[don't know whether (it's)] a he or a she*	unmarked
3e	it	*[refer to (it) as] it*	unmarked
3f	offended	*will be very offended*	unmarked
4a	family	*in your family*	unmarked
4b	she	*either he or she*	unmarked
4c	up	*[when (it)] grows up*	unmarked
4d	is	*[what (it)] is*	unmarked
5a	do	*[suggest (you)] should do*	unmarked
5b	baby	*[has] a baby*	unmarked
5c	girl	*a boy or a girl*	unmarked
6	didn't	*didn't*	unmarked
7	knew	*[I don't suppose (she)] knew*	unmarked
8	the	*the*	unmarked
9	hello the	*hello the*	unmarked
10a	oh	*oh*	unmarked
10b	I know	*I know*	unmarked
11	baby	*baby*	unmarked

In the "New" column, the focal element is outside the brackets. Square brackets enclose other New material; within this, the items shown within curved brackets are those previously mentioned.

The New is what the speaker presents as being for the listener to attend to: 'this is what's news'. It may be previously unknown, or contrary to expectation, or picked out for special prominence. It is realized by means of the tonic accent.

Phonologically, spoken discourse in English consists of a linear succession of tone groups, each characterized by one intonation contour or 'tone'. The tone group, in turn, consists of a tonic segment that carries the characteristic tone contour: 1, falling; 2, rising; 3, level (phonetically realized as low rising); 4, falling–rising; 5, rising–falling; 13, falling plus level; 53, rising–falling plus level. The tonic segment begins with the tonic accent, which embodies the distinctive pitch movement. Optionally, the tonic segment may be preceded by a pretonic segment that also forms part of the same tone contour. Both tonic and pretonic segments display a range of more delicate options within each tone: wide fall, narrow fall, low pretonic, high pretonic, and so on.

Grammatically, the tone group realizes a unit of information, which is one piece of news, so to speak. It consists of a New component optionally accompanied by a component that is Given. Typically, the New comes at the end; but unlike thematic structure, information structure is not realized by the order in which things are arranged, but by tonic prominence—the New is the element containing the tonic accent. The particular word on which the tonic accent falls is said to carry the information 'focus'. Anything after the focal element is thereby marked as Given, while anything preceding it may be Given or may be New (there are rather subtle intonational and rhythmic variations serving as signals).

An information unit is not necessarily coextensive with a clause, but that is its unmarked status: Each ranking clause (i.e., independent or dependent, but not embedded) is typically one information unit. The principal systematic variants are (1) two clauses / one information unit: falling dependencies, that is, $\alpha \ ^\frown \ \beta$ sequences; (2) one clause / two information units: thematic focus, that is, // Theme // Rheme // information patterns.

Analysis of the New elements will reveal the 'main point' of the text. In the example it is to do with babies, what sex they are, and how they are to be referred to in cases of doubt. Subsidiary points of attention are the baby's growing up, the children's understanding and obligations, and the adult world's possible displeasure.

The Theme in a clause is what is prominent for the speaker; it is 'what I am on about'. The New in an information unit is what is made prominent (by the speaker) to the listener; it is 'what you are being invited to attend to'. When clause and information unit are mapped on to each other, the result is a wavelike movement from speaker to listener, the diminuendo of the speaker's part being as it were picked up by the crescendo of the listener's part.

The effect of this movement is cumulative over the text as a whole. The present text is typical in the way that the sequence of Themes

represents the 'method of development' of the dialogue, while the sequence
of News represents the 'main point' of the discussion, with each speaker
contributing her part to the construction of the overall pattern—all un-
consciously, of course.

This interplay of two distinct waves of prominence is possible because
Theme–Rheme and Given–New are not (as often conceived) one single
structure, but two distinct structures that interpenetrate. As a result,
they can vary independently, allowing for all possible combinations of
the two kinds of texture. In unit 2h, for example, Elsie might have chosen
a different distribution by combining thematic and information prominence
(mapping New onto Theme):

*'cause you've got //.1. so / **used** to / calling it / she //*

This would have strongly highlighted *used to,* as a marked focus, and
marked *calling it she* as Given; the effect of the latter would have been
to bring out the repetitive facet of *calling it she,* thus reinforcing its
cohesion with 2e; but by the same token to deprive it of its status as a
main point for attention. The interaction of the thematic and informational
systems is the clause grammar's contribution to the creation of texture
in discourse.

MOOD

Each finite clause is analyzed for mood; its Subject and Finite element
are shown, together with any modality:

Clause	Subject	Finite	Mood	Modality
1.1	*you*	*have*	β declarative	
1.2	*you*	*do*	interrogative: yes/no	
1.3	*you*	*do*	interrogative: yes/no	
2.1	*you*	*don't*	β declarative	
2.2	*it*	*is*	β interrogative: WH-	
2.3	*you*	*ought*	declarative, modulated	probability, obliga-tion: median
2.4	*you*	*don't*	β declarative	
2.5	*you*	*are*	β interrogative: yes/no	
2.6	*it*	*gets*	β declarative	
2.7	*you*	*start*	β declarative	
2.8	*you*	*find*	β declarative	
2.9	*it*	*is*	β declarative	
2.10	*you*	*can't*	declarative	ability: high/negative
2.11	*you*	*have*	β declarative	

Clause	Subject	Finite	Mood	Modality
3.1	*Mrs. Siddons*	*says*	declarative	
3.2	*some neighbour*	*has*	β declarative	
3.3	*you*	*don't*	declarative	
3.4	*it*	*is*	β interrogative: alternative	
3.5	*you*	*refer*	β declarative	
3.6	*the neighbour*	*will*	declarative	
4.1	*it*	*is*	β declarative	
4.2	*you*	*should*	declarative, modulated	probability, obligation: median
4.3	*the poor thing*	*won't*	declarative	
4.4	*it*	*grows*	β declarative	
4.5	*it*	*is*	β interrogative: WH-	
5.1	*you*	*should*	β interrogative: WH-, modulated	obligation: median
5.2	*Mrs. Siddons*	*did*	declarative	
5.3	*your neighbour*	*has*	β declarative	
5.4	*you*	*don't*	β declarative	
5.5	*it*	*is*	β interrogative: alternative	
6.1	*she*	*didn't*	declarative	
7.1	*she*	*knew*	declarative	probability: median
8.1			imperative	
9.1			minor	
10.1	*I*	*know*	declarative	
11.1			imperative	

The system of mood expresses the speech function of the clause. Typical patterns of realization are as shown in the following chart (where ↘ means 'is typically realized as').

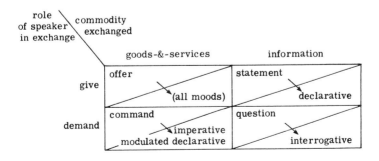

In addition there are the minor speech functions of exclamation, greeting, and call, realized by minor clauses, and by exclamatory declaratives.

Offers, commands, and statements may be tagged, for example, *I'll help you, shall I?* The tag makes explicit the speaker's request for the listener to perform his complementary role: accept offer, carry out command, acknowledge and confirm statement. There are no tagged clauses in the text under consideration.

The Subject expresses the participant in respect of which the particular speech function is validated: performer in the case of goods-&-services, bearer of the argument (i.e., the one on whom the validity is made to rest) in the case of information. In a declarative, the Subject is typically also the Theme (hence 'unmarked Theme'; see the discussion of Theme above); but whereas the Theme is a discourse (textual) function, displaying patterns over the text as a whole, the Subject is an interpersonal function having significance just for the particular exchange. Here it is frequently the impersonal *you,* showing that these statements are to be arguable as statements that are valid in general; in other cases, it is the baby, Mrs. Siddons, or the hypothetical neighbor.

The Finite element expresses the deicticity of the process, by reference to either (1) speaker–now (primary tense: past, present, or future) or (2) speaker judgment (modality: probability, usuality, obligation, inclination, or ability; high, median, or low value). Almost all the finiteness in this text is combined with present tense; the children's text proceeds as a series of declaratives, some independent and some dependent, the mood-bearing constituent of which consists of generalized Subject plus Finite present (and there is very little secondary tense). This is typical of logical argument; and it is interspersed with interrogatives as the adult prompts the children to explore further.

There is very little modality in the text. In the Finite element, apart from one 'ability' form *can't,* in *you can't stop yourself,* there are just three expressions of obligation (*ought* and two instances of *should*). Other than in combination with finiteness, there are again only three modalities, in this case expression of probability: (*I suppose* and two instances of *I think*). As it happens, in two paired instances the two kinds of modality are associated: Where the speaker expresses a judgment of obligation, she qualifies it with a judgment of probability, 'it may be that it should be so'. Thus when the children are making rules, they are also being tentative about them.

TRANSITIVITY AND PROCESS TYPES

Each clause is analyzed for transitivity, showing process type, Process, Medium, other participant functions, and circumstantial elements:

Clause	Process type	Process	Medium	Other participants or circumstances
1.1	III poss/attr	have	you	Atte *a small baby* Loc *in the house*
1.2	III int/ident	call	it	Ag *you* Tok *'it'*
1.3	III int/ident	call	it	Ag *you* Tok *'she or he'*
2.1	II cog/mid	know	you	
2.2	III int/attr	be	it	Atte *what*
2.3	III int/ident	call	it	Ag *you* Tok *'it'*
2.4	II cog/mid	know	you	
2.5	III int/ident	call	it	Ag *you* Tok *a boy or a girl*
2.6	I mat/mid	get on	it	
2.7	III int/ident	call	it	Ag *you* Tok *'she'*
2.8	II cog/mid	find out	you	
2.9	III int/attr	be	it	Atte *a boy*
2.10	III int/ident	[call]	[it]	Ag *you* Tok [*'she'*]
2.11	III int/attr	get	you	Atte *used* [[*to calling it she*]]
3.1	II verb/mid	say	Mrs. Siddons	
3.2	III poss/attr	have	some neighbour	Atte *a new baby* Loc *next door*
3.3	II cog/mid	know	you	
3.4	III int/attr	be	it	Atte *a he or a she*
3.5	III int/ident	refer to	it	Ag *you* Tok *'it'*
3.6	II aff/effec	offend	the neighbour	
4.1	III circ/attr	be	it	Loc *in your family*
4.2	III int/ident	call	it	Ag *you* Tok *either 'he' or 'she'*
4.3	II cog/mid	know	the poor thing	
4.4	I mat/mid	grow up	it	
4.5	III int/attr	be	it	Atte *what*
5.1	I mat/mid	do	you	Ra *what*
5.2	II verb/mid	suggest	Mrs. Siddons	
5.3	III poss/attr	have	your neighbour	Atte *a baby*
5.4	II cog/mid	know	you	
5.5	III int/attr	be	it	Atte *a boy or a girl*

Clause	Process type	Process	Medium	Other participants or circumstances
6.1	II verb/mid	[suggest]	she	
7.1	II cog/mid	know	she	
8.1	III int/ident	call	it	Tok 'the'
9.1	—			
10.1	II cog/mid	know	I	
11.1	III int/ident	call	it	Tok 'baby'

Key to abbreviations:

Process types (features)

aff	affect (= reaction)
attr	attributive
cog	cognition
effec	effective (= non-middle)
ident	identifying
int	intensive
mat	material
mid	middle
poss	possessive
verb	verbal

Participants or circumstances (functions)

Ag	Agent
Atte	Attribute
Loc	Location
Ra	Range
Tok	Token

Transitivity is the representation, in the clause, of the experiential component of meaning: specifically the processes, the participants in them, and the attendant circumstances.

This text is a discussion of a problem: what to do if a certain situation arises. The majority of the clauses in it relate to the situation, the problem, its solution, and the process of problem-solving:

(i) possessive / attributive:	*have + baby*	(× 3)
(ii) intensive / attributive:	*be + male / female*	(× 5)
(iii) intensive / identifying:	*call + baby + he / she*	(× 11)
(iv) cognitive:	*know, find out*	(× 8)
(v) verbal:	*say, suggest*	(× 3)

The remaining six clauses include three characterizing the baby (two material: *grow, get on;* one circumstantial: *be in + family*), one characterizing the neighbour (affective: *be offended*), and two others, one minor (greeting: *hello*) and one a WH- process (*do what*).

There are three major types of process in English: Type I, doing (material and behavioral); Type II, sensing/saying (mental and verbal); Type III, being (relational and existential). They are distinguished in the grammar in various ways; the principal distinctions are as follows:

	Pro-verb	Direction (active)	Participants		Unmarked present tense	Verb accent
			Medium	Other		
I Doing					present in present	+
1 material	do, happen, do to, do with	one	thing	thing		
2 behavioral	do	one	conscious being			
II Sensing/saying					present	+/−
3 mental	—	two:	conscious being	thing or fact		
	(do to)	a likes x, x pleases a				
4 verbal	—	one	signal source			
III Being					present	−
5 relational	—	one	thing or fact			
attributive				class of thing or fact		
identifying				identity of thing or fact		
6 existential	—	one	thing or fact			

In the example text, the clauses in (i–iii) above are all type III, relational; the issue is one of being, partly attribution (having a baby, which in this text means possessing it, not bearing it; being male or female) and partly identification (being the name of). Of these, (i) and (ii) are middle—there is a Medium (the neighbor, the baby) but no Agent; (iii) however is effective—there is an Agent in the identification process, always represented as *you,* but moving from personal 'you' in clause complex 1 to impersonal 'you' thereafter. The clauses in (iv) and (v) are type II, mental–verbal; (iv) are cognitive, with the Medium (Senser) being you, I, Mrs. Siddons or the baby when it grows up; (v) are verbal, the Medium (Sayer) being Mrs. Siddons. All interactants, real and hypothetical, are involved in thinking about the problem—including the baby, at some future date, if a solution is not reached now; and the teacher has put the problem into words.

A summary of process types and the relevant participant functions follows:

Process type	Specific role of Medium	Other roles	
		Obligatory	Optional
I doing			
1 material	Actor, Goal		
2 behavioral	Behaver		
a middle (action/event)	Actor, Behaver		Range/Scope
b effective (action on)	Goal	Agent/Actor	Beneficiary/Recipient
II Sensing/saying			
3 mental	Senser		
i perception			
ii affect			
iii cognition			
a middle ('like' type)		Range/Phenomenon	
b effective ('please' type)		Agent/Phenomenon	
4 verbal	Sayer		Beneficiary/Addressee
III Being			
5 relational			
i intensive		Identity	
ii possessive		Possession	
iii circumstantial		Circumstance	
a middle (attributive)	Carrier	Attribute	Agent/Attributor
b effective (identifying)	Token/Value	Value/Token	Agent/Nominator
6 existential	Existent		

OTHER GROUP FEATURES

Groups and phrases are analyzed with respect to features that are relevant to the inquiry:

Verbal Group

Clause	Verbal group	System/tense	Other features
1.1	*have*	F Ø present	
1.2	*do . . . call*	F Ø present	
1.3	*do . . . call*	F Ø present	
2.1	*don't know*	F Ø present	polarity: negative
2.2	*is*	F Ø present	
2.3	*ought to call*	N Ø present	modality: obligation/median
2.4	*don't know*	F Ø present	polarity: negative
2.5	*are calling*	F Ø Ø pres. in pres.	
2.6	*gets on*	F Ø present	
2.7	*start calling*	F Ø present	phase: inceptive, + imperf.
2.8	*find out*	F Ø present	
2.9	*is*	F Ø present	
2.10	*can't stop*	N Ø	modality: ability/high/negative

(continued)

Clause	Verbal group	System/tense	Other features
2.11	*have got*	F Ø − past in pres.	
	[[*calling*	N Ø	nonfinite: imperfective]]
3.1	*says*	F Ø present	
3.2	*has*	F Ø present	
3.3	*don't know*	F Ø present	polarity: negative
3.4	*is*	F Ø present	
3.5	*refer*	F Ø present	
3.6	*will be offended*	F + future	voice: passive
4.1	*is*	F Ø present	
4.2	*ought to call*	N Ø	modality: obligation/median
4.3	*won't know*	F + future	polarity: negative
4.4	*grows up*	F Ø present	
4.5	*is*	F Ø present	
5.1	*should do*	N Ø	modality: obligation/median
5.2	*did . . . suggest*	F − past	
5.3	*has*	F Ø present	
5.4	*don't know*	F Ø present	polarity: negative
5.5	*is*	F Ø present	
6.1	*didn't* [*suggest*]	F − past	polarity: negative
7.1	*knew*	F − present	modality: probability/median [meta]/negative
8.1	*call*	N Ø	nonfinite: perfective (imper.)
10.1	*know*	F Ø present	
11.1	*call*	N Ø	nonfinite: perfective (imper.)

Key to verbal group categories:

System: F (finite; 36 tenses); N (nonfinite/modalized; 12 tenses) [A third system, S (sequent; 24 tenses) is not represented]
Tense: Ø (present); − (past); + (future); Ø − (past in present); Ø Ø (present in present)
Finiteness: finite [not shown]; nonfinite
Aspect: [nonfinite only] perfective; imperfective
Polarity: positive [not shown]; negative
Phase: [time phase] inceptive; durative
Voice: active [not shown]; passive
Modality: probability; usuality; obligation; inclination; ability / high; median; low

The English verbal group carries a recursive three-term (past/present/future) tense system of the type 'present in past in . . .' where any tense selection may become the point of reference for another one, subject to certain restraints that limit the total number of possible combinations. In the 'full' (finite) system of tenses the number is 36; from this is derived, by a neutralizing of certain tenses in the 'past' series (*he said she had arrived* corresponds to *she arrived, she has arrived,* and *she had arrived*), the 24-tense 'sequent' system; and from this in turn, by a parallel neutralization in the 'future' series (*to be about to depart* corresponds to

will depart, is going to depart, and *will be going to depart*), is derived
the 'nonfinite' system which has just 12. This last is also the system that
applies if the Finite verbal element is a modality (e.g., *should, must*),
since that eliminates the primary tense choice.

Most of the verbal groups in this text are simple present tense; not
only because of the general nature of many of the propositions, but
because most of the processes are other than 'doing' ones, and therefore
have simple present, not present in present, as their unmarked choice.
Furthermore, even the material ones are dependent (*if it gets on, when
it grows up*), which again requires simple present.

Nominal Group. The only nominal groups with structure other than
simply Head/Thing are the following:

Clause	Deictic	Epithet	Classifier	Thing
1.1	*a*	*small*		*baby*
1.1	*the*			*house*
2.5	*a / a*			*boy / girl*
2.9	*a*			*boy*
3.2	*some*			*neighbour*
3.2	*a*	*new*		*baby*
3.2			*next*	*door*
3.6	*the*			*neighbour*
4.1	*your*			*family*
4.3	*the*	*poor*		*thing*
5.3	*your*			*neighbour*
5.3	*a*			*baby*

Just as the verbal group further specifies the process, in respect of
tense, polarity, and so on, the nominal group further specifies the entity
represented by the Head noun. There are similarities between the two
types of word group; but the nominal group has much more lexical
material, since entities have a more developed taxonomic organization.
Hence the nominal group has a functional structure Deictic–Numerative–
Epithet–Classifier–Thing–Qualifier, with left–right ordering from the most
instantial, situation-bound to the most permanent characteristic, modified
by a purely syntactic principle which puts anything that is embedded at
the end.

There is little elaboration of nominal groups in the text. Most of them
are simply personal pronouns, functioning cohesively; those that have
noun as Head contain just enough specification to establish the general
point being made, for example, *a small baby, your neighbour, the house*.

The only Qualifier is the nonfinite clause *to calling it she* following the Attribute *used*; and this is a metaphor for a modality 'have so usually been calling it she'.

Adverbial Group. None.

Prepositional Phrase. The following occur in the text:

Clause	Preposition	Complement	Function
1.1	*in*	*the house*	Locative/Spatial (= Place): rest
3.5	*to*	*it*	Matter (representing Medium)
3.5	*as*	*'it'*	Role (representing Value)
4.1	*in*	*your family*	Place: membership/rest

GRAMMATICAL AND LEXICAL COHESION

The text is analyzed for grammatical and lexical cohesion:

A: Do you—when you have a small baby in the house do you

call it 'it' or do you call it 'she' or 'he'?

E: Well if it's just—if you don't know what it is I think you
        C   R   R
      cont pers   pers
ought to call it 'it', because you don't know whether you're
              L   R L
            rep pers rep
calling it a boy or a girl, and if it gets on and if you start
      L   R   L   L   R
    rep pers hyp   hyp   pers
calling it 'she' then you find out that it's a boy you can't stop
      L   R L   L   R
    rep pers rep   syn   pers
yourself 'cause you've got so used to calling it 'she'.
                                              L   R L
                                            rep pers rep

L: Em—Mrs. Siddons says that if—if some neighbour has a new

baby next door and you don't know whether it's a he or a
  L   L   L   R   L
rep   coll   rep   pers syn
she, if you refer to it as 'it' well then the neighbour will be
 L   L   R   L
syn   syn   pers rep
very offended.

T: Well if it's in your family I think you should call it either
          C   R   L
        cont   pers   coll

     'he' or 'she' or else the poor thing when it grows up won't
       L   L   L   L
      rep   rep   hyp   syn

     know what it is.
       L   R
      rep   pers

A: Well what did Mrs. Siddons suggest you should do if . . .
          C   L
        cont   rep

     your neighbour has a baby and you don't know whether it's
            L   L   L
           rep   rep   rep

     a boy or a girl?
       L   L
      rep   rep

T: She didn't. I don't suppose she knew.
       R   E   R   L   E
      pers verb   pers rep claus

E: Call it 'the'.
       L   R
      rep pers

L: Hello, The!
             L
            rep

E: Oh, I know. Call it 'baby'.
       L   L   R   L
      rep   rep pers rep

Key to categories of cohesion:
R Reference: personal (pers); demonstrative; comparative
S Substitution: [none in text]
E Ellipsis: clausal (claus); verbal (verb); nominal
C Conjunction: continuative (cont); appositive, additive, adversative, temporal, causal,
                  conditional, concessive [none in text]
L Lexical: repetition (rep); collocation (coll); synonymy (syn); hyponymy (hyp)

The headings given in the key are the basic lexicogrammatical resources for creating texture between clause complexes. In fact they function also within the clause complex—they are simply indifferent to grammatical boundaries; but they have greater force when linking one clause complex with another because of the absence of structural links. In this example, therefore, only inter-complex instances have been noted.

What all types of cohesion have in common is that every instance presumes some other element in the text for its interpretation; and hence a tie is set up between it and what it presumes. In reference, what is presumed is some semantic representation: of a participant, for example, as when *it* refers back to 'a small baby', but also of a semantic construct of any extent. In substitution and ellipsis, on the other hand, what is presumed is a lexicogrammatical representation, some piece of wording that has to be retrieved, as when *she didn't* requires the restitution of *suggest* (anything); this is a different kind of textual retrieval and rarely extends beyond one clause complex. Conjunction refers to the nonstructural representation of logical–semantic relations that may also be expressed structurally; for example, *on the other hand,* semantically related to paratactic *but* and hypotactic *although.* Lexical cohesion is created by the repetition of a lexical item (e.g., *call . . . call*); the use of a synonym (e.g., *call . . . refer to*); the use of a high-frequency collocate (e.g., *house . . . family*); or the use of a hyponym or superordinate—an item within the same lexical set but differing in generality (e.g., *baby . . .* [*poor*] *thing, baby . . . boy, girl*).

The sample text is characterized by dense lexical repetition and personal reference; the discourse unfolds around a small number of entities that are constantly being referred to. When a new instance is brought in, the link is achieved by collocation: *in the house . . . next door.* There is very little conjunction, because the logical–semantic relations are realized by the hypotactic organization of the clause complex: The reasoning is systematic and explicit. There is also little ellipsis, which comes in only when the reasoning gives way to a more dialogic pattern with shorter exchanges.

GRAMMATICAL METAPHOR

Grammatical metaphors are identified, reworded, and reanalyzed.

Most examples of adult English contain some instances of grammatical metaphor: Clauses in which one type of process is represented in the grammar of another; for example, *the fifth day saw them at the summit* 'on the fifth day they arrived at the summit', or *guarantee limited to refund of purchase price of goods* 'we guarantee only to refund the price for which the goods were purchased'.

Children's speech is largely free of grammatical metaphors of this kind; this is in fact the main distinction between child and adult language. There are no examples of it in the present text.

There are however certain grammatical metaphors that have been built into the language, so that the metaphorical version has become the norm; for example, *she gave a nod* 'she nodded', *he has a long nose* 'his nose is long'. One very common type of these is the use of a mental process (cognitive) clause to express a modality, such as *I think, I don't believe.* It was pointed out above that the tagged form of *I think it's broken* is *I think it's broken, isn't it?*, not *I think it's broken, don't I?*, showing that this is a metaphor for *it's probably broken*. We can use one of these as an example:

||| *I don't suppose* || *she came* ||| $\alpha \,\hat{}\, '\beta$
    mental: cognitive   material
    negative   positive

reworded as:

||| *she probably didn't come* ||| (single clause)
    material
    modalized: probability/median
    negative

In cases like this it saves time if the analysis moves directly to the nonmetaphorical version, since the rewording is quite automatic. In other instances, however, the principle is as follows:

1. Analyze the clause as it stands.
2. Reword it, in nonmetaphorical form.
3. Analyze the reworded version.

Both analyses figure in the interpretation. Sometimes it takes several steps in rewording to reach a nonmetaphorical version, and there may be more than one possible route; all are potentially relevant to an understanding of the text.

CONTEXT OF SITUATION

The 'context of situation' of the text is described in terms of field, tenor, and mode. The 'field' is what is going on: the nature of the social–semiotic activity. The 'tenor' is who are taking part: the statuses and mutual roles of the interactants. The 'mode' is what part the language is playing: the rhetorical and communicative channels. This description is then used to interpret the lexicogrammatical features of the text.

Field.   A general, imaginary problem of verbal behavior: how to refer to a baby whose sex is unknown, without offending against the parents, the baby (later in life), or the language.

Tenor.   Adult and three children: adult (neither teacher nor parent) interviewer, informal; children self-conscious but relaxed. Speech roles: adult questioning, children suggesting.

Mode.   Informal spontaneous speech. Dialogue: question–and–answer exchanges. Exploratory; hypothetical and logical in orientation, moving towards (partly humorous) resolution.

These features determine the choice of 'register': that is, the kinds of meanings that are likely to be exchanged. Like the rest of the linguistic system, the patterns are probabilistic: Given these features of the context of situation, we can make semantic (and therefore lexicogrammatical) predictions with a significant probability of being right—that, after all, is precisely what the interactants themselves are doing all the time.

What makes this possible is what makes it possible for a child to learn the language in the first place: the systematic relationship between these categories of the situation and the 'metafunctions' of the content system. By and large, characteristics of the field predict experiential meanings, those of the tenor predict interpersonal meanings, and those of the mode predict textual meanings.

In analyzing a text, we identify those features of the lexicogrammar which in a text-generation program might reasonably be expected to be called upon if the situation was represented in this way.

Situation	*Lexicogrammar*
Field	Experiential metafunction
general nature of problem	present tense; *you* impersonal as Agent
imaginary	*if, when,* in sense of 'supposing'
how to behave	modulations: *should, ought*
verbal: referring to	identifying process + Agent
problem: lack of knowledge	cognitive process, negative
. . . of sex, and linguistic difficulties	lexical items marked for sex: *boy, girl*
thus caused	grammatical system of gender: *he, she, it*
Tenor	Interpersonal metafunction
adult interviewing children: informal	personalized *you* as Subject
children self-conscious and hesitant	reinterpreted as impersonal *you* modalities: *I think*
but relaxed	absence of markers of formality, e.g., politeness forms
adult questioning	interrogative: *yes/no,* WH-, alternative
children suggesting	modulated declarative, imperative
Mode	Textual metafunction
spontaneous and informal	elaborate clause complexes
dialogue	exchanges, e.g., question–and–answer; continuative *well* ('I'll now take my part')
exploratory: hypothetical and logical	hypotactic dependent clauses as Theme: *if* with tone 4
orientation towards and resolution of problem ('main point')	names as 'New' information: *it, he or she, baby*
exploratory ('method of development')	protagonists as Theme; no first person Themes

CONCLUSION

Three final points should be made about an outline of this type. One is that it is just an outline: Obviously, the analysis under every heading could be developed much further in delicacy, and other headings could be added. The guiding principle is to select and develop whatever is needed for the particular purpose in hand. There are many different purposes for analyzing a text, and the scope and direction of the analysis will vary accordingly. Often we may want to scrutinize only one or two features, but to follow them through to a considerable depth.

Secondly, a text analysis is a work of interpretation. There are relatively few absolute and clearcut categories in language; there are many tendencies, continuities, and overlaps. Many actual instances can be analyzed in two or more different ways, none of which can be ruled out as impossible; some may be less sensible than others, and so can be discarded, but we may still be left with valid alternatives. Especially in a literary text it is to be expected that we will find clauses with multiple grammars; but this is not a distortion of the system—it is a richer use of its natural resources. All analyses may need to figure in the interpretation.

Thirdly, the lexicogrammatical analysis is only a part of the task. It is an essential part; all text is made of language, and the central processing unit of the linguistic system is the lexicogrammar. But just as the grammatical system does not itself create text—text is a semantic creation, with the grammar functioning largely (though not entirely) as the automatic realization of the semantic choices—so the analysis of the grammar does not constitute the interpretation of a text. (There has been some misunderstanding on this point, for example in the use of cohesion as a method of text analysis. Cohesion is an essential property of texts, but it is the way the cohesive resources are deployed that makes the difference between text and non-text, and between one text and another.)

For the systemic treatment of some other aspects of text interpretation, see the items listed in the Bibliography.

BIBLIOGRAPHY

Benson, J. D., & Greaves W. S. (1981). Field of discourse: Theory and application. *Applied Linguistics, 2*(1), 45–55.

Berry, M. (1981a). Systemic linguistics and discourse analysis: A multi-layered approach to exchange structure. In R. M. Coulthard & M. M. Montgomery (Eds.), *Studies in discourse analysis* (pp. 120–145). London: Routledge & Kegan Paul.

Berry, M. (1981b). Towards layers of exchange structure for directive exchanges. *Network, 2*, 23–32.

Butler, C. S. (1979). Recent developments in systemic linguistics. *Linguistics and Language Teaching: Abstracts, 12*(1).

Ellis, J. (in press). *The contrastive analysis of language registers*. Tübingen: Narr.
Fawcett, R. P. (1980). *Cognitive linguistics and social interaction* (Exeter Linguistic Studies 3). Heidelberg and University of Exeter: Julius Groos.
Fawcett, R. P. (in preparation). *A grammar for textual analysis: Proposals derived from a systemic model of language.*
Fries, P. (1981). On the status of theme in English: arguments from discourse. *Forum Linguisticum*, 6(1), 1–38.
Gregory, M. J. (1983). Towards "communication" linguistics: A framework. In J. Morreall (Ed.), *The Tenth LACUS Forum*. Columbia, SC: Hornbeam Press.
Gregory, M. J., & Malcolm, K. (in preparation). Generic situation and discourse phase: An approach to the analysis of children's talk. In J. D. Benson & W. S. Greaves (Eds.), *Systemic perspectives on discourse: Selected theoretical papers from the Ninth International Systemic Workshop*. Norwood, NJ, Ablex.
Halliday, M. A. K. (1959). *The language of the Chinese "Secret History of the Mongols"* (Philological Society Publications 17), Oxford: Blackwell.
Halliday, M. A. K. (1971). Linguistic function and literary style: An inquiry into the language of William Golding's *The Inheritors*. In Seymour Chatman (Ed.), *Literary style: A symposium* (pp. 330–365). New York: Oxford University Press. Reprinted in M. A. K. Halliday (Ed.), (1973). *Explorations in the functions of language* (pp. 103–138). London: Edward Arnold.
Halliday, M. A. K. (1977). Text as semantic choice in social contexts. In A. van Dijk & J. Petöfi (Eds.), *Grammars and descriptions* (pp. 176–225). Berlin: de Gruyter.
Halliday, M. A. K. (1981). Text semantics and clause grammar: Some patterns of realization. In J. E. Copeland & P. W. Davis (Eds.), *The seventh LACUS Forum* (pp. 31–59). Columbia, SC: Hornbeam Press.
Halliday, M. A. K. (1982). The de-automatization of grammar: From Priestley's *An Inspector Calls*. In John Anderson (Ed.), *Language form and linguistic variation: Papers dedicated to Angus McIntosh* (Current Issues in Linguistic Theory 15) (pp. 129–159). Amsterdam: John Benjamins B.V.
Halliday, M. A. K. (1985). *A short introduction to functional grammar*. London: Edward Arnold.
Halliday, M. A. K., & Hasan, R. (1976). *Cohesion in English*. London: Longman.
Halliday, M. A. K., & Hasan, R. (1980). *Text and context: Aspects of language in a social-semiotic perspective* (Sophia Linguistica 6). Tokyo: Sophia University Graduate School of Linguistics.
Hasan, R. (1965). *The language of nine-year-old children*. Nuffield Foreign Languages Teaching Materials Project, Child Language Survey (Transcript No. 2d).
Hasan, R. (1978). Text in the systemic-functional model. In W. U. Dressler (Ed.), *Current trends in textlinguistics* (pp. 228–246). Berlin: de Gruyter.
Hasan, R. (1979). On the notion of text. In J. Petöfi (Ed.), *Text versus sentence: Basic questions of text linguistics* (pp. 369–390). Hamburg: Helmut Buske.
Hasan, R. (1983). Coherence and cohesive harmony. In J. Flood (Ed.), *Understanding reading comprehension*. Newark, DE: International Reading Association.
Hasan, R. (1984). The structure of the nursery tale: An essay in text typology. In L. Coveri (Ed.), *Linguistica testuale* (pp. 95–114). Roma: Bulzoni.
Hasan, R. (in press). Situation and the definition of conversation. In A. D. Grimshaw (Ed.), *Perspective on discourse: Multidisciplinary study of naturally occurring conversation.*
Huddleston, R. D., Hudson, R. A., Winter, E. O., & Henrici, A. (1968). *Sentence and clause in scientific English* (Report of the O.S.T.I. Programme in the Linguistic Properties of Scientific English). University College London, Communication Research Centre.

Lemke, J. L. (in press). The language of science teaching. In S. B. Heath (Ed.), *Language in the Professions*. Cambridge: Cambridge University Press.

Malcolm, K. (1983). *Communication linguistics: A sample analysis*. In J. Morreall (Ed.), *The Tenth LACUS Forum*. Columbia, SC: Hornbeam Press.

Mann, W. C. (1982). *Generating text: The grammar's demands* (Report No. RR-82-106). Los Angeles: Information Sciences Institute, University of Southern California.

Martin, J. R. (1980). How many speech acts? *University of East Anglia Papers in Linguistics, 14–15*, 52–77.

Martin, J. R. (1983a). The development of register. In R. O. Freedle & J. Fine (Eds.), *Developmental issues in discourse* (pp. 1–39). Norwood, NJ: Ablex.

Martin, J. R. (1983b). CONJUNCTION: The logic of English text. In J. Petöfi (Ed.), *Micro and Macro Connexity of Texts* (pp. 1–72). Hamburg: Helmut Buske.

Martin, J. R. (1984). Process and text: Two aspects of human semiosis. In J. D. Benson & W. S. Greaves (Eds.), *Systemic perspectives on discourse: Selected theoretical papers from the Ninth International Systemic Workshop*. Norwood, NJ: Ablex.

Martin, J. R., & Rothery, J. (1980–1981). *Writing project: Report 1980, 1981* (Working Papers in Linguistics Nos. 1 & 2). Sydney: Linguistics Department, University of Sydney.

Martin, J. R., & Rothery, J. (in preparation). What is good writing?—the school's view. In R. Hasan (Ed.), *Five to nine: Children's language from home to school*.

Matthiessen, C. M. I M. (1981). A grammar and a lexicon for a text production system. In *The Nineteenth Annual Meeting of the Association for Computational Linguistics*. Palo Alto, CA: Sperry Univac.

Rochester, S., & Martin, J. R. (1977). The art of referring: The speaker's use of noun phrases to instruct the listener. In R. O. Freedle (Ed.), *Discourse comprehension and production* (pp. 245–269). Norwood, NJ: Ablex.

Rochester, S., & Martin, J. R. (1979). *Crazy Talk: A study of the discourse of schizophrenic speakers*. New York & London: Plenum Press.

Ure, J. (1971). Lexical density and register differentiation. In G. E. Perren & J. L. M. Trim (Eds.), *Applications of linguistics: Selected papers of the Second International Congress of Applied Linguistics, Cambridge 1969* (pp. 443–452). Cambridge: Cambridge University Press.

Ure, J. (in press). *Patterns and Meanings: An introduction to systemic grammar and its application to the description of registers in contemporary English*. London: Allen & Unwin.

Ventola, E. (1979). The structure of casual conversation in English. *Journal of Pragmatics, 3*, 267–298.

Ventola, E. (1983). Interactive play of signalling discourse element boundaries in service encounters. *Grazer Linguistische Studien, 20*, 171–192.

CHAPTER 4

Phonology: Intonation in Discourse

David Brazil

THE AREA DEFINED

It is customary to make a distinction in linguistics between segmental and suprasegmental phonology. Thus any vocalization of the word "man" can be represented as a concatenation of three segments but also as the carrier of some other feature, say a rising or a falling pitch, that can best be described as a property of the whole word. The peculiar significance of phonological matters for an understanding of discourse organization can best be appreciated by making a somewhat different distinction, that between word-level phonology on one hand and discourse phonology on the other.

Word-level phonology takes as its field of investigation the way sound patterns define particular words. When we say that *man* is realized by the segments /m/, /a/, and /n/, we are making perhaps the most self-evident statement about its phonology. If the word has more than one syllable—as, for instance, *manage*—we can say additionally that there is a difference between the two syllables not adequately accounted for by describing the segments, a difference most commonly spoken of as the presence of greater stress in the first syllable than in the second. It is the defining feature of word-level phenomena that they are determined once for all by the conventions of whatever dialect the speaker uses. In the act of selecting from the lexicon, the speaker commits himself to certain aspects of its realization: He cannot substitute any other segment for /m/ and still be saying *man* or reverse the stress pattern of *manage* and still be speaking any recognized dialect of English. Since word-level features are inherent in the word, the speaker cannot exploit them in a meaningful way. If meaning is regarded as the consequence of choice,

HANDBOOK OF DISCOURSE ANALYSIS, Vol. 2
Dimensions of Discourse

Copyright © 1985 by Academic Press London.
All rights of reproduction in any form reserved.
ISBN 0-12-712002-5

then meaning accrues only to the choice of the word with all its phonological appurtenances attached. The study of word-level phonology belongs to general linguistics and is referred to here only to make the distinction between it and discourse phonology.

Discourse phonology is concerned with features over which the speaker does have independent control, features that are the consequence of separate—and therefore separately meaningful—choices. In the sentence *I can do it,* one feature that can evidently be varied without disturbing the acceptable realization of any of the words is the vowel in *can.* With /kən/, the sentence might be a response to "We need someone to fetch the beer." With /kan/, it might be a response to "Why can't you do it?" The vowel alternation is, of course, only one of the ways in which the two responses would be differentiated phonetically. It is not, as a matter of fact, a way that will receive any more treatment in this chapter. Pointing it out here simply makes clear, in a fairly nontechnical way, that a speaker may act within the constraints imposed by word phonology and still make further decisions that make their own contribution to the discourse value of the utterance.

The notion of independent choice needs further elaboration. It may appear that, in the examples cited, the speaker must necessarily match his utterance to the preceding one. A lengthy exposition was avoided by representing the utterance as meshing with a preexistent set of discourse conditions. Most utterances, however, do not follow upon explicit questions that make relevant aspects of the discourse conditions transparently obvious. The more general case is one in which the speaker makes clear what he is taking the discourse conditions to be. Although speakers and hearers normally cooperate, it is the way each utterance makes a presumptive projection of what these conditions are that has to be attended to when considering the communicative significance of features dealt with here.

THE TONE UNIT

The task of making a mental separation between those phonological features that are an inherent property of the word and those that affect its discourse value is complicated somewhat by the fact that when words are spoken aloud they already have features that indicate their status as constituents of a discourse. The practice of speaking of a number of degrees of stress, which has long been widespread in linguistics, tends to obscure this fundamental fact. Dictionaries and grammars say of words like *suggest, safely,* and *preceding* that they have primary stress in *-gest, safe-,* and *-ced-.* For present purposes, it is better to regard the phenomenon in question as a feature of discourse phonology that just happens—because the word is quoted in isolation—to be associated with a word. The same pattern is often associated with phrases:

sug¹gest	*¹safe ly*	*pre¹ceding*
you¹jest	*¹save me*	*he's ¹leading*

It is one of two patterns that are of special interest.

The second is also exemplified in the citation forms of words. The dictionary representations of the following have secondary stress in a syllable preceding the one that carries primary stress:

²phono¹logical	*²separ¹ation*	*²differ¹entiated*

Phrases that exhibit a similar pattern are

²Joan is ¹logical	*²see the ¹nation*	*²this is ¹activated*

The two patterns exemplify what is referred to in this chapter as 'minimal' and 'extended' 'tone units'. Their occurrence in connected speech is demonstrated in the following example, which is used as a basis of discussion throughout this chapter:

(1) *// in ²order to have some ¹picture // of ²how the brain ¹works // it is ²useful to ¹think of it // as a gi ²gantic ¹government office // an enormous ¹ministry // whose ²one aim and ¹object // is to preserve in¹tact // the ²country for which it is res ¹ponsible //*

In the recorded data of which this is a transcription—it is the careful reading of printed matter—there are clearly identifiable pauses at the points marked //. This is not, however, a defining criterion of the tone unit. The features that have been specified are regarded as sufficient reason for recognizing a meaningfully separate unit whether there are phonetic reasons for saying there is a break or not.

One advantage of beginning with the citation forms of words and of seeing the tone unit as a possible expansion of the two basic forms they take is that the ability to identify primary and secondary stress can be assumed to be part of the untrained competence of the language user: No special phonetic expertize is presupposed by dictionary entries. What is useful for expository purposes, might, however, be misleading in an examination of the communicative value of the phenomena. For this latter purpose, it is necessary to recognize both a functional similarity and a functional dissimilarity between what have been referred to as two kinds of stress and at the same time to show that they are not part of word specification. The similarity is acknowledged by using the term 'prominent syllable' for the location of both kinds of stress. The final prominent syllable in the tone unit is also a 'tonic syllable.' In transcriptions, prominent syllables have upper case type and tonic syllables are bold. Minimal and extended tone units are thus transcribed as

// to preserve inTACT //
// in ORder to have some PICture //

Experimentation has shown that what hearers perceive as prominence is a complex acoustic variable in which loudness, pitch, and duration can play parts of differing significance. In the present enterprise of seeking to capture and characterize a set of meaningful oppositions, there is no alternative to speaking of the physical correlates of this and other categories in a rather loose way. In practice, perhaps the most important thing is to distinguish prominence from word stress. The difference is best appreciated by considering cases like

(2)   a. // *SUperCILious* //
      b. // *a SUpercilious MANner* //
      c. // *his MANner was superCILious* //
      d. // *VERy supercilious inDEED* //

In the citation form (a) both *su-* and *-cil-* have prominence as well as word stress. In (b) and (c), they both retain word stress but only one has prominence (which one is determined automatically on the basis of whether it is the first or last prominent syllable in the tone unit). In (d), they both have word stress only. (It is the practice of referring to cases like the last as instances of tertiary stress that particularly encourages the mental conflation of phenomena that need to be kept separate.)

The tonic syllable is distinguished by being the location of a speaker choice that has been variously spoken of as a 'pitch movement,' 'glide,' 'nucleus,' or 'tone.' The last-mentioned term is adopted here. Once more, we have to say that the precise physical correlates of each of the tones have yet to be investigated. An adequate working characterization describes the five tones as a 'fall,' a 'rise,' a 'fall–rise,' a 'rise–fall,' and a 'level' tone, the movement always starting in the tonic syllable and continuing to the end of the tone unit. Instrumental analysis provides a characterization in terms of fundamental frequency somewhat as in the diagrams on page 61.

Dialectal and many other factors can result in modification of this pattern and no doubt affect perceptually important variation on the other parameters of loudness and duration. It is essential to keep in mind that the tones—and indeed all the phonological categories referred to here—realize meaning oppositions in the language system, and it is the stability of these oppositions rather than of their exact acoustic realizations that has to be assumed.

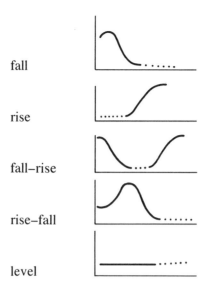

fall

rise

fall–rise

rise–fall

level

The description of the tone unit presented in outline attributes two kinds of meaningful choice to the speaker: He must decide about the distribution of prominence (a decision that has to be taken at least with respect to each word) and he has to make a once-for-all choice of tone for each tone unit.

PROMINENCE AND SENSE SELECTION

The significance of assigning or not assigning prominence to a particular syllable can be appreciated by comparing the tone unit

(3)   a. // of HOW the brain WORKS //

with an alternative version that might well have taken its place

b. // of HOW the BRAIN works //

The first version projects an assumption that 'the brain' is already established as a topic of interest: It is 'how this-thing-we-are-concerned-with works'' that the speaker proposes to enlarge upon. The second projects a different assumption: That it is the working of things—possibly human organs—that is already engaging his listener's interest, and it is the working of the brain rather than any other organ that he proposes to focus upon. Note the importance of the concept of 'projection' in all this. For the speaker, the reason for choosing one way or the other will almost certainly be attributable to earlier events. In reality, this sentence opened a talk in a series in which each lecture was concerned with some aspect of the brain. Given the distribution of prominence proposed for the alternative version, it might have been part of a series devoted to the functioning of various organs in the body. But the meaning of the distribution of prominence does not depend on either of these circumstances existing or being known to exist. It is fully accounted for by saying that each version projects its own assumptions about what the prevailing discourse conditions are.

Spoken discourse occurs in real time, and discourse conditions change from moment to moment. Observations made in the last paragraph can be given greater generality if the here-and-now circumstances in which *brain* does or does not have prominence are examined systematically. If the fragment of speech is considered as a left-to-right sequence of elements, then it can be seen that the language system allows selection from a very large set of words at the slot filled by *brain*:

$$
\textit{of how the}\ \left|\begin{array}{l}\textit{brain}\\ \textit{heart}\\ \textit{engine}\\ \text{etc.}\end{array}\right|\ \textit{works}
$$

In virtually any discourse, many members of the set would not be possible options, but the situation of most immediate interest is that in which the discourse conditions reduce the possibilities to one. The set of possibilities that the language system makes available will be referred to as the 'general paradigm' to distinguish it from the set that the here-and-now circumstances actually justify, the 'existential paradigm.' It can then be said that by assigning no prominent syllable to a word, the speaker projects discourse conditions in which there is no alternative in the existential paradigm. More briefly, the word is presented as being nonselective.

The key concept of 'selection' can be elaborated in a number of ways by examining the treatment of specific words in the transcribed sentence.

In some places, there is no alternative to the word used, even in the general paradigm. The operation of the language system alone is enough to preclude the possibility of anything but *in* and *to* occupying the first and third slots in *in order to have*. Since no normal discourse conditions could be contrived in which either of these would be selective, it is virtually certain that they will never be prominent.

In *whose one aim and object*, nonprominent *aim* projects the expectation that, in the context of the idiomatic frame *one ——— and object, aim* will be regarded as the only word that could fill the vacant slot. Note that if aims and objects were conceived of as being existentially differentiated—as in another context they might be—they could be presented as independently selecting in their own paradigm; thus,

(4)   // whose *AIM* and *OBject* are //

In *is to preserve intact,* the notion of preservation is largely subsumed by *intact.* It would be difficult to substitute a verb that was semantically incompatible with *preserve* and still be left with a sensible combination. To introduce the idea of compatibility is, however, to modify the concept of selection in an important way. There certainly do seem to be verbs that could replace *preserve,* most obviously *keep.* If the discourse conditions are such that both *preserve* and *keep* are nonselective, it follows that they must be existential synonyms. Similar conditions obtain in

(5)   // as a *giGANtic* *GOVernment* office//

where the substitution of nonselective *department* for nonselective *office* makes little difference to the state of understanding that is projected. It turns out that *brain* represents the rather less common case where it is proper to speak simply of word selection, because the word happens to be the unique realization of an existential sense. More often it is necessary to think in terms of sense selection and, if the absence of sense is signaled by absence of prominence, to entertain the possibility of its being realized by one of a number of existential synonyms.

In the first tone unit, *in order to have some picture, have* could be replaced by *get* and *some* by *a,* but the implication of the prominence distribution is that, in the world of understanding the hearer is invited to share, these are merely word selections whose values fall together as the same sense selection. If *some* had prominence, as for instance in

(6)   // in *ORder* to have *SOME* picture //

it would invite interpretation in a different way. There would then be projected an understanding that the choice between *some* (rough-and-ready) picture and *a* (possibly definitive) picture was an existentially significant one. And with the probable treatment of *picture* as nonselective, it would be the approximateness of the analogy that would be foregrounded.

The nonprominent treatment of *enormous* in *an enormous ministry* seems fairly predictable when the phrase is introduced as a gloss on *a gigantic government office.* The case is worth examining, however, for a number of reasons. First, since the speaker decides which words have prominence, he has the option of presenting a word as selective even if there seem to be textual reasons for thinking it is not. *Enormous* might have prominence if the speaker wanted, simply by reiterating reference to size, to insist upon it. Furthermore, any relation of synonymy between *gigantic* and *enormous* would itself be an existential relationship: That is to say, the two words are realizations of the same sense selection only in the state of speaker–hearer understanding that the former presently assumes. In another situation, where the taken-for-granted scale of magnitude was differently constituted, the two adjectives might represent different selections on that scale (consider // *it's NOT just giGANtic* // *it's eNORmous* //).

Finally, note that the general paradigm from which *enormous* is selected includes words like *efficient, impersonal, overstaffed* and very many more. An office might, in a general way, be enormous, impersonal, efficient, and overstaffed at one and the same time. Clearly, what is projected by nonprominent *enormous* is a here-and-now world in which there are no alternatives on the same sense dimension. In the specimen sentence, for instance, it seems likely that the exclusion of any adjective referring to a different size is assumed to have been negotiated, but not necessarily any adjective that does not refer to size. The "not necessarily" is crucial in the last sentence, however. The speaker may think he is justified in exploiting an ongoing understanding that largeness and efficiency, or largeness and friendliness, are incompatible attributes of ministries. Nonprominent *enormous* might then have the existential value 'not efficient' or 'not friendly' (= *impersonal*) as the case may be. Thus both synonymy and incompatibility have to be viewed as having validity in the here-and-now of the utterance and not in the abstract lexicon of the language.

A fact that has been glossed over in the foregoing is that choices in the prominence system are associated with syllables, while sense selections are normally realized by words. This simplification is possible because of the empirical fact that speakers normally distribute prominence on the assumption that indicating selection once in a word is sufficient to uniquely specify the appropriate sense. In *a gigantic government office,* there are no other words, and therefore no other senses that can result from substitution in the first and last places of *gi GAN tic;* the general paradigm provides the alternative *governing* to *government,* but even if this is a viable choice of word in the context, it realizes no different existential sense. Adequate demonstration of this particular point would require reference to a large amount of data and so cannot be attempted here. One consequence is worth remarking on: Words whose quotation forms have two prominent syllables (see above) normally have only one prominent syllable in connected discourse. With two, they are heard as quotations. Compare

(7)   a.   // *he SAID he was disap-*   =   "He said he was
             POINTed //   disappointed"

b. *// he said he was DISap-*   =   "He said he was
    POINTed //   'disappointed' "

THE TONIC SEGMENT

Selective value attaches to each and every occurrence of a prominent
syllable, in the manner just described. Not all the significance of prominence
can be accounted for on a syllable-by-syllable basis, however. In addition,
prominence serves to delimit the stretch of speech to which other meaning
increments are attached. In extended tone units there is a stretch that
begins with the first prominent syllable and ends with the last, to which
the term 'tonic segment' will be applied:

$$in \left| \begin{array}{l} ORder\ to\ have\ some\ PIC \\ HOW\ the\ brain\ WORKS \end{array} \right| ture$$
$$of$$
$$\longleftarrow \text{tonic segment} \longrightarrow$$

In minimal tone units, the tonic segment is coterminous with the single
prominent syllable:

$$to\ preserve\ in \left| TACT \right|$$
$$an\ enormous \left| MIN \right| stry$$

It is to the tonic segment that attention has to be given in ascribing
communicative value to the choice of tone. In the case of the extended
tone unit, this segment can usefully be thought of as constituting a larger
sense unit to which values derived from the tone system attach.

PROCLAIMING AND REFERRING TONES

The central opposition in the part of the meaning system realized by
tone is that associated with end-falling tones on the one hand and end-
rising tones on the other. There are alternative versions of each—the
fall and rise-fall are both end-falling and the rise and fall-rise are both
end-rising. Although these alternatives are themselves systematically opposed to each other and thus carriers of a further meaning distinction,
present purposes are best served by disregarding that distinction and
focusing upon the binary opposition. Since the fall and the fall-rise occur
more frequently as realizations of their respective terms in the system,
these are assumed in what follows.

In the sample sentence examined earlier, there is an end-falling tone
in the two tone units marked ↪, and an end-rising tone in those preceding
them:

(8)   // in ORder to have some PICture // of HOW the brain WORKS
       // it is USEful to THINK of it // as a giGANtic GOVernment
       office // an enormous MINistry //

A paraphrase that makes explicit the significance of this set of choices
might be "If you want to know what it is useful to think of in order to
have some picture of how the brain works, well (I suggest) a gigantic
government office, that is to say an enormous ministry." What this makes
clear is that the first three tone units do no more than articulate an
assumption the speaker makes about the present state of understanding
he has with his hearer: "Assuming this is what you want, well. . ."
Tones in tonic segments that have this value are "referring" tones, the
term serving as a reminder that the content makes reference to what is
taken to be common ground. The fall in *a gigantic government office*
marks its content as something the hearer is told. It will be labelled
"proclaiming" tone. One way of conceptualizing the distinction between
the two tone types is to say that matter associated with a referring tone
proposes no modification to the hearer's here-and-now world, invoking
only background with respect to which speaker and hearer are already
matched. By selecting proclaiming tone, on the other hand, the speaker
projects an assumption that the matter is not yet accommodated in the
hearer's world.

The importance of continuing to think in terms of projection rather
than of objectively verifiable circumstance is underlined by the treatment
of *an enormous ministry*. Dispassionate assessment of the situation might
lead to the conclusion that, once someone had been told that "a gigantic
government office" was a useful analogy, the fact that *an enormous
ministry* was also one would be self-evident, and therefore likely to be
presented as common ground. The assumption underlying the practice
of glossing is, however, that the equivalence of the two formulations
may not be self-evident. It is a here-and-now decision on the part of the
speaker that *an enormous ministry* should be presented as potentially
world-changing that leads to the allocation of a proclaiming tone.

Tone choices in the continuation are

(9)   // whose ONE aim and OBject // is to preserve inTACT // the
       COUNtry for which it is resPONsible //

It is clear that the notions of 'preservation' and 'responsibility' are integral
to the analogy the speaker proposes and therefore predictably have proclaiming tones. Allocation of a referring tone to *whose one aim and
object* seems to be the result of a speaker decision that could easily have
gone either way: He elects to attribute to his hearers the understanding

that ministries—and by implication brains—have a single raison d'etre, but could equally well have projected an assumption that they needed to be told.

Proclaimed tone units can be thought of as increments in the furtherance of whatever communicative business is currently in hand, while those with referring tones are marked as making no such progress. The following diagram of loops and lines makes this clear, each loop being an excursion into the already negotiated common ground that ends with the speaker and hearer in the same state of understanding as they were in before it was made:

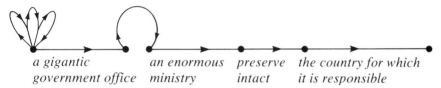

a gigantic   an enormous   preserve   the country for which
government office   ministry   intact   it is responsible

The earlier paraphrase can now be reduced to "(Given our present state of understanding, think of) a gigantic government office, an enormous ministry, that preserves intact the country for which it is responsible."

Both absence of prominence and presence of a referring tone are sometimes interpreted as indicating that something is given (as opposed to new) in a discourse. It helps to clarify the peculiar significance of each if the difference underlying this superficial similarity is demonstrated. In

(10)   // in ORder to have some **PIC**ture // of HOW the brain
          WORKS // . . .

it was pointed out that lack of prominence in *brain* projected an assumption that it was nonselective, the brain being presumed to be the already established focus of interest. Compare this with *The various organs of the human body function in quite different ways. In order to have some picture of how the brains works, it is* . . . Here, *brain* has been anticipated in *organs*. It therefore refers to common ground, but it obviously does so selectively: the existential paradigm probably comprises all the bodily organs. We can expect that *brain* will be prominent but will be part of a tonic segment that has a referring tone, perhaps as in

(11)   // of HOW the **BRÃIN** works //

Many choices in the proclaiming–referring system can be related to events in the co-text in the way that has just been demonstrated. Many others illustrate how the speaker can presume understandings that have their origin outside the present conversation, including some whose currency can be taken to be culturewide. The most general characterization of the system is not, in fact, in textual terms but in social terms. In making the referring choice, the speaker invokes the togetherness aspect of the conversational relationship, speaking as it were for the "we" who are the participants. In making the proclaiming choice, he adopts the stance of the "I" who is set over against the "you" in a situation of unassimilated viewpoints. In some cases, the choice of either tone can be associated with a word that appears not to realize a sense selection:

// PERsonǎlly // I'd RATHer not TRY //

The choice has then to be interpreted as an underlining—for broadly social reasons—of one or an other aspect of the relationship. Its effect in an example like this, for instance, would be to insinuate a generalized element of intimacy as a prelude to the following assertion.

ORIENTATION

Consideration of the proclaiming–referring system probably provides the best background against which to discuss briefly the significance of speaker orientation for discourse phonology. The speaker has been represented as making moment-by-moment assumptions about how parts of his discourse relate to a putative state of conversational play. This presupposes a putatively identified hearer (if not an actual one) whose capacity and willingness to assimilate his viewpoint to that of the speaker can be assessed. We can speak of "direct orientation" towards a hearer. Language may, however, be spoken simply as language sample. One can, for instance, vocalize a sample as a "well-formed English sentence" or even as an "ill-formed" one without having any regard to its significance as part of a communicative (and hearer-sensitive) event. When the speaker's set is towards the language sample in this way rather than to an assumed recipient of a message, it is useful to speak of "oblique orientation."

Two particular features serve as indicators of oblique orientation.

1. Allocation of extra-prominent syllables in the tonic segment:

// in ORder to have SOME PICture of HOW the BRAIN WORKS // . . .

> The occurrence of two prominent syllables in the citation form of some words (see p. 59 above) is a special case of this.

2. Choice of level tone:

// in ORder to have some PICture // of HOW the BRAIN // WORKS //

Some ritualized, precoded language events are marked by the features of oblique orientation thoughout. Sometimes, the nature of a precoded sequence inserted in a predominantly direct discourse (such as a lecture or other monologue type) is acknowledged in this way. In most kinds of spontaneous discourse, on-line changes to oblique orientation can be attributed to a particular cause. Hesitations, occasioned by what may be informally spoken of as the need for planning time, often occur in close association with a level tone. If the lecture were not scripted, we might expect one of the following:

(13)   a.   // it is USEful to THINK of it // AS . . . // a giGANtic
             GOVernment office //
        b.   // as a giGANtic . . . // GOVernment office //

The momentary disengagement from interaction with a hearer could be attributed to the fact that the lecturer was searching for an appropriate analogy.

THE PITCH SEQUENCE

Prominent syllables in direct discourse are the place of operation of two other speaker options whose communicative values have to be described independently of the referring–proclaiming system, although they also attach to the whole of the tonic segment in which the choice is made. They are associated for diagnostic purposes with relative pitch level (and thus distinguished from tone choices that are characterized in terms of pitch movement). In an extended tonic segment, pitch level at the first prominent syllable realizes a choice of key; that at the last prominent syllable (the tonic syllable) realizes a choice of termination. Both key and termination constitute a three-term system: high, mid, and low. In a minimal tonic segment, both choices are necessarily made in the same syllable, so that high key automatically involves high termination, and so on.

In most discourse of any length, key and termination work together to define a unit of greater extent than a tone unit: the 'pitch sequence'. An example is

(14)// inORder to have some PICture // of HOW the brain WORKS // it is USEful to THINK of it // as a giGANtic GOVernment office // an enorMOUS MINistry // whose ONE aim and OBject // is to preserve inTACT // the COUNtry for which it is resPONsible //

In this transcription, displacement above or below the mid line indicates merely the choice of key and termination; it has no other phonetic implications. All the relevant information is retained in a reduced form of the transcription:

(15)   // in ᴼᴿ PIC // HOW WORKS // USE THINK // GAN GOV //
        MIN // ONE OB // TACT // COUN ₚₒₙ //

A pitch sequence is defined as any stretch of speech ending in low termination (here realized in -*pon*-) and having no occurrence of low termination within it. This example begins with high key and has a mid choice at all intermediate occurrences of both systems. Though this provides a convenient baseline for exposition, neither of the latter are necessary conditions.

This pitch sequence is coterminous with a grammatical sentence, and in much monologue there is a marked tendency for this to be the case. There is no deterministic relationship between the two modes of organization, however. A sentence may comprise two or more pitch sequences, and a pitch sequence may comprise two or more sentences. In two-party discourse, the pitch sequence may span a number of consecutive utterances or there may be several pitch sequences within the utterance. To begin to explore the effects of differential segmenting on the two levels would require a fairly elaborate examination of discourse structure. To appreciate that it is significant it is necessary to do no more than consider the possibility of a pitch-sequence boundary after

(16)   // in *ORder to have some* PICture // *of* HOW *the brain*
        WORKS //

The clause is now heard as setting up a topic for subsequent discussion. In spite of its grammar, the introductory sequence has a kind of discreteness not unlike

(17)   // LET'S *try to* PICture // HOW *the brain* WORKS //

A little more is said about the implication of pitch sequence boundaries below.

Quite apart from bringing about a variation in the grammatical constituency of pitch sequences, key and termination choices affect communicative value in two other ways.

Intrasequential Choices

Inside the pitch sequence, either key or termination, or both, may depart from the pattern of repeated mid choices represented in the transcript.

Key

An internal choice of high key gives contrastive value to the tonic segment. The special way in which this term is used can be stated as follows: The assumption projected is that the sense selected is one side of a binary opposition, the other side of which is expressly excluded. Often the implication is that the side chosen is contrary to some ongoing expectation. A small alteration in the model sentence produces

(18)   // in $^{ORder \ to \ have \ some}$ **PIC**ture // of HOW the brain **WORKS**
         // it is $^{USEful \ to \ think \ of \ it}$ // as a . . .

Here, *useful* is not merely selective; it carries some such additional implication as "It is not useless (as might be supposed)." If selectivity is thought of as the process of choosing sense value X from the existential paradigm, then the contrastive value deriving from internal high key modifies this to choosing X by explicitly rejecting Y, the value of the excluded member being assumed to be known to the hearer: being part, that is to say, of the understanding that the speaker takes for granted.

The opposition 'X versus Y' may be a notionally symmetrical one, like 'useful' versus 'useless', or it may be the result of the speaker projecting upon the existential paradigm a distinction between one member on the one hand and all other possible members on the other. Given appropriate discourse conditions,

(19)   // a gi^{GANtic} // GOVernment office //

might have the implication "Of all the ways the government office could be described, this is the only one that fits the facts."

Low key gives equative value to its tonic segment. In

(20)   // a giGANtic GOVernment office // an enormous MINistry //

the matter of the first tone unit and that of the subsequent gloss are presented simply as two successive world-changing increments. With a low-key choice in *min-*, the second segment carries the additional projection that what is here proclaimed is existentially equivalent to—and agreed to be equivalent to—the first.

The use of key is of special interest when the choice is associated with a minimal response *yes* (or any synonym for *yes*). Contrastivity now carries the explicit value 'not *no*', a value that can be captured approximately by speaking of an "adjudicating *yes*." By producing high-key *yes* after, say,

(21)   // perHAPS he'll come LATer //

the speaker assumes the role of the one who knows, and whose knowledge enables him to decide whether he'll come later or not. This can be compared with the value of a mid-key concurring *yes*. The most likely interpretation of this, if it occurred in the same context, would be "(yes) perhaps he will," the speaker being understood to do no more than indicate his willingness to go along with the other's comment. In such circumstances the opposition between *yes* and *no* is not an issue. Low-key *yes* also occurs, but when it does so its function can best be described as bringing about pitch-sequence closure.

Termination

Distinguishing between adjudicating and concurring *yes* provides a way in to establishing the communicative value of termination. The central point is illustrated in the following:

	Speaker A	Speaker B
(22) a.	// perHAPS he'll come LATer //	// YES //
b.	// perHAPS he'll come LATer //	// YES //

In (a), the mid termination at the end of speaker A's contribution anticipates—and elicits—a mid-key (concurring) response. We can say that by making this choice, speaker A projects an expectation that speaker B will concur. In (b), the expectation projected is that speaker B will adjudicate, an expectation that writing conventions would be likely to indicate thus: "Perhaps he'll come later?" (Will he, or will he not?).

To broaden this account so that it will apply to all cases requires elaboration of the distinction that has been made between adjudicating and concurring. Some clarification is achieved if the second speaker is thought of as being invited either to make an active response (of which adjudicating is one possible form) or a passive response (to which category concurring belongs). It is possible, however, to avoid such conceptual problems once the patterns represented by (a) and (b) have been recognized, by saying simply that high termination anticipates a response beginning with high key and mid termination anticipates one beginning with mid key.

Two further points need to be made here. The first is that expectations are not necessarily fulfilled. An anticipation of a particular kind of response that is built into the discourse value of A's utterance leaves B with the option of matching or not matching key to termination. If he declines to do so, however, he is heard as taking a conspicuously independent or nonacquiescent line. The other point is that high and mid termination have comparable values even when they do not occur at the end of an utterance. Speakers can be said to invite active and passive responses in much the same way in the course of an extended monologue, as careful attention to any orator's performance will confirm. Some of these responses have audible or visible realizations as sotto voce *yes* or *mm,* as headnods or other nonvocal behavior.

A new interpretation can now be given to the low-termination choice that regularly closes the pitch sequence. While high and mid terminations set up expectations of particular kinds, low termination carries no assumption that the other participant will react in one way rather than another. The total range of possibilities at utterance end can be summarized as follows.

High termination   expects high key
Mid termination   expects mid key
$$\text{Low termination}\quad\text{permits}\begin{bmatrix}\text{high key}\\\text{mid key}\\\text{low key}\end{bmatrix}$$

The formal significance of pitch sequence closure is summed up as follows: It is the point at which a set of constraints inherent in the organization of the unit come to an end. In this respect, it resembles the close of the grammatical sentence, though the constraints in question are of very different kinds. The fact that moments of maximum relaxation in the two different kinds of organization tend to come together but do not necessarily do so is of considerable interest to anyone concerned with how the two units function, separately and in cooperation, in discourse structure.

Intersequential Choices

It follows from what was said in the last paragraph that a speaker beginning a new pitch sequence may open it with high, mid, or low key. The significance of this choice is not explained by what was said about key choices within the pitch sequence; it is, nevertheless, possible to characterize it in roughly comparable terms. An example of sequence-initial low key might be:

(23)   // the COUNtry for which it is res*PONsible* // *the* BRAIN *and*
        the office are SIM*ilar* // *in* MANy WAYS //

A relationship similar to that which was described as equative exists here as well. The fact that brain and office have noteworthy similarities can legitimately be presented as a restatement, in existentially equivalent terms, of the sense of the preceding pitch sequence. But note that it is the second pitch sequence as a whole that is now presented as an existential synonym for the preceding sequence as a whole. The step up to mid termination in // . . . SIMilar // opens up the possibility of indefinite prolongation of the second sequence but does not affect the truth of this statement. In practice, most low opening sequences seem to comprise not more than two tone units.

Mid key opening is exemplified by:

(24)   // the COUNtry for which it is res_{PON}sible
        // A VAST NUMber // of TELephone lines //
        bring inforMAtion to the office //

The purpose of the new sequence here is to expand upon the assertion made in the first: The speaker sets out to enlarge upon the analogy he has just proposed. In this kind of intersequential relationship, too, it is the sense of the whole of the second that expands the sense of the first.

The third possibility, the high-key opening, is best thought of as marking maximal disjunction between sequences. Negatively, it can be said that the new pitch sequence is presented as neither paraphrasing, nor expanding upon, the content of the previous one. No other relationship is implied than that this sequence comes after—and is therefore to be heard in the light of—its predecessor. Such a relationship might be exemplifed by

(25)   // the COUNtry for which it is res_{PON}sible
        // be^{FORE} deVELoping this analogy however // I WISH
        to conSIDer //

THE CONTEXT OF INTERACTION

It is not possible in this brief exposition to bring out the consequences of such an approach to discourse phonology for a general theory of interactive discourse. Two general points ought, however, to be made explicitly, since it is easy to overlook them in preoccupation with the detailed application of analytical categories. The first is that these categories are necessarily conceived as meaning oppositions inherent in the language system and that lack of precise statement about phonetic exponence is therefore to be expected. It must be assumed from the start that there will be as much variation in the possible physical correlates of a given speaker choice here as there is in the case of word-defining segments. Second, the notion of existential value, touched upon in the paragraphs on prominence, must be applied to the whole of the meaning system. The distinguishing fact about discourse phonology is that it consistently relates to a projected state of speaker–hearer convergence, as it exists in the here-and-now of the utterance, the context of interaction.

REFERENCES

Brazil, D. C. (1975). *Discourse intonation I* (Discourse Analysis Monographs No. 1). Birmingham: University of Birmingham English Language Research.
Brazil, D. C. (1978). *Discourse intonation II* (Discourse Analysis Monographs No. 2). Birmingham: University of Birmingham English Language Research.
Brazil, D. C., Coulthard, M., and Johns, C. (1981). *Discourse intonation and language teaching*. London: Longman.

CHAPTER 5

Morphology

Wolfgang U. Dressler

INTRODUCTION

Morphology, the study of the smallest meaningful forms (units) of
language, plays only a subordinate role in production and reception of
texts, and therefore its role is in general completely overlooked in textual
and discourse analysis. Morphology can be divided into inflectional morphology (the declension or conjugation of words as in *dog-s, work-ed*
and word formation (the formation of complex words from simpler ones)
with its subparts derivational morphology (usually by affixation as in
affix-ation) and compounding (word combination as in *discourse analysis*).

INFLECTIONAL MORPHOLOGY

. The use of inflectional forms is governed by the syntactic structures
in which the inflected words occur, and this holds for textual structures
as well (Zubin, 1979; Halliday, Chap. 3, this Volume). Such inflectional
forms may also have specific pragmatic functions (Gazdar, 1980). And
they can mark the beginning or end of episodes or paragraphs (Beaugrande
& Dressler, 1981; pp. 69–70). But inflectional morphology can produce
textual effects of its own in cases of inflectional variation in anaphoric
lexical recurrence, for example, in the Latin sequence:

(1)   *Regem occid**unt**. Occis**um** sepeliunt.*
       'They killed the king. The killed (king) they bury.'

Resumptive participles and gerunds of this type are also frequent in
Sanskrit and Saramaccan (Grimes & Glock, 1970).
    In some languages prefix recurrence can be accompanied by lexical

77

HANDBOOK OF DISCOURSE ANALYSIS, Vol. 2
Dimensions of Discourse
Copyright © 1985 by Academic Press London.
All rights of reproduction in any form reserved.
ISBN 0-12-712002-5

deletion. Several Slavic languages and Hungarian can corefer anaphorically to an inflectional prefix-verb in the question with the prefix alone in the answer (Isačenko, 1965), for example, the Hungarian perfective pre-verb *meg* in:

(2)   Q: *Meg-nezted a könyvet?*
          'Did you see the book?'
       A: *Meg.*
          'Yes'

In processing, the hearer or reader may use inflectional morphemes— similar to other grammatical forms—as strategic cues for interpretation (Marslen-Wilson, Levy, & Komisarjevsky-Tyler, 1982).

WORD FORMATION

Cohesion

Morphological Recurrence

Recurrence is the simplest means of achieving cohesion of neighboring sentences. One type is syntactic recurrence, that is, repetition of syntactic constructions (see Halliday, Chap. 3, this Volume); in a subtype of syntactic recurrence derivational affixes are repeated as well. Lev (1978, pp. 112–113) cites German texts where many adjacent sentences and clauses contain verbal adjectives ending in *-bar* (English *-able*), for example, in an advertisement: *bearbeitbar—prägbar—aushärtbar* 'workable—embossable—hardenable'.

Partial Lexical Recurrence: Anaphora

Lexical recurrence, that is, repetition of lexical items, not only contributes to cohesion but also minimizes effort in production and facilitates reception, since identification of coreferents is most transparent if identical concepts referred to are signaled by identical lexical items. This has been demonstrated by Merlini and Schianchi (1978) in the following sentence sequence:

(3)   *The two developing countries have thus decided to introduce containers. This involves complete reorganization of ports and terminals.*

Anaphoric *This* is ambiguous, whereas its replacement by *Their decision* would exclude the possible interpretation of *This* as meaning 'The introduction of containers.' Both *decision* and *introduction* are instances of anaphora by means of partial lexical recurrence where the lexical root or stem is repeated but a different derivationally related word is used: *decided—decision, introduce—introduction.*[1] An example with an agent noun from P. D. Wolfkind's *Zwischen Böschung und Bach* is

(4)   *. . . mich vielleicht dem Tod zutreiben wollte. Ein Zutreiber des Todes*
         '. . . maybe wanted to push me to death. A pusher of death.'

Partial Lexical Recurrence: Variation

Partial lexical recurrence instead of total lexical recurrence (that is, identical recurrence of whole words) is a means of variation that avoids repetitiveness, a property of style proscribed in many school systems. In sentence chains, where the same concept must be referred to many times, the introduction of morphological derivatives is a means of variation (Wildgen, 1980, p. 6). This may conduce the text producer to form neologisms, particularly ad hoc compounds in languages with productive compound formation such as English, Russian, and German. A short text cited by Wildgen (1980, 1981) from the German news magazine *Der Spiegel* contains a chain of 13 coreferent noun phrases (in addition to coreferent pronouns): (1) *das Wahl-Schiedsgericht* 'the court of arbitration for the election', (2) *dieser Spruchkörper* 'this verdict body', (3) *der Fünfer-Rat* 'the council of five (arbiters)', (4) *das Schiedsgericht* 'the court of arbitration', (5) *das Gremium* 'the assembly', (6) *die Schieds-kommission* 'the commission of arbitration', (7) *die Schiedsstelle* 'the authority of arbitration', (8) *die Kommission* 'the commission', (9) *die Schiedsstelle*, (10) *ein Gremium*, (11) *die Sommer-Instanz* 'the summer-court', (12) *das Kunst-Gremium* 'the assembly (headed by Mr.) Kunst', (13) *die Schiedsstelle*.

In this text *Gremium* occurs twice (5, 10), and *Kommission* (8) occurs once; both are non-compounded nouns. Eight compounds, of which only one recurs in an identical form (7, 9, 13), appear, but this lexical recurrence is always interrupted by one or more different coreferent nouns. With the help of such anaphoric variation the text producer can stress different aspects of the designated object and enrich its conceptual properties. Of the compounds used in the text cited, two are neologistic in the sense of marginally stored new items that one would not find in any dictionary

---

[1] More on this type in Beaugrande & Dressler, 1981, pp. 56–57; Dressler, 1982; Herbermann, 1981, pp. 294 ff. (criticized by Wildgen, 1981); Merlini & Schianchi, 1978; Panagl, 1982; Vladovaja, 1978.

(6, 7, 9, 13), whereas four have been created by the text producer for this text (1, 3, 11, 12).

Wildgen (1980, p. 6) has shown an inverse relationship between the frequency of repetitions of coreferent nouns and the frequency of ad hoc compounds in German newspapers.

Elliptic Coreference: Word Formation as a Device for Condensation in Coreference

Word formation (both derivation and compounding) is a technique of identifying or labeling concepts (Seiler, 1975). Thus it can serve, as we have seen, the textual needs of coreference (Dressler, 1982). Complex words can fulfill this function more succinctly than more descriptive techniques such as multilexical phrases, clauses, or sentences (Seiler, 1975). In other words, as has been remarked by most authors on the subject, word formation is a means of condensing the expression of content. It is thus an economical means of resumption, that is, of elliptic coreference such as pronouns or substitution by zero (see Halliday, Chap. 3, this Volume). This reduction of information renders the meaning of complex word forms ambiguous or vague unless their meaning is fully lexicalized or supplied by the extralinguistic context or by the linguistic cotext.

Elliptic Coreference: Derivational Ellipsis in Anaphora

The examples given above show the compacting of redundant information, that is, material known from the previous cotext in cases of anaphora. This condensation is not only economical in production but also respects the needs of the receiver by following Grice's (1975) maxim of quantity: "Make your contribution as informative as (but not more informative than) is required."

A relevant instance of condensation by means of a prefix derivation is to be found in Carlo Emilio Gadda's *Prima Divisione nella notte:*

(5)   *che l'aveva piantata dopo due anni per andare a combattere nel Marocco stufo di litigare con lei*
        '(her husband) who left her in the lurch in order to go fighting in Morocco, weary of quarreling with her'

This paragraph is resumed three pages later by

(6)   *nel corso dei loro litigi pre-Marocco*
        'in the course of their pre-Morocco quarrels'

Since anaphoric coreference is unambiguous here, Grice's maxim is respected.

Certain languages (see, e.g., Watkins, 1966) can delete derivational prefixes in anaphorically recurrent prefixed verbs. A Latin example is in Catullus (beginning of Carmen 62):

(7)   verse 1:   *Vesper adest: iavenes* **consurgite**. . . .
                   'Evening is here: Lads get up!'
       verse 3:   **Surgere** *iam tempus* . . .
                   'It is time to get up'

Elliptic Coreference:
Condensating Compounds

Anaphoric Transformations.[2]   In languages with productive compound formation, compounds can be used to corefer anaphorically to larger noun phrases, clauses, or sentences (Beaugrande & Dressler, 1981, pp. 56–57; Dressler, 1982; Herbermann, 1981; Lev, 1978; Vladovaja, 1978; Wildgen, 1980, 1981). If the antecedent noun phrase consists of an adjective and a simplex noun, the noun is repeated as the second part of the coreferring compound, whereas the adjective is transformed into the first part of the anaphoric compound, as in the following German example from Wildgen (1981):

(8)   *das grammatische Telefon—das Grammatiktelephon*
       'the grammatical telephone'—'the grammar telephone'

If the antecedent phrase consists of a noun with a subordinate nominal or prepositional phrase, the subordinate phrase is transformed into the first part of the compound, for example,

(9)   *cuts in education—education cuts* (Lev, 1978, p. 124)

or from E. Strittmatter's *Der Wundertäter* (Vladovaja, 1978, p. 104)

(10)   *Die Frau des Lehrers—Die Lehrersfrau*
       'The wife of the teacher—The teacher's wife'

If an antecedent noun is itself a compound, this compound is usually shortened, for example,

(11)   *the campaign against the tuition fees proposals—tuition fees campaigning* (Lev, 1978, p. 122)

---

[2] Transformation is used in the sense given by Z. S. Harris, not as a technical term of transformational generative grammar.

or from P. D. Wolfkind's *Zwischen Böschung und Bach:*

(12)   *Ein schwarzer Schutzengel. Schwarzengel.*
        'A black protector angel. Black-angel.'

A whole clause is paraphrased by an anaphoric compound in E. Strittmatter's
Die Eiskuh:

(13)   *Nur eine Jungkuh ging auf das Eis. . . . Die Eiskuh*
        'Only a baby cow went on the ice. . . . The ice cow'

and

(14)   *Immer wenn sommers die großen Regen über das Land gehen
        . . . An solchen Sommer-Regentagen.*
        'Always when in summer the big rains go over the land . . . On
        such summer raindays.'

If, in German, the antecedent compound consists of three members, the
middle member is deleted in anaphoric coreference (irrespective of the
situation of the major morphological boundary to the left or to the right
of the deleted member), as in the following examples discussed in Wildgen
(1980, 1981):

(15)   *Geldtransportauto—Geldauto*
        'money transport car—money car'
        Sportbrieftauben—Sporttauben
        'sport letter pigeons (i.e., carrier pigeons)—sport pigeons'.

Of course, more complicated sequences are also possible, such as

(16)   *die winzigen Ski-Matadore—die Ski-Winzlinge*
        'the tiny ski matadors—the ski tinies' (Wildgen, 1981).

Compare Wildgen's example of variation (p. 79).

Cataphoric Compounds.   Condensing compounds can precede their more
descriptive coreferents. Such compounds remain vague and need their
more descriptive coreferents in order to be understood by the text receiver,
that is, they are cataphoric. Therefore the distance between these cataphoric
compounds and their later explication must be quite short (Dressler,
1982; Wildgen, 1980, pp. 9–10, 1981). Many writers use this device in
titles or text initially in order to arouse interest in the text following
the title, whereas such cataphoric compounds occur very rarely in oral
(orally composed) texts, where they occur mostly in cases of unplanned
speech production difficulties (Wildgen, 1981, §5). Since existing compounds
are stored in the lexicon, that is, are lexicalized with a specific meaning

and lack the vagueness needed for cataphoric usages, such titles typically contain neologistic compounds, most of them nonce forms that do not survive their original usage in the text for which they are coined. An invention of a text-initial compound by a journalist is cited by Wildgen (1981):

(17)   *eine Christbaum-Fällaktion. . . . Der Tourist bringt seine eigene Axt mit und wählt seinen Lieblingsbaum aus.*
         'a Christmas-tree-felling activity. . . . The tourist brings his own axe and chooses his favorite tree.'

Examples of such cataphoric compounds in titles abound in literature (Beaugrande & Dressler, 1981, p. 57; Dressler, 1982). One work by the Nobel Prize winner Elias Canetti is called *Der Ohrenzeuge. 50 Charaktere (The Auricular Witness. 50 Characters).* Here the author describes 50 rather weird characters. In order to label each of these invented characters each description is preceded by a title that is usually a neologistic compound, for example, *Der Heroszupfer,* 'The hero tugger'. In the very first sentence of the text this title is explained by using both the noun *hero* and the verb *to tug:*

(18)   *Der Heroszupfer macht sich an den Denkmälern zu schaffen, und zupft Heroen an den Hosen*
         'The hero tugger potters about the monuments, and tugs heroes' trousers'

But the explanation may also consist of a total paraphrase (in one or more sentences), for example,

(19)   *Die Sultansüchtige*
         'The sultan addict' (fem.)
         Die Sultansüchtige leidet unter dem Verschwinden der Harems
         'The sultan addict suffers from the disappearance of harems'

Ad hoc compounds are also used in intermediate titles or summaries where they can serve the function of segmenting a text into smaller parts (see Wildgen, 1981).

Knowledge Frames.   As elsewhere in text linguistics (see Beaugrande & Dressler, 1981), the concept of frames and other global patterns of knowledge can be usefully applied to word compounding (Wildgen, 1980, pp. 71ff). In cases of anaphorically used word formation, the anaphoric compound or derivative corefers to a frame established in the preceding cotext. In the case of cataphoric compounds, a new frame is announced and the text receiver is eager to complete this frame starting with the fragmentary information given by the cataphoric compound. In the case of variation, different parts of the frame are referred to in succession.

Advertisements often use the strategy of building up a new frame (with positive connotations) for a new product and then labeling it with a neologistic, anaphoric compound that is intended to stick in the memory of the text receiver (so that it can be reused in later advertisements of a promotion campaign). For example, a one-page German ad[3] starts with the title *Im Ziegelhaus bleibt alles lebendig* 'In the brick house everything remains alive'. Then it praises the qualities of bricks, such as *Wärme-dämmung* 'warmth insulation' and healthy and pleasant warmth (*Wärme*), and ends with the sentence in big, boldface letters; *Ziegelwärme ist gute Wärme* 'Brick warmth is good warmth'. In isolation the nonce form *Ziegelwärme* is many-ways ambiguous (as tested by Benedikt Lutz with informants), but at the end of the advertisement the intended frame is firmly established, even if only temporarily. The anaphoric and cataphoric usage of word formation in longer texts can be fruitfully analyzed using the concepts of frames and plans.

Anaphoric Compounds In Conversation.   In conversational turn taking (see Volume 3 of this handbook), a partner may corefer anaphorically to previous utterances with a neologistic compound (or derivative) if this compound is adequate in evoking the correct knowledge frame of the conversation partner(s). From the material analyzed by Wildgen (1981, §5) I cite the following turns:

(20)   Theo: *Kannst du den Himbeergeist einschleppen?*
                 'Can you bring the raspberry liqueur?'
        Lissa: *Nein nicht den Himbeergeist, Kirschwasser*
                 'No, not the raspberry liqueur, cherry brandy'
        Theo: *den Kirschwassergeist*
                 'the cherry-brandy liqueur'

Macrostructures

Cohesion and Macrostructures

In much of his work, van Dijk (e.g., 1977, p. 6) has elaborated the notion of macrostructures as "a global level of semantic description; they define the meaning of parts of a discourse and of the whole discourse on the basis of the meanings of the individual sentences." At various

---

[3] Brought to my attention by my student Benedikt Lutz.

points of our discussion we have seen a cohesive use of word formation that affects a text as a whole: A cataphoric title refers to the macrostructure of the whole text, an anaphoric chain with varying compounds reflects the thematic structure of the text, and neologistic compounds may summarize a knowledge frame established by a text. However, word formation may contribute to determining the structure of a whole text in a more direct way.

Syntactic and Morphological Parallelism

Sometimes poems are constituted by symmetrical parallelisms throughout their texts. For example, the poem "Ahnenkult" by Bernhard (Dressler, 1981, p. 429) repeats the following structure over and over again:

(21)   *Es steigt der Steiger, Bis er nicht mehr steigt*
        'The climber climbs, until he no longer climbs'

The regular recurrence of such agent nouns ending in *-er* (many of them are neologistic) enhances the parallel structure of the text.

Similarly in M. Cvetaeva's poem "Tak vslušivajut'sja" (analyzed by Revzin, 1971), nearly all sentences start with a verb (optionally preceded by *tak* 'thus') consisting of the prefix *v,* the root, the iterative suffix, third person present (singular or plural), and reflexive enclitic. (Many of these verbs are nonce forms.)

And the constructivist poem "Four Seasons" by V. Kamenskij has the same series of inflectional and derivational forms (many nonce forms) for all seasons, for example,

(22)   *Vesna*   'Spring'
         Pesnijanka   'Woman from the song country'
         Pesnijannaja   'song-ing' (fem. nom. sg.)
         Pesnijannyh   'of the song-ing' (masc. gen. pl.)
         Pesnijan   'men from the song country' (masc. gen. pl.)

Thematic Word Families

Aphek and Tobin (1981) signal the use of the Modern Hebrew root *X–L–R* 'to return, revert, repeat, regret, reconsider, court, woo, retreat' as a leitmotif in S. Y. Agnon's short story "The Lady and the Peddler." By simply using the rich derivational possibilities of Hebrew word formation, the author achieves a macrostructural semantic coherence. Such a strategy is feasible in a Semitic language whose lexical stock consists of a limited number of roots that are the basis of large word families, derived by productive word formation.

BIBLIOGRAPHY

Aphek, E., & Tobin, Y. (1981). S. Y. Agnon: Word systems and translation. *Text, 1,* 269–277.

Beaugrande, R. de, & Dressler, W. (1981). *Introduction to text linguistics.* London: Longman.

Dressler, W. (1981). General principles of poetic license in word formation. In *Logos Semantikos, Fs. E. Coseriu II* (pp. 423–431). Berlin: de Gruyter.

Dressler, W. (1982). Zum Verhältnis von Wortbildung und Textlinguistik. In J. Petöfi (Ed.), *Text vs. sentence continued* (pp. 96–106). Hamburg: Buske.

Gazdar, G. (1980). Pragmatic constraints on linguistic production. In B. Butterworth (Ed.), *Language production I: Speech and talk* (pp. 49–68). New York: Academic Press.

Grice, P. (1975). Logic and Conversation. In P. Cole & J. Morgan (Eds.), *Syntax and semantics III: Speech acts* (pp. 41–58). New York: Academic Press.

Grimes, J. E., & Glock, N. (1970). A Saramaccan narrative pattern. *Language, 46,* 408–425.

Herbermann, C.-P. (1981). *Wort, Basis, Lexem und die Grenze zwischen Lexikon und Grammatik.* München: Fink.

Isačenko, A. V. (1965). Kontextbedingte Ellipse und Pronominalisierung im Deutschen. *Beiträge zur Sprachwissenschaft, Volkskunde und Literaturforschung. Fs. W. Steinitz* (pp. 163–174). Berlin: Akademie-Verlag.

Lev, L. S. (1978). *O vzaimnyh otnošenijah imenyh slovosočetanij v tekste. Turkulevič,* 120–127.

Marslen-Wilson, W., Levy, E., & Komisarjevsky-Tyler, L. (1982). Producing interpretable discourse: The establishment and maintenance of reference. In R. J. Jarvella & W. Klein (Eds.), *Speech, place and action* (pp. 339–378). New York: Wiley.

Merlini, L., Schianchi, A. M. (1978). Soluzioni coesive lessicali e morfosintattiche nez testo tecnico-scientifico inglese. *Studi e Ricerche della Facoltà di Economia e Commercio dell' Università di Parma 14.*

Panagl, O. (1982). Produktivität in der Wortbildung von Corpussprachen. *Folia Linguistica, 16,* 225–239.

Revzin, I. I. (1971). Grammatičeskaja pravil'nost', pöètičeskaja reč' i problema upravlenija. *Trudy po znakovym sistemam, 5,* 224–231.

Seiler, H. (1975). Die Prinzipien der deskriptiven und der etikettierenden Benennung. *Linguistic workshop, 3,* H. Seiler (Ed.), 2–57.

Šved, V. I. (1978). Tekstoobrazujuščie potencii slovoobrazovatel'nyh edinic. *Turkulevič* 109–113.

Turkulevič, T. A. (Ed.). (1978). *Lingvistika teksta i obučenie inostrannym jazykam.* Kiev: Višča Škola.

van Dijk, T. A. (1977). *Text and context.* London: Longman.

Vladovaja, E. V. (1978). Odnokornevye raznostrukturnye sinonimy kak sredstvo svjazi meždu komponentami teksta. *Turkulevič* 102–108.

Watkins, C. (1966). An Indo-European construction in Greek and Latin. *Harvard Studies in Classical Philology, 71,* 115–119.

Wildgen, W. (1980). Textuelle Bedingungen der Einführung und Verwendung Ad Hoc Gebildeter Komposita. Linguistic Agency, University of Trier, A.

Wildgen, W. (1981). Makroprozesse bei der Verwendung nominaler Ad-Hoc-Komposita im Deutschen. *Deutsche Sprache, 3,* 237–257.

Zubin, D. (1979). Discourse function of morphology: The focus system in German. In T. Givón (Ed.), *Syntax and semantics 12* (pp. 469–504). New York: Academic Press.

CHAPTER 6

Lexicon

János S. Petöfi

PRELIMINARY REMARKS

The term 'lexicon' as it is used in linguistic theory generally refers to a monolingual dictionary constructed in a particular way so that it can function as a component of a theory. We can thus speak about the lexicon component of a transformational grammar or of a Montague grammar. The structure of a lexicon understood in this way is determined by (1) the object domain to be analyzed and described by the theory that contains the lexicon as its component, (2) the goal of this analysis and description, and (3) the methodology underlying the structure and function of the theory in question.

In this chapter I am concerned with some aspects of the nature and use of a lexicon that has been conceived as a component of a theory designed to analyze and describe texts. Instead of the terms 'text' and 'disourse', I simply use the term 'text'. I stress that I do not consider textuality to be an inherent property of verbal objects. In a given context, an interpreter may consider an object to be a text independently of whether any other interpreter shares this opinion. Moreover, the same interpreter may consider a verbal object to be a text in one context while he may not consider it to be a text in some other context. Whether or not an interpreter considers a given verbal object to be a text in a given context depends, roughly speaking, on whether or not he judges the given object to be a complete functional whole in its communication context. 'Complete' and 'functional whole' are categories related primarily to the communication situation in which the given verbal object has come into being rather than to the verbal object itself.

With respect to the definition of textuality, I want to point out, without

HANDBOOK OF DISCOURSE ANALYSIS, Vol. 2
Dimensions of Discourse

Copyright © 1985 by Academic Press London.
All rights of reproduction in any form reserved.
ISBN 0-12-712002-5

going into details, that textuality as understood above does not depend on the size of the verbal object in question and that it is a property that is independent of connexity and coherence. These properties can either be assigned to a given verbal object or not, depending on whether the interpreter considers the object to be a text. I return to connexity and coherence later.

When we investigate the lexicon component of a theory designed for text analysis and text interpretation, the following questions seem to be crucial:

1. What is the most expedient way to interpret the meaning of 'word meaning'?
2. What pieces of information should be represented in a lexicon entry (and in what form)?
3. What role do lexicon entries play in the analysis and description of the connexity and in the interpretation of texts?

THE MEANING OF A WORD

The problems involved in the investigation of word meaning have wide ramifications and the literature on this topic is very extensive. I deal here with only the most relevant aspects.

Let us take the so-called triangle of signification (sometimes referred to as the semiotic triangle) as a starting point (Lyons, 1968, p. 404, shown here as Figure 6.1). This representation with a slight alteration in terminology mirrors the views of the medieval grammarians that Lyons characterizes as follows:

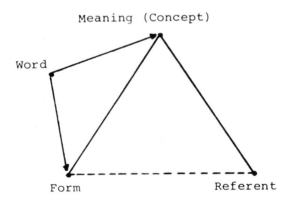

Figure 6.1   The Semiotic Triangle

As the distinction was formulated by the medieval grammarians: the form of a word (the *vox*-part of a *dictio*) signified 'things' by virtue of the 'concept' associated with the form of the word in the minds of the speakers of the language; and the 'concept', looked at from this point of view, was the meaning of the word (its *significatio*). (1968, pp. 403–404)

Lyons uses the more general term 'referent' to replace the original term 'thing' in the semiotic triangle.

Discussions about the nature of word meaning have been and continue to be centered around the following three questions: (1) Does signifying things actually take place by virtue of the concept? In other words, does the concept (the sense, the intension) determine the referent (the denotatum, the extension, the extralinguistic correlate)? (2) What is the character and structure of the concept assigned or assignable to a word? (3) Is it the concept, the referent, or both together that should be considered as the meaning of a word.

Some philosophers such as Kripke and Putnam prove convincingly that the intension does not determine the extension. In dealing with proper names and species' names, Kripke (1972) criticizes those theories of meaning that consider proper names or species' names as abbreviations for feature combinations that determine the extensions. Kripke considers proper names and species' names to be 'rigid designators' by means of which the referents are established. With respect to species' names, this conception implies—according to Stegmüller's summary—the following:

The first step in establishing a species does not involve qualitative determination, rather it involves *paradigmatical single cases*. It is only in the second step that one arrives at the conviction that these cases have some features in common and there is *at least one* combination of features that can be assigned to all of them. However, this conviction is only a belief which *could prove to be wrong*. The feature theories of species' names lay considerable stress upon features *we have come across by chance* and which we assume to be features of examples of a species. (1979, p. 335)

Thus, to generalize Kripke's view, we do not learn words but pairs consisting of words and their referents (extensions). Concepts are only secondary products.

Putnam takes the same view as Kripke. For Putnam (1975), the central aspects of meaning are stereotype and extension. Basically, stereotype represents the theory that members of a language community associate with a word in an ordinary context. The stereotype thus does not determine the extension; it need not even be true in a scientific sense. It follows that the meaning of a word must also contain the extension itself, although, in general, the knowledge of the extension need not exist as a part of the word's meaning in an ordinary context, nor does the extension really have to be known to every member of the language community. For them it is sufficient to know that there is someone among them who knows the extension, who is able to decide whether an x is really an x. In this connection, Putnam mentions the fact that the social dimension of cognition has so far been ignored, and he proposes the hypothesis of the universality of the division of linguistic labor. It is quite clear, however, that the theories of experts may be wrong and may change. Therefore, it is sufficient in every context that speakers, instead of knowing the extension (having an adequate theory about the extension), all have the intention to speak about the same thing.

With reference to the analyses of Kripke and Putnam, the consequences of which are far reaching both for philosophy and linguistics, the above three questions can be answered briefly: (1) signifying things does not generally take place by virtue of the concept; the concept does not determine the referent unequivocally; (2) a concept belonging to a word represents the set of knowledge that is assigned to the word in question by the average members of a language community and also by the experts in that community; (3) it is expedient to consider the concept and the referent together as meaning. These considerations also make it expedient to substitute a semiotic pyramid (Figure 6.2) for the semiotic triangle. (In what follows, I use the terms in boldface in Figure 6.2.)

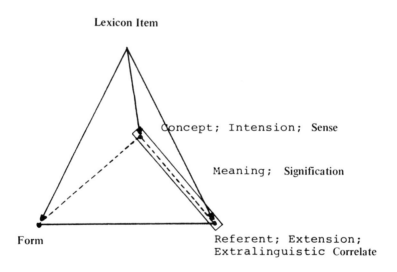

Figure 6.2   The Semiotic Pyramid

THE STRUCTURE AND COMPONENTS
OF LEXICON ENTRIES

The semiotic pyramid represented in Figure 6.2 contains the following elements: lexicon item (since, in general, lexica need to contain not only single words but also expressions (idioms) consisting of more than one word, it is more expedient to use the term 'lexicon item' instead of 'word'), form (also called 'formative'), sense, correlate, and signification.

A lexicon item is the manifestation of relations existing among the form, sense, and correlate. These relations are as follows:

1. the relation between form and correlate, which we may call denotation: The form is the denotans, the correlate is the denotatum or denotandum, depending on whether the form or the correlate is considered as the starting point;
2. the relation between form and sense, which we may call designation: The form is the designans, the sense is the designatum or designandum, depending on whether we consider the form or the sense as starting point;
3. the relation between sense and correlate, which we may call correspondence: This relation exists in both directions; however, it cannot be considered as a mutual and unequivocal relation;
4. the relation between form and meaning (i.e., sense plus correlate), which we may call signification (in an extended sense of the word): The form is the significans, the meaning is the significatum or significandum, depending on whether we consider the form or the meaning as starting point.
5. the representation of the sense, the explication–definition relation: The one-word representation of a sense is the explicandum–definiendum, the paraphrastic textual representation of the same sense is the explicans–definiens. Definition is a mutual and unequivocal relation, while explication is not. The definiendum is an abbreviated version of the definiens, thus the definiendum and the definiens can be substituted for one another. The explicandum implies the explicans; the implication does not hold in the other direction.

It is expedient to structure the lexicon entries according to these elements and relations so that the lexicon entries will have the macrostructure represented in Table 6.1. It is not necessary to represent the correspondence and signification relations separately; they are already represented by virtue of the fact that the form in the denotation and designation relations is a common element between the sense and the correlate. The subscripts of the sign " = " ("den," "des," "exp," or "def") are placed on the same side of the sign " = " as that on which the element ending with "-ans" or "-ens" of the relation concerned is placed.

In the following section I discuss those pieces of information that must be assigned to the individual components of the lexicon entry. In so doing, I am aiming at neither completeness nor at theoretical adequacy in the representations. The sole function of the example is to illustrate the structure of the individual components.

Lexicon Item

A lexicon item is a word or an idiom of a natural language in written form (a so-called graphic item), to which it is practical to assign the following information:

1. a phonetic representation indicating such information as pronunciation, stress, and word division;
2. specification of those registers in which the lexicon item can occur as an element (i.e., stylistic level, sociolect, dialect) and specification of technical sublanguages in which the item is used as a technical term;
3. a list of items that have, in some register or technical sublanguage, a synonymous or antonymous relation to the item concerned;
4. idiomatic expressions.

Table 6.2 illustrates the information that should be contained in each of these components for *filter, copy, subject,* and *square.*

Form

The kernel of the representation of form(ative)—considered both as denotans and as designans—is a canonical syntactic representation. (In this way, it is possible to guarantee that the formatives of all natural languages can be represented in the same way.) The representation of form should contain

1. a phonological representation,
2. a natural-language specific syntactic category,
3. a semantic (classificatory) category.

An example of such a representation for *write* and *filter* is given in Table 6.3.

Correlate

Rather than present a detailed discussion of how to represent the correlate (denotatum–denotandum), I only comment on one aspect of correlate representation.

Table 6.1

Lexicon item	Form(ative)	Correlate		Sense	
	denotans	den =	denotatum, denotandum	designatum, designandum des =	
	designans		explicandum or definiendum	= exp = def	explicans definiens

Table 6.2

	filter	copy	subject	square
Phonetic representation	/ˈfil-tə/	/ˈkop-1/	/ˈs ə b-ʤekt/	/skwe ə (r)/
Registers	term in chemistry engineering photography physics	term in journalism	term in British law linguistics psychology music	term in mathematics botany games
Synonyms, antonyms	screen	manuscript imitation reproduction	theme citizen	open place conservative person
Idioms			on the subject of	on the square

Table 6.3

#	[[s]	filter]	{sp:x}
1.		$filter_{PhR}$	
2.	adj.	subst.	
	syn.c_i	syn.c_k	
	sem.c_j	sem.c_m	
3.			o_r

#	[[s]	write]	{cp:x,	eo:y,	to:z,	im:u}
1.		$write_{PhR}$				
2.	adv.	verb				
	syn.c_i	syn.c_k				
	sem.c_j	sem.c_m				
3.			ø	ø	about	with
			$(case_l)$	$(case_j)$	$(case_k)$	$(case_m)$
			o_r	o_s	o_v	o_z

The symbols in the examples of representations are to be read as follows:

s: specifier variable.

x, y, z, u: object variables.

(sp), (cp), (eo), (to), (im): argument role indicators (elements which are analogous to the deep case elements of the case grammar); for example, (cp) indicates the role of the object that writes; (eo) the object that comes into being as the result of writing, (to) the object that is the topic of y, (sp) indicates the role of the object that has a property. (im) the tool by means of which the writing has been carried out.

The subscript (PhR) refers to the phonological representation.

(adj.), (adv.), (subst.), and (verb) are natural-language specific syntactic categories.

The symbols (c_x) indicate different syntactic (syn) or semantic (sem) subclasses; about and with indicate prepositions.

(ø) indicates the lack of prepositions.

The symbols $(case_l)$ indicate the case where it is necessary.

Correlate representation can be fulfilled by an element standing for (pointing deicticly to) the correlate. This insures the representation of the fact that in a given communication situation the participants in the communication are speaking about the same object without necessarily having the same knowledge or opinion as to what the object actually is (more exactly, what properties it has). In the case of a lexicon including pictures—assuming the pictures are unambiguous—the role of correlate representation can be fulfilled by either the picture itself or a symbol referring to the picture.

Sense

The representation of the sense (designatum–designandum, explication–definition) is the representation of the commonsense knowledge of the average speaker and the technical knowledge of the experts in the given language community. It is necessary to represent these as two different sets of knowledge even if in most cases single persons have a specific configuration of elements taken from both sets of knowledge in their knowledge about the object or state of affairs concerned.

In the formal respect, the representation of the individual components of these two sets of knowledge is the same kind of canonical representation as in the canonical representation of the form. In order to guarantee that different natural-language texts can be compared adequately, it is useful to represent these sets of knowledge not only by means of natural-language specific elements but also by means of an interlingua that is canonical in the semantic respect. Space restrictions do not allow a detailed treatment of this question here.

The representation of the individual subsets of the commonsense knowledge and of the experts' knowledge must have a well-defined macrostructure. This means that it is necessary to define these categories for all object and state-of-affairs classes with respect to which the elements of the given class are to be characterized. Let us consider some examples.

1. *Pineapple, apple, apricot,* and *banana* should be characterized within the commonsense knowledge sector with reference to the following categories: class (genus proximum), parent plant, native climate, shape, color, taste, seed type, characteristics of fruit pulp, characteristics of outer surface, manner of harvesting.
2. *Railway station, airport,* and *seaport* should be characterized within the commonsense knowledge sector with reference to the following categories: class (genus proximum), transportation category, purpose, installations, vehicle of transportation.

Finally, concerning the structure of the explicans–definiens, it is important to consider how circularity can be avoided. In other words, we must consider how to select the elements of the language of explication (i.e., those elements that are not to be explicated, but are to be defined or taken as semantic primitives within the lexicon). At the same time, the lexicon must contain information about how these elements may be paraphrased in the given natural language. This information must, however, be distinguished unambiguously from the explicantia–definientia (see Heydrich, 1981; Neubauer, 1980; Wilks, 1977).

LEXICON ENTRY, CONNEXITY, INTERPRETATION

The term 'connexity' designates a property that may be assigned by an interpreter to a verbal object that he considers to be a text if, in his opinion, the sentences of the text constitute a single sentence chain. (It is not necessary for the text sentences to be connected to a sentence chain in their linear order.) The term 'interpretation' indicates an operation in the course of which the interpreter first constructs a model suitable for interpreting the text (if he can construct such a model at all), and then, on the basis of this model, constructs the configuration of states of affairs (the extralinguistic correlate) that he, on the basis of his model, assumes to be represented in the text.

There are three sets of knowledge that play an essential role in the analysis and description of connexity, and in the construction of the model and in the interpretation:

1. general common sense and expert knowledge concerning the classes of objects and the classes of potential states of affairs (e.g., the knowledge of the average and expert members of a language community of what an *author,* a *king,* a *palace,* a *nuclear power station,* and a *trade union* are, and what it means that someone *paints, builds, fights*);
2. general knowledge concerning individual objects and individual states of affairs (e.g., knowledge concerning Thomas Mann, Charlemagne, the Palazzo Vecchio, the trade union called "Solidarność," the painting of the Sistine Chapel, the building of the cupola of Saint Peter's Basilica, the battle at Borodino);
3. special knowledge concerning the object classes, potential classes of states of affairs, and individual objects and states of affairs constructed by (expressed in) the text T_i under analysis.

Let us use 'lexicon' to refer to the apparatus that systematizes the knowledge in the first category, 'encyclopedia' for that which systematizes the knowledge in the second, and 'T_i' (specific thesaurus) for that which systematizes the knowledge in the third.

Obviously, it is not possible to imagine the construction of either a lexicon or an encyclopedia by means of which the connexity of all texts could be revealed and described in an intersubjective way and all texts could be interpreted. However, it would be desirable to construct a lexicon and an encyclopedia that could serve as a reference basis in the course of the analysis and interpretation of connexity. Then, by means of this reference basis, one would be able to construct in every case the T_i-specific lexicon and T_i-specific encyclopedia that, together with the T_i-specific thesaurus, could render it possible to provide an explicit description of the structure and meaning of the text T_i according to a given interpreter.

A T_i-specific lexicon, encyclopedia, and thesaurus must, of course, be constructed (or reconstructed) even if a lexicon and an encyclopedia suitable for serving as a reference basis are lacking. An explicit, interpreter-specific description of the structure and meaning of a given text T_i would otherwise be impossible.

The structure of a lexicon entry as described above can represent not only the structure of an entry in a general lexicon but also the structure of entries in any kind of lexicon, encyclopedia, and thesaurus.

A sentence sequence will appear to be a sentence chain (i.e., a connex) to an interpreter, if the sentences of this sequence are connected to each other by relations that he considers to be connexity relations. The carrier of these relations can be (1) some aspect of the formal linguistic formation of these sentences (e.g., the length of a sentence measured by the number of syllables, the configuration of the grammatical categories assignable to the sentences), (2) some aspect of the grammatical structure of these sentences, (3) some aspect of the lexical structure of these sentences, and (4) some aspect of the factual or fictitious relation that the interpreter considers as existing among the states of affairs represented by the sentences. The relations belonging to the last type manifest themelves for the interpreter either in what he assumes to be the relations among the objects involved in the individual states of affairs on the basis of his knowledge (e.g., in his opinion, these objects may belong to one and the same class, or they may be functionally or in some other way connected to each other), or in the fact that he considers, for example, one of the states of affairs a cause, consequence, or accompanying phenomenon, with respect to some other state of affairs. (See Beaugrande & Dressler, 1980; Halliday & Hasan, 1976; Harweg, 1968.)

These relations can be made explicit in an intersubjective way if the explicans components of the respective lexicon–encyclopedia–thesaurus entries are detailed enough and can be described explicitly, if adequate T_i-specific lexicon–encyclopedia–thesaurus entries can be constructed.

Let us illustrate the types of connexity relations of the classes (3) and (4) by some examples taken from Halliday and Hasan (1976). They use the term 'lexical cohesion' for indicating these relations.

Halliday and Hasan give the term 'reiteration' to the type of lexical cohesion that corresponds to the relations I have classified as belonging to class (3). The term 'reiteration' and the types of reiteration are explained by them as follows:

> When we talk about REITERATION . . . we are including not only the repetition of the same lexical item but also the occurrence of a related item, which may be anything from a synonym or near synonym of the original to a general word dominating the entire class. . . . any instance of reiteration may be (a) the SAME WORD, (b) a SYNONYM or NEAR-SYNONYM, (c) a SUPERORDINATE or (d) a GENERAL WORD. For example:
>
> There's a boy climbing that tree.
> a. The boy's going to fall if he doesn't take care.
> b. The lad's going to fall if he doesn't take care.
> c. The child's going to fall if he doesn't take care.
> d. The idiot's going to fall if he doesn't take care. (Halliday & Hasan, 1976, pp. 279–280, reprinted by permission from Longman Group Limited)

In all of these examples lexical cohesion also involves identity of reference indicated by the definite article *the*. (This connexity type appears, as a consequence, to be in tight connection with the connexity type (2) of my classification.) However, the identity of reference is no necessary condition for the establishment of lexical cohesion.

> A lexical item . . . coheres with a preceding occurrence of the same item whether or not the two have the same referent, or indeed whether or not there is any referential relationship between them. . . . The second occurrence may be, as far as reference is concerned, (a) IDENTICAL, (b) INCLUSIVE, (c) EXCLUSIVE or (d) simply UNRELATED. So for example:
>
> There's a boy climbing that tree.
> a. The boy's going to fall if he doesn't take care.
> b. Those boys are always getting into mischief.
> c. And there's another boy standing underneath.
> d. Most boys love climbing trees.
>
> In (a) *the boy* has the same referent as *a boy* has; the reference item *he* could be used instead. In (b) *those boys* includes the boy referred to previously, and others as well; here we could have a reference item *they* on the basis of the weak coreferentiality. . . . In (c) *another boy* excludes the boy referred to in the first sentence; here there is explicit NON-identity of reference, and in such instances we cannot have a reference item to replace *boy*—we can however have a substitute or elliptical form, *another one* or *another*. In (d) *most boys* bears

no referential relation at all to the boy previously mentioned; we cannot gather from (d) whether the boy in question likes climbing trees or not, and the speaker does not necessarily know, or care. (Halliday & Hasan, 1976, p. 283, reprinted by permission from Longman Group Limited)

In order to render it possible to disclose and describe these connexity manifestations in an explicit way, the lexicon entries have to contain the necessary syntactic and semantic information.

The type of lexical cohesion corresponding to connexity relations classified by me as belonging to class (4) is called by Halliday and Hasan 'collocation', and they use the following examples:

There is cohesion between any pair of lexical items that stand to each other in some recognizable lexicosemantic (word meaning) relation.

This would include not only synonyms and near-synonyms such as *climb . . . ascent, beam . . . rafter, disease . . . illness*, and superordinates such as *elm . . . tree, boy . . . child, skip . . . play*, but also pairs of opposites of various kinds, complementaries such as *boy . . . girl, stand up . . . sit down*, antonyms such as *like . . . hate, wet . . . dry, crowded . . . deserted*, and converses as *order . . . obey*.

It also concludes pairs of words drawn from the same ordered series. For example, if *Tuesday* occurs in one sentence and *Thursday* in another, the effect will be cohesive; similarly *dollar . . . cent, north . . . south, colonel . . . brigadier*. Likewise with any pairs drawn from unordered lexical sets, like *basement . . . roof, road . . . rail, red . . . green. . . .* They may be related as part to whole, like *car . . . brake, box . . . lid*, or as part to part, like *mouth . . . chin, verse . . . chorus* (or *refrain*); they may be cohyponyms of the same superordinate term, i.e., both members of the same more general class, such as *chair . . . table* (both hyponyms of furniture),*walk . . . drive* (both hyponyms of *go*); and so on. . . .

We will find a very marked cohesive effect deriving from the occurrence in proximity with each other of pairs such as the following, whose meaning relation is not easy to classify in systematic semantic terms: *laugh . . . joke, blade . . . sharp, garden . . . dig, ill . . . doctor, try . . . succeed, bee . . . honey, door . . . window, king . . . crown, boat . . . row, sunshine . . . cloud. . . .*

This effect is not limited to a pair of words. It is very common for long cohesive chains to be built up out of lexical relations of this kind, with word patterns line *candle . . . flame . . . flicker, hair . . . comb . . . curl . . . wave, poetry . . . literature . . . reader . . . writer . . . style, sky . . . sunshine . . . cloud . . . rain* weaving in and out of successive sentences. . . .

We . . . group together all the various lexical relations that do NOT depend on referential identity and are NOT of the form of reiteration accompanied by *the* or a demonstrative—in other words, all lexical cohesion that is not covered by what we have called 'reiteration'—and treat it under the general heading of COLLOCATION, or collocational cohesion. (Halliday & Hasan, 1976, pp. 285–287, reprinted by permission from Longman Group Limited)

I want to emphasize that the word pairs brought as examples by Halliday and Hasan guarantee—taken by themselves—only the formal connexity of a given sentence chain. Their occurrence does not allow any conclusions to be drawn as to whether there also exists some kind of relevance relation between the states of affairs described by the sentences of this sentence chain.

As to the single sets of knowledge, the interpretation of a verbal object considered to be a text requires the fulfilment of other criteria than is the case for the discovery and description of connexity. Connexity is neither a necessary nor a sufficient condition for interpretability, and the depth of the explication required for interpretation is not necessarily the same as the depth required for discovering and describing the connexity.

The interpretation conditions required from the sets of knowledge (more precisely, from their systematic representations: the lexica, the encyclopedia, and the thesauri) are the following: (1) that they also contain and systematize that type of knowledge representative of frame-, scene- and script-semantics which apply in the course of discourse analysis (Metzing, 1980); and (2) that they render it possible to select from or construct on the basis of the lexicon, encyclopedia, and thesaurus the explicans-configuration relevant to the given cotext for one and the same word occurring in different cotexts. These are the requirments that have to be taken into consideration when the explicans is constructed (Neubauer & Petöfi, 1981; Petöfi, 1982a).

CONCLUDING REMARKS

There are a number of researchers dealing with sentence structures who speak of lexicogrammar, by which they mean a grammar whose operations are controlled by the structure of the lexicon entries. Inter-relations between lexicon and grammar may exist, however, not only in a sentence grammar but in a text grammar as well; in the latter case this is even more evident, since the structure of an explication is a text structure itself.

Research in word meaning, sentence meaning, and text meaning are equally vital objects of interest in linguistics and philosophy, as well as in psychology. A consequence of this fact is that questions concerning the lexicon can only be discussed and solved as interdisciplinary questions if the present requirements of research are to be met (Eikmeyer & Rieser, 1981).

BIBLIOGRAPHY

Agricola, E. (1972). *Semantische Relationen im Text und im System*. The Hague: Mouton.
Beaugrande, R. A. de, & Dressler, W. U. (1981). *Introduction to text linguistics*. London: Longman. *Einführung in die Textlinguistik*. Tübingen: Niemeyer, 1981.

Cahiers de Lexicologie. (1976). Vol. 29.

Eikmeyer, H.-J., & Rieser, H. (Eds.). (1981). *Words, worlds, and contexts. New approaches in word semantics.* New York: de Gruyter.

Greimas, A. (1965). *La sémantique structurale.* Paris: Larousse.

Halliday, M., & Hasan, R. (1976). *Cohesion in English.* London: Longman.

Harweg, R. (1968). *Pronomina und Textkonstitution.* München: Fink.

Heydrich, W. (Ed.). (1981). *Lexikoneinträge. (Grundelemente der semantischen Struktur von Texten V.)* Hamburg: Buske.

Katz, J. J. (1972). *Semantic theory.* New York: Harper & Row.

Kripke, S. A. (1972). Naming and Necessity. In D. Davidson & G. Harman (Eds.), *Semantics of natural language.* (pp. 253–355). Dordrecht: Reidel.

Lehrer, A. (1974). *Semantic fields and lexical structure.* New York: American Elsevier.

Lyons, J. (1968). *Introduction to theoretical linguistics.* Cambridge: Cambridge University Press.

Lyons, J. (1977). *Semantics* (Vols. 1–2). Cambridge: Cambridge University Press.

Metzing, D. (Ed.). (1980). *Frame conceptions and text understanding.* New York: de Gruyter.

Models of lexical structuring. (1983). *A Roundtable Discussion. Quaderni di Semantica, 4,* 89–177, 273–366.

Neubauer, F. (1980). *Die Struktur der Explikationen in deutschen einsprachigen Wörterbüchern. Eine vergleichende lexiko-semantische Analyse.* Hamburg: Buske.

Neubauer, F., & Petöfi, J. S. (1981). Word semantics, lexicon systems and text interpretation. In H.-J. Eikmeyer & H. Rieser (Eds.), *Words, worlds, and contexts* (pp. 343–380). New York: de Gruyter.

Norman, D. A., & Rumelhart, D. E. (Eds.). (1975). *Explorations in cognition.* San Francisco: Freeman.

Petöfi, J. S. (1982a). Exploration in semantics: Analysis and representation of concept systems. In F. W. Riggs (Ed.), *The CONTA Conference. Proceedings of the Conference on Conceptual and Terminological Analysis in the Social Sciences* (pp. 100–118). Frankfurt: Indeks.

Petöfi, J. S. (1982b). Meaning, text interpretation, pragmatic-semantic text classes. *Poetics, 11,* 453–492.

Petöfi, J. S., & Bredemeier, J. (Eds.). (1977). *Das Lexikon in der Grammatik, die Grammatik im Lexikon.* Hamburg: Buske.

Putnam, H. (1975). The meaning of 'meaning'. In H. Putnam, *Mind, language and reality. Philosophical papers* (Vol. 2), (pp. 215–271). Cambridge: Cambridge University Press.

Rozencvejg, V. (Ed.) (1974). *Essays on lexical semantics* (Vols. 1–2). Stockholm: Skriptor.

Stelzer, S. (Ed.) (1972). *Probleme des 'Lexikons' in der Transformations-grammatik.* Frankfurt/Main: Athenäum.

Stegmüller, W. (1979). *Hauptströmungen der Gegenwarts-Philosophie* Vol. 2. Sixth, revised edition. Stuttgart: Kröner.

Wettler, M. (1980). *Sprache, Gedächtnis, Verstehen.* Berlin: de Gruyter.

Wilks, Y. (1977). Good and bad arguments about semantic primitives. *Communication & Cognition, 10,* 181–221.

CHAPTER 7

Semantic Discourse Analysis

Teun A. van Dijk

WHAT IS SEMANTIC DISCOURSE ANALYSIS?

Before we try to specify how to give a semantic analysis of discourse,
we must define what semantic analysis is and what kinds of semantic
analysis can be distinguished. Such a definition will be as complex as
the number of semantic theories in the various disciplines involved in
the study of language: linguistics and grammar, the philosophy of language,
logic, cognitive psychology, and sociology, each with several competing
semantic theories. These theories will be different according to their
object of analysis, their aims, and their methods. Yet, they will also
have some common properties that allow us to call them semantic theories.
In this chapter I first enumerate more or less intuitively a number of
these common properties, then select some of them for further theoretical
analysis, and finally apply the theoretical notions in actual semantic
analyses of some discourse fragments.

In the most general sense, semantics is a component theory within a
larger semiotic theory about meaningful, symbolic, behavior. Hence we
have not only a semantics of natural language utterances or acts, but
also of nonverbal or paraverbal behavior, such as gestures, pictures and
films, logical systems or computer languages, sign languages of the deaf,
and perhaps social interaction in general. In this chapter we consider
only the semantics of natural-language utterances, that is, discourses,
and their component elements, such as words, phrases, clauses, sentences,
paragraphs, and other identifiable discourse units. Other semiotic aspects
of verbal and nonverbal communication are treated elsewhere in this
Handbook.

Probably the most general concept used to denote the specific object

HANDBOOK OF DISCOURSE ANALYSIS, Vol. 2
Dimensions of Discourse
Copyright © 1985 by Academic Press London.
All rights of reproduction in any form reserved.
ISBN 0-12-712002-5

of a semantic theory is the concept of 'interpretation'. Interpretation may be of various kinds, depending on the discipline or theory involved. For the sake of clarity, we first distinguish between abstract and concrete types of interpretation. Thus, grammar (see Lyons, 1977) and logic (see Carnap, 1956; Cresswell, 1973; Lehrer & Lehrer, 1970; Linsky, 1952, 1967, 1971; Montague, 1974), have semantic theories that specify abstract interpretations, whereas a cognitive model in psychology (see Clark, 1976; Clark & Clark, 1977; Cotton & Klatzky, 1978; Kintsch, 1974, 1977; Lindsay & Norman, 1972; Norman & Rumelhart, 1975; Tulving & Donaldson, 1972) will be about concrete interpretations. The first are interpretations of discourse and discourse elements by systems and by rules of such systems, whereas the latter are interpretations by language users. The two kinds of interpretation are not unrelated: An abstract linguistic (grammatical) semantics usually has empirical claims that it intends to model at least some aspects of the concrete interpretations of language users as they are accounted for in psychological models.

Interpretations are processes or operations of assignment: to objects of kind X they assign objects of kind Y. The objects of kind X to which we assign something are usually called expressions. Thus words, or rather word forms (morphemes), and sentences, or rather sentence forms (syntactic structures), are objects of which interpretations are provided in semantic theories. What is assigned by operations of interpretations are typically semantic objects of various kinds. A first semantic object of this kind is meaning. Hence the interpretation of a discourse, as it is explicated in a semantic theory of discourse, is the assignment of meaning(s) to the expressions of a discourse. This is more or less the kind of semantics that is usual in linguistic theory. Roughly speaking, meanings are conceptual objects of various degrees of complexity, depending on the complexity of the corresponding expressions. Again depending on the kind of semantics, such meanings may be described in abstract or more concrete terms; the latter are the cognitive representations of language users associated with the expressions of natural language in general or with actual discourses in particular. The kind of interpretation whereby meanings are assigned to expressions is usually called 'intensional'. Besides such intensional interpretations we also have extensional interpretations, which depend on (are a function of) intensional interpretations: Expressions with a given meaning may refer to or denote some object or property in "the world." Hence, to provide an extensional interpretation of a discourse is to specify what such a discourse is about, that is, the individuals, properties, or states of affairs that constitute its various referents in some formal model of a possible world. This kind of referential semantics is the one traditionally explored, in rather formal terms, in philosophy and especially logic. It is shown below that a discourse semantics should be both intensional and extensional, that is, about meanings and about reference. Also, it is seen that a discourse semantics is not only abstract but also involves the kind of semantic notions used in the cognitive models of psychology and artificial intelligence. For instance, in order to be able to interpret a discourse, that is, to assign it meaning and reference, we also need a substantial amount of world knowledge, and such knowledge can only be partly specified within linguistics or grammar, namely, in the lexicon.

A first principle of semantics is 'functionality', which says that the meaning of discourse expressions is a function of the meanings of their component expressions. Thus the meaning of a sentence must be calculated on the basis of the meanings of its component words. A second major principle is 'structural', which holds that the structures of expressions are interpreted as structures of meanings. We are not here concerned with the specific rules that specify how the meaning of sentences can be derived from the meanings of words and phrases. We merely assume (1) that discourse expressions can be analyzed as sequences of sentences and (2) that the meaning units assigned to sentences are propositions, which consist of a predicate and a number of arguments that may have various (case) roles. Hence a first aspect of semantic discourse analysis is to investigate how sequences of sentences of a discourse are related to sequences of underlying propositions and how the meaning of such sequences is a function of the meaning of the constituent sentences or propositions.

At the same time, though, semantic discourse analysis has an extensional or referential dimension. That is, we want to know what sequences of sentences in a discourse can refer to. Traditionally, philosophy and logic identified the object of reference for a sentence with a truth value, for example, "true" or "false." Compound propositions were then also assigned a truth value on the basis of the specific meaning of the connectives linking propositions (e.g., logical *and, or, if . . . then*). In that tradition we could then demand that discourse semantics specify the rules that assign a truth value to the discourse as a whole on the basis of the truth values assigned to individual sentences. Although to a certain extent that would be a legitimate aim, there are several reasons not to follow that logical approach here, because, for instance, sentences and propositions in a discourse are not only linked by logical connectives. Also, a truth functional approach is too limited and would be relevant only for discourses used in affirmative contexts, that is, as speech acts of assertion, and would not be relevant for questions, orders, promises, congratulations, and accusations. Hence, we assume that the objects of reference for meaningful sentences are facts, namely the facts that constitute some possible world. A pragmatic theory will specify whether such facts are part of a given possible world or not, whether such a fact will be or should be brought about, according to the speech act performed when uttering and using the discourse in some specific social context. Hence, whereas intensionally we link sequences of sentences with sequences of propositions, these are in turn linked, at the extensional level, with configurations of facts, such as states of affairs, events, actions, or complex episodes of these. Note, by the way, that facts, just like tables or properties like 'hot' and relations like 'to love', are ontologically real only with respect to social and cognitive norms and conventions, principles of identification and distinction, or other operations that may be culturally variable. Finally, it should be added that not only are the facts denoted by a discourse dependent on the meanings of the expressions of the discourse; conversely, the meaningfulness of a discourse depends on the actual or possible facts (or complexes of facts or episodes) denoted by the discourse, a dependence that may be assessed only on the basis of our knowledge or beliefs about the actual or possible facts in some world or situation. This is one reason why a purely abstract semantics of meaning and reference should be extended in a cognitive framework.

Although most semantic theories involve notions such as 'interpretation', 'meaning', 'reference', 'intension', 'extension', 'truth values', or 'facts', and have as their main aim to specify the rules whereby, for example, meaning units, such as propositions, are assigned to natural or formal-language expressions, we need not limit ourselves to these well-established notions of abstract linguistic, philosophical, or logical theories. We have emphasized above that real interpretation is a mental act, or rather a cognitive process, of language users. The result of this process is a conceptual representation of the discourse in memory. If such a representation satisfies a number of properties, we say that a language user has understood the discourse (see Beaugrande, 1980; Freedle, 1977, 1979; Just & Carpenter, 1977; Kintsch, 1974; Kintsch & van Dijk, 1978; van Dijk & Kintsch, 1983; and the references in Bower & Cirilo, Vol. 1, this *Handbook*; Kintsch, Vol. 2, this *Handbook*). Such representations, however, in general consist not only of the conventionalized meanings as they are specified in the lexicon for a given language. The language user, as we stressed before, brings to bear her knowledge of the world, and many relevant aspects of this very extensive world knowledge may therefore become part of the conceptual representation. Similarly, language users have had previous experiences, such as having read other discourses about the same kinds of facts, and traces of the representations of these experiences gradually build and update models of the situation in episodic memory. These models provide the knowledge and referential basis for the interpretation process. And finally, individual language users may also generate opinions, that is, evaluative beliefs, about individual objects or facts, based on their attitudes and ideologies. That is, the representation of the discourse will not only be objective in the sense of being socially normalized or conventional, but will also have subjective dimensions. Such subjective interpretation will also depend on contextual factors such as personal motivations (wishes, desires, preferences, purposes, intentions), goals, interests, tasks, obligations, or social aspects of the communicative setting. These will determine which meanings receive special attention, which meanings will be disregarded, how knowledge, beliefs, and opinions are activated and used, which associations are activated, and how meanings may be transformed to more special, personal, or contextual meanings.

In the rest of this chapter we abstract from these cognitive and subjective aspects of discourse meaning and focus our attention on more general properties of semantic interpretation. We do not, however, respect the usual boundaries between linguistic or grammatical semantics and cognitive semantics. Thus if we speak about the meaning or reference of discourse elements, such as sentences, this is meant as a generalization and abstraction with respect to the cognitive properties of discourse understanding, which are dealt with in separate chapters of this *Handbook* (Bower & Cirilo, Vol. 1; Kintsch, this Volume).

SOME SPECIFIC PROPERTIES OF DISCOURSE SEMANTICS

Against the background of the more general notions of natural-language semantics mentioned in the previous section, we are now able to specify what additional notions are relevant in the semantic interpretation of discourse. That is, what aspects of meaning and reference of discourse cannot simply be described in terms of the meanings of words, phrases, or sentences (in isolation) alone?

Discourse Coherence

A first aspect that requires our attention is the fact that discourses usually consist of sequences of sentences that express sequences of propositions (see Beaugrande, 1980; Beaugrande & Dressler, 1981; Östman, 1978; Petöfi, 1979; Petöfi & Rieser, 1973, 1974; van Dijk, 1972, 1977). Just as we want to know how the meanings of words and phrases within a sentence are related so as to form the meaning of the sentence as a whole, we want to know how the meanings of sentences are related so as to form the meaning of the sequence as a whole. In other words, how are the propositions of a discourse linked up in a sequence, and how do they add up to more complex meanings? And conversely, how does the meaning of one sentence depend on the meaning of a sequence as a whole? The same questions can be asked for the referential dimension of the discourse. One important aspect of this latter dimension is, for instance, the issue of the respective orderings or organization involved. Sentences follow each other, in both written and oral discourse, in a linear fashion. The underlying semantic structures, that is, the propositions, may—according to many theories—have an additional hierarchic organization. The facts denoted by the discourse, for example, states of affairs, actions, or events, however, have spatial, conditional (e.g., causal), or temporal organization. Hence it is an important cognitive task for a speaker or writer to represent these relations between the facts as relations within or among propositions and to express these again in the linear ordering of words, phrases, and sentences (Levelt, 1981; van Dijk, 1977), whereas the hearer or reader has the task of establishing these relations the other way around (with the additional knowledge about the usual ordering of facts). Hence a discourse is not just a set of sentences but an ordered sequence, with conventional constraints on the possible orderings if it is to be meaningful and if it is to represent certain fact structures, for example, episodes. But not only is the ordering of propositions in a discourse constrained by rules of meaningfulness; their content, that is, their conceptual meanings and reference, is also subject to certain principles or rules. In general, then, the proposition sequence underlying an acceptable discourse must satisfy various conditions of what is called 'coherence'.[1] Similarly, the surface structure expressions, that is, the morphonological, syntactic, and lexical structures of the respective sentences, must appropriately signal this coherence, by, for instance, word order, sentence order, the use of connectives, sentential adverbs, verb tenses, or pronouns; these devices are often subsumed under the concept of (surface structure) 'cohesion'. These surface-structure expressions of semantic coherence are not dealt with here.

---

[1] Instead of 'coherence', other terms have been used to denote semantic relationships defining the unity of discourse, for example, 'cohesion' and 'connectedness'. Following usage now being established in much of the literature, we here distinguish between semantic coherence, as a general principle, and surface-structural cohesion, taken as the system of coherence expressions. 'Connection' is used as a particular aspect of coherence, namely as the local, linear semantic relationship between subsequent propositions. See Beaugrande and Dressler (1981) for a discussion of these various terms.

Before we analyze some natural discourse examples, a simple constructed example may illustrate some of the conditions of what we call 'local coherence' in discourse:

(1)   a.   *Next month we will be in Berkeley.*
        b.   *We will be staying with friends.*

For this sample discourse we may first observe that the reverse order of the sentences would result in a much less meaningful discourse. That is, we apparently should first have the specification of some more global action or state of affairs, possibly with indication of time and place, and then we may have details of the action or state mentioned. There seems to be a principle requiring that the sentence or proposition ordering may reflect the general–particular ordering of facts. This means that (1b) will be interpreted relative to the interpretation of (1a): That is, "we will be staying in Berkeley" and "the friends we are staying with live in Berkeley." These latter propositions may be inferred from (1b) given the previous sentence (1a) in the same discourse. Similarly, spatial ordering between facts may require the same linear ordering in the expression of propositons:

(2)   a.   *They have a big house on the hill.*
        b.   *It has at least 10 rooms.*

Again, we find that objects must be introduced before properties, such as 'contents', can be properly specified. It would be rather funny to have: *They are living in ten rooms. These are in a big house on the hill,* so there are constraints on the representation of space or possession relations. Similar ordering principles exist for the representation of the perception or understanding of facts: In general, what is discovered first should be mentioned first. This is also why we should rather have *There was a table in the corner. On it was a large vase of flowers.* than *In the corner was a large vase of flowers. It was standing on a table.* Some of the principles involved are more or less conventionalized rules, whereas others are stylistic strategies that are often followed but may be ignored to obtain special effects.

The most conspicuous coherence constraints hold for the representation of temporal and conditional relations between events or actions. Possible, probable, or necessary conditions (e.g., causes) should in general be mentioned before their consequences:

(3)   a.   *This morning I had a toothache.*
        b.   *I went to the dentist.*

(4)   a.   *We went to an expensive restaurant.*
        b.   *John ordered trout with almonds.*

In (3) we first have the condition, namely, a reason, and then a consequent action, whereas in (4) we first have an action that allows another action as its consequence or as its specification. In the latter case we may not reverse the order of the sentences, because then it would not be clear when and where John performed that specific action. In (3) however, we may put the second sentence in first position, but then we obtain a different meaning: Having a toothache no longer is presented as a reason for an action; the sentence functions as an explanation rather than as a description of a sequence of events. That is, sentence ordering in discourse may indicate a conditional ordering between represented facts but also may indicate the use of the sentence as an explanation. Such uses would require further pragmatic analysis of sentence sequences (van Dijk, 1981). In general, therefore, it makes sense to distinguish between two large classes of semantic coherence conditions, conditional coherence and functional coherence.[2] A sequence of propositions is conditionally coherent if it denotes a sequence of conditionally related facts, such as causes and consequences, whereas a sequence of propositions is functionally coherent if the respective propositions have themselves a semantic function defined in terms of the relation with previous propositions. Thus a proposition may function as a specification, explanation, example, comparison, contrast or generalization with respect to a previous proposition. Whereas discourses (1), (3), and (4) are conditionally coherent, (2) is functionally coherent. Note that the two kinds of coherence may also overlap to a certain degree: In (1), going to some town may be a possible condition for the act of staying with friends (and not, say, going to the movies). At the same time there is a functional aspect: To be in some town, taken as the equivalent of staying in some town, can be specified by the information that we are staying with friends.

We have argued that coherence is provided not only by the ordering of sentences, but also by their meaning and reference. Thus, we do not in general have sequences like (5) in stereotypical situations:

(5)   a.   *We went to an expensive restaurant.*
       b.   *John ordered a big Chevrolet.*

Although (5b) is a meaningful sentence in isolation, it does not meaningfully relate to the previous sentence if it is interpreted as an action performed at the restaurant. Our world knowledge about eating in restaurants—

---

[2] For conditional coherence, see van Dijk (1977); for work on artificial intelligence and discourse see Schank and Abelson (1977). Functional coherence is studied in van Dijk (1977, 1981) after earlier work done by Grimes (1975) and B. Meyer (1976), who speak of 'rhetorical relations'. See also P. G. Meyer (1975) on functional links between sentences, and Reichman (1981) for such relations in dialogue.

organized in so-called scripts (Schank and Abelson, 1977)—tells us that ordering a car is not a normal thing to do in restaurants. Hence the meaningfulness of discourse also depends on what we assume to be the normalcy of the facts, episode, or situation described. In other words, understanding a discourse presupposes understanding the world. For a discourse like (5), understanding is restored as soon as we know that John is crazy or just trying to be funny. (5b) could also be interpreted as the first sentence of a sequence that, as a whole, specifies the restaurant event: John ordered a car (e.g., a taxi) to take us to the restaurant.

Coherence relations connect sentences or propositions as wholes, and not just elements of propositions. Thus in (1) through (3) we may note that in the sentence pairs we find referential expressions denoting identical referents: we in (1), the house and it in (2), and I in (3). It should be stressed that such forms of cohesive coreference are neither a sufficient nor a necessary condition for discourse coherence. (In many early studies this coreferential criterion is the major condition for coherence, as seen by the attention to phenomena such as pronouns.) In (4) there is no strict coreference, although it is understood that John is a member of the set denoted by we. But (4a) may be preceded by sentences like It was a beautiful night or There was no food in the house, and such sentences would be perfectly coherent with (4). This is because such sentences, as wholes, denote a condition, reason, or background for the actions mentioned later in the discourse. Mere coreferential identity would not be sufficient, as we can see if we substituted John for the pronoun we in (5a), or if I was born in New York were substituted for (3b). It follows that the basis for assessing discourse coherence is not the individual word meanings or referents but rather whole propositions as they relate to facts. Since identity of referents is often concomitant with the relatedness of facts, coreference is a frequent aspect of coherence: for at least some stretch of a discourse we are speaking about the same object or the same person, or introduce new objects or persons related to previously mentioned ones. Surface cohesion markers such as pronouns, pro-verbs, articles, demonstratives, names, or lexical identity signal this property of underlying semantic coherence (Halliday & Hasan, 1976).

The relations between propositions as wholes, denoting relations between facts, are expressed not only by sentence ordering as discussed above, but also by various kinds of connectives such as the conjunctions and, but, although, if . . . then, for, because, or, unless, and despite, the sentence adverbs therefore, however, consequently, and by adverbial compounds such as on the contrary, as a consequence, or on the one hand and on the other hand. They express both conditional and functional coherence types, although it seems that the conditional uses predominate.

In the examples given above we can easily imagine the use of the connectives in the conditional readings, whereas functional coherence is
simply signaled by clause or sentence coordination and subordination.
We assume that the semantics of connectives can at least partly be
accounted for in terms of conditional relations of various strengths (possibility, probability, and necessity) between the facts denoted by connected
clauses or sentences (van Dijk, 1977). Thus, *and* has a general function
of connection, which allows it to be used instead of other conditional
connectives, and also may function as the weakest conditional connective
(*A* allows *B*), whereas *because, for,* and *so* express stronger conditional
relations. *But, however,* and *yet* presuppose this conditional relation but
indicate that an inference or expectation does not hold for a particular
case: *Normally A conditions B, but not-B is the case.* This indicates that
the meaning of connectives needs explanation in terms of language users'
expectations (see Ducrot, 1980). The formal details and the specific meaning
and reference conditions of the various connectives are not discussed in
this chapter. It should be added, however, that connectives have pragmatic
as well as semantic functions (van Dijk, 1981). In addition to expressing
relations between propositions and thereby denoting relations between
facts, they may also be used to express relations between the speech
acts performed by the utterance of the respective sentences in some
context. In that case, *and* may signal additional information, *but* a protest
against a previous speech act, *or* a correction of previous speech acts
or their appropriateness conditions, and *so* a conclusion. Pragmatic uses
are often signaled by sentence-initial position in independent new sentences,
whereas the semantic use of the connectives may also be interclausal.

Information Distribution

Above we have reviewed some of the conditions for discourse coherence
at the level of sentence and proposition sequences. We have seen that
there are rules and strategies for ordering sentences and expressing spatial,
temporal, and conditional relations between propositions and facts. We
have distinguished between conditional and functional coherence types
and have emphasized that coherence always should be defined in terms
of full propositions and the facts they denote and that coherence is
relative to the world knowledge of speaker and hearer. Connectives may
be used to express these connections between propositions, whereas
other surface phenomena (e.g., definite articles, pronouns, verb tenses,
or demonstratives) may be used to indicate that the same time, place,
action, event, or individual participate in the subsequent facts. This latter
we saw as a frequent but not necessary or sufficient condition for coherence.

There is a second aspect of the semantics of discourse involved in the definition of coherence. Discourse is not simply a representation of related facts; it also must respect various information processing constraints, from both a cognitive and an interactional or social point of view. Used in social contexts, discourses are performed as speech-act sequences (and as one global speech act—see below), and they therefore have as their first function to establish some semantic representation, and on that basis some pragmatic representation, in the memory of the hearer or reader. In this perspective a discourse should respect a number of very general communicative principles: It should be informative enough (not too little but not too much), it should be relevant with respect to the topic of discourse or conversation (see below) or with respect to the interactional context, it should be brief, and it should be sufficiently clear (Grice, 1967). For each sentence of the discourse, as well as for the discourse as a whole, it should be indicated to the hearer, at both the semantic and surface structural levels, how each sentence relates to previous and possibly following sentences, how the information of each sentence is tied in with the information of other sentences, and what information the hearer or reader is supposed (by the speaker or writer) to have about the context and about the world. This means, among other things, that at each point of the discourse there should be at least some new information (we may not repeat the same sentence over and over again), and that this new information should be appropriately linked with old information, which may be textual (introduced before in the same discourse) or contextual (derivable from the hearer's knowledge about the communicative context and about the world in general). At several levels this informational aspect of the discourse as a form of communicative interaction shows up. One prominent way of organizing the informational structure of discourse is the distinction, within the semantics of each sentence, between a topic function and a comment function.[3] These are extremely intricate notions, which still have not been fully understood, but it is here assumed that they are textually dependent functions assigned to fragments of the semantic structure of the sentences in a discourse. The topic function may be assigned to the semantic information that is "old" in various senses, that is, already introduced by the text or already

---

[3] For some references from the vast literature on topic–comment relations in sentences and on functional analyses in general, see Dik (1978), Givón (1979b), Li (1976), Sgall, Hajičová and Benešová (1973). See van Dijk (1972, 1977, 1981) for the textual dimensions of topic–comment structures. There is some terminological and theoretical confusion in this area; sometimes the term 'focus' is used instead of 'comment', although 'focus' is also used in different ways. For cognitive aspects, see Clark and Haviland (1977), Reichman (1981), and van Dijk and Kintsch (1983).

known to the hearer (also from context), and therefore somehow given or presupposed. The old information is selected and placed in the foreground as an anchorpoint for the new information of the sentence. We see from this intuitive characterization that the notion of topic requires grammatical, pragmatic, cognitive, and interactional explication. Within our restricted semantic point of view we can only define it in terms of semantic relations between propositions; for example, in terms of identity or other relations (implication, entailment) or in terms of proposition fragments (predicates, individuals). The most typical means of topic assignment derives from the identity of previously introduced individuals: The sentence provides further information (the comment) about an object or person that has been mentioned before. Such a topic function is signaled in various ways by the surface structure features of languages, such as word order, grammatical functions (e.g., subject), pronouns, definite articles, demonstratives, or hierarchical clause ordering. In English, for example, the topic function of an underlying semantic fragment can be expressed by an unstressed, initial-position definite noun phrase or pronoun with subject function and often semantic agent role. These different indications need not always coincide: Other positions are possible, and the topic may also be combined with other semantic roles. If some of these markers are not available as in the case of free word order or no special grammatical marking of subjects, languages may have an additional lexical or morphological expression for topic-expressing sentence segments. If the preferred ordering is not followed, then special arrangements might become necessary. Thus in English, initial noun phrases (definites or pronouns) that are not assigned topic function are assigned special stress or organized in cleft sentences (*It was John who . . .*). Depending on cognitive constraints (short-term memory capacity, focus of attention, etc.) topic function in surface structure may be marked by semantic identity at the referential level expressed by pronouns instead of full definite noun phrases (Marslen-Wilson, Levy, Komisarjevsky-Tyler, 1981).

The so-called topic–comment articulation of sentences is not restricted to elements of propositions but may also extend to whole propositions. In that case we usually make a distinction between the presupposition and assertion parts of a sentence (Kempson, 1975; Petöfi & Franck, 1973; Wilson, 1975). A presupposition, having topical function, is a proposition assumed to be known to the hearer from previous text or from the context. Formally speaking, such a proposition is entailed by both the presupposing sentence and by the negation of that sentence. Presupposed propositions are typically expressed by initial subordinate clauses but may also be signaled by a number of predicates or adverbs, such as *to know* (of which the object proposition is assumed to be true by the speaker), *to pretend* (of which the object proposition is doubted by the speaker), or *even* (presupposing that the negation of the proposition would have been more likely, just as in the use of *but*), as in:

(6)   *Even the professors participated in the student rally.*

Note that the assertion part of sentences exhibiting presuppositions is relevant only for affirmative sentences used as assertions; presuppositions also occur in questions, threats, promises, or other speech acts, although their presupposed nature then is outside the scope of such speech acts (we need not question what we already know to be the case, nor promise or command that information).

Global Coherence: Macrostructures

Until now we have discussed the semantic properties of discourse only for relations between sentences or between propositions, that is, for pairwise, linear connections between elements in a sequence. We have summarized these properties under the term 'local coherence'. There is, however, a third major aspect of discourse semantics that needs our attention. The meaningfulness of discourse resides not only at this local (or microstructural) level of immediate clause and sentence connections but also at a global level. We should also explain the properties of the meaning of the larger fragments of a discourse, such as paragraphs, as wholes. Paragraphs may be connected even though their respective last and first sentences are not connected according to the conditions mentioned above. Similarly, we make statements about the meaning of larger discourse fragments or whole discourses that cannot simply be defined in terms of the local coherence conditions mentioned above. We talk about the topic, the theme, the subject, the upshot, the point, or the outline of a discourse, and such notions do not apply to individual sentences or propositions. We therefore assume that, besides the local semantic structure, a discourse also has a global semantic structure or macrostructure (Jones, 1977; van Dijk, 1972, 1977, 1980). Thus a macrostructure is a theoretical reconstruction of intuitive notions such as 'topic' or 'theme' of a discourse. It explains what is most relevant, important, or prominent in the semantic information of the discourse as a whole. At the same time, the macrostructure of a discourse defines its global coherence. Without such a global coherence, there would be no overall control upon the local connections and continuations. Sentences might be connected appropriately according to the given local coherence criteria, but the sequence would simply go astray without some constraint on what it should be about globally:

(7)   *This morning I had a toothache.*
       I went to the dentist.
       The dentist has a big car.
       The car was bought in New York.
       New York has had serious financial troubles.

The above facts may be related locally, but they are not related to one central issue or topic. The macrostructure is the semantic information that provides this overall unity to a discourse. Often such underlying macrostructures are expressed by the text itself, for example, in announcements, titles, summaries, thematic sentences, or the expression of plans for action. According to the fundamental principle of semantics, that of functionality, a macrostructure of a discourse should be a function of the respective meanings of its sentences. This function, however, is not given by an added connectivity at the local level of the sequence, that is, the sum of all pairwise coherence links between sentences. Rather it is a kind of semantic transformation, mapping sequences of propositions of the text on sequences of macropropositions at more abstract, general, or global levels of meaning. Intuitively, such mappings are operations that select, reduce, generalize, and (re-)construct propositions into fewer, more general, or more abstract propositions. These transformations or operations are called 'macrorules'. They are second-order semantic interpretation rules: After the interpretation of sentences and sentence pairs, they allow a further interpretation of sequences as (global) propositions that characterize the meaning of a sequence or discourse as a whole. Thus a description of the sequence of actions performed by John going on a ski vacation to Switzerland may be reduced by macrorules to the macroproposition 'John went skiing in Switzerland'. The macrorules delete all propositional information of only local relevance that is not necessary for understanding the rest of the discourse; they generalize and collect individuals in terms of groups and various characteristics of persons in terms of global personality traits, and they group conditions, components, or consequences of some action or event together as one overall action or event concept ('Going to the station', 'Buying a ticket', 'Going to the platform', would thus together result in the macroproposition 'Taking the train to . . . '). Obviously, such macrorules can operate only on the basis of world knowledge: We must know or have assumptions about what is relevant and important in some communicative context, we must know how to group individuals and properties, and we must know what stereotypical aspects are involved in global events and actions such as accidents or train trips, so that we can, as hearers, activate the relevant scripts and have a global representation of the communicative context and goals of the speaker.

Macrorules operate recursively. They may derive a sequence of macropropositions from the sequence of propositions expressed by the discourse (for instance, those of a page in a novel), which may again be the input for the rules so that higher-level topics or themes are derived. We thus arrive at a hierarchic structure, with the most global topic or theme at the top. In newspapers, for instance, such a highest topic is often expressed (at least partially) by the headlines, as in *TORNADO KILLS 500 PEOPLE*, or *PRESIDENT WILL MEET SOVIET LEADER*. More fully, a macrostructure is typically expressed by the summary of a discourse (Kintsch & van Dijk, 1978; Reder & Anderson, 1980; van Dijk & Kintsch, 1978). Operationally speaking, discourses that do not allow summarizing have no macrostructure or only a very fragmentary one (e.g.,some modern poems).

What has been observed for the analysis of meaning in the beginning of this chapter also holds for macrostructures. As theoretically described here, macrostructures are only abstractions relative to more concrete cognitive operations and representations. That is, since the world knowledge, beliefs, opinions, attitudes, interests, and goals of speech participants may vary, they may also assign different global meanings (macrostructures) to the same discourse as they may have different evaluations about what is relevant or important information for the discourse (and the communicative context) as a whole. Despite these individual and subjective variations, there is often enough overlap to guarantee successful communication and interaction.

SEMANTIC STRATEGIES

The kinds of semantic properties that have been dealt with in the previous section are typically described, as we suggested earlier, in more or less abstract, structural semantics. That is, semantic interpretations and coherence are assigned ex post facto to the discourse or discourse fragment as a finished verbal utterance. We have emphasized that real interpretation, that is, understanding by a language user, does not proceed only by working systematically from one unit or from one level to another by systematic rules. Rather, language users apply effective strategies to arrive as soon as possible at the intended interpretation, making use of various kinds of textual, contextual, and cognitive information at the same time. These cognitive processes cannot be dealt with here (but see

Bower & Cirilo, Vol. 1, this *Handbook*; Kintsch, this Volume of the *Handbook*; and especially van Dijk & Kintsch, 1983).

Nevertheless, as we also have seen, there is no strict boundary between these different kinds of semantics, that is between the kind of abstract, structural semantics of a linguistic theory of discourse and the processual and strategic semantics of a cognitive model. In order to establish local and global coherence, we should at least take into account that missing link propositions should be derived from world knowledge (scripts).

There is also another reason why a more dynamic reformulation should be given of the semantic principles discussed above. We have seen that discourses do not simply "have" meanings, but that such meanings are assigned to them by language users (on the basis of the cognitive processes mentioned above) in some concrete interaction and context. This means that the interpretation of discourse is also something people "do," both cognitively and socially. In everyday conversation (of which the major principles are discussed in Vol. 3 of this *Handbook*) this implies that conversational partners are permanently busy interpreting ongoing talk, that is, a current turn or move of another speaker, with the goals of semantically linking this turn or move to their own previous contribution to the conversation and acquiring the information needed to make next moves in the conversation. In other words, local semantic coherence assignment may be both backwards and forwards. At the same time, though, an actual speaker in such a conversation must monitor his or her own contribution to the conversation for its semantic coherence with previous turns of previous speaker(s) and must probably also anticipate possible interpretations by the hearer (a strategy usually called 'recipient design'). In other words, actual speakers and hearers not only follow general rules of local and global coherence but also use a number of efficient strategies in doing so. These cognitive and social strategies may involve, for instance, interpretative short cuts or the effective solution of interpretative puzzles when the other speaker apparently speaks "out of topic" or when some turn or move seems inconsistent with a previous one. These are examples of conversational interpretation strategies. The speaker also uses production strategies to remain coherent or to motivate apparent deviations from coherence principles. If some ongoing topic (macrostructure) is interrupted for a good personal, contextual, or interactional reason, this should be signaled in the surface structures of the turn (such as in *By the way* . . . or *Speaking about John* . . .). Similarly, there are a large number of anticipating semantic strategies. Thus, when some speaker A is expressing a proposition p, he or she may realize that maybe conversation partner B might draw the inference q from p. If that inference is not intended, A may use a strategy to block such an inference, for example, by denying q with a subsequent sentence or clause beginning with *but* and a negation. In talk where participants are particularly interested in prohibiting wrong conclusions by speech partners, there are many such strategies, including hedgings, corrections, additions, and mitigations. That is, a move in a turn of a speaker may be given a special strategic semantic function with respect to previous moves (or their underlying propositions): The speaker may hedge when a previous move was too harsh or decisive, may add some detail explaining why some belief or opinion was expressed or use a correction move to take back what was asserted. Such semantic strategies are part of the overall communicative and interactional strategies used to maintain or establish certain goals, such as face keeping or self-presentation (for details and lists of strategies see Kreckel, 1981).

The hearer in a conversation must analyze and interpret such semantic strategies. He or she must determine not only what is propositionally meant by some expression but also why such a proposition is expressed at a particular point in the conversation.

Let us give some examples from data we have collected in the context of an investigation into the ethnic opinions of people in Amsterdam as these are expressed (or not) in nondirected interviews (van Dijk, 1983, 1984). It is obvious that in such interviews people take care to monitor rather attentively what they say or imply so as to establish or maintain the wanted self-representation of a kind, responsible, tolerant, and "nice" citizen and at the same time to provide information about beliefs, opinions, attitudes, or experiences. In the following (approximately translated) interview fragment, for instance, we find a typical correction move:

(8)   *. . . they do not work, well, don't work, they just mess around with cars and sell them*

We see that the meaning of the expression *they do not work* may imply a too far-reaching proposition (such as 'they do not want to work' or 'they are lazy'), which could be interpreted as a negative opinion or even as a prejudice, so a semantic correction is necessary, signaled here by *well*, the reviewing repetition of the wrong statement, and then the correct statement. This is an example of a typically strategic semantic move (and therefore has conversational and interactional functions as well) in which the relation between the two propositions can be accounted for by the functional link of a correction. Similarly, we often find different forms of explanation. Thus, the same speaker tries to account for the fact that he has few contacts with ethnic minorities first by a series of arguments about his own actual condition and actions and then by attributing some cause or reason to the other group. He first says

(9)   *. . . don't think that one of those people is trying to establish contact*

in which a direct cognitive blocking strategy in an appeal to the hearer is performed. The speaker wishes to prevent the conclusion that he is the only one responsible for lack of contact. In order to argumentatively sustain that general proposition the speaker then resorts to several explanatory moves:

(10)   *because they terribly need their own community.*

in which we find not only a strategic–rhetorical use of an exaggeration (*terribly*) but also, semantically, reference to a possible reason for their (lack of) actions, and such postponed references to reasons or causes usually function as explanations. That these semantic strategies and their communicative goals are often at the same time rhetorical, we see in the following fragment, in which a semantic contrast is expressed between subsequent propositions:

(11)   *we couldn't sleep, and **my** husband works, and my neighbors don't, so **they** could have a party*

Here we have the semantic opposition between the unpleasant 'not being able to sleep' and the pleasant 'having a party', and between 'my husband works' and 'they don't'. The semantic contrast operates as a rhetorical antithesis so as to make more effective (and therefore more defensible) the negative opinion about the other group (black neighbors).

In the same way, people in their conversational turn establish a large number of strategic semantic connections between sentences or moves or between underlying propositions. They use apparent denials (*I don't hate them, but . . .*), displacement (*I don't care so much, but the others in the street do*), attribution (as in [9], which illustrates the well-known strategy of 'blaming the victim'), denial of presuppositions or implications (*but that does not mean they are inferior*), and so on. In other words, semantic relations between sentences or propositions may be used strategically in order to convey precise meanings or to prevent wrong inferences by the hearer, and these strategies are part of more general strategies of conversation and interaction. Hence they need further conversational, pragmatic, rhetorical, and interactional analysis; their semantic analysis is just one dimension (van Dijk, 1984).

SEMANTIC ANALYSIS: SOME EXAMPLES

We now have some of the theoretical notions that allow us to provide a semantic analysis, description, or interpretation of discourse. It should be stressed, however, that theories do not immediately fit the empirical phenomena they try to account for. Instead of giving a lengthy methodological discussion of the sometimes very intricate problems involved, we simply summarize some of them in the following points as they apply to semantic discourse analysis:

1. Theories, and hence also their component statements (about rules, laws, principles, units, categories, levels, and so on), are general and relatively abstract. Hence the various properties of a general discourse semantics, for example, the conditions of local and global coherence, sometimes do not apply or only indirectly apply to the discourse data we obtain in some context of observation.

2. Our theoretical assumptions about the local and global coherence of discourse in principle should have a more or less universal nature. However, our data base allows only generalizations for some languages and cultures (e.g., English, Dutch, German, and other western cultures). Since knowledge and beliefs are so deeply involved in understanding, the assignment of local and global meanings is often dependent on cultural variation, and the various surface manifestations of coherence, as discussed above, may vary from one language to another.

3. We have not made a systematic distinction between written and oral discourse. Although our observations particularly hold for monological discourse, the various coherence constraints also hold for dialogical discourse. Additional semantic principles of connection, information distribution, and topics may be necessary for dialogues and particularly for everyday conversation, in which strategic moves are especially important.

4. We also abstracted from differences among discourse types, that is, genres. Although the most general principles hold for each discourse type, there may be differences in surface marking of coherence, additional constraints on local or global coherence, or specific meaning properties holding only for some discourse types (e.g., stories vs. poems vs. advertisements).

5. Although we have stressed the importance of personal differences in understanding due to different cognitive sets, memory capacity, and strategies, the principles we have formulated have abstracted from them. Both participants in textual communication and analysts root their semantic interpretation of concrete discourse in personal episodic models.

6. Meaning and reference are just one aspect of discourse, closely intertwined with surface structural, pragmatic, cognitive, and interactional features, so that also in this respect any semantic analysis exhibits the disadvantages of a partial description.

7. In addition to the cultural, personal, and interactional variation in the semantic principles discussed, there are a number of social constraints,

such as specific social setting, participant roles, conventions, age, sex, status, and power. Each may give specific or additional features to the conditions of meaningfulness of discourse.

8. Generalization and abstraction also involve presuppositions about normalcy. Specific uses and users may not satisfy this condition for reasons of pathological conditions (e.g., in aphasic or schizophrenic discourse), lack of control (e.g., in drugged or hypnotized language users), or intentional deviations having specific functions (esthetic, as in literary discourse; didactic, as in examples; or rhetorical and stylistic deviation or variation for special purposes).

9. Finally, the theory is simply far from complete. There are still many aspects of discourse meaning we simply do not know yet or know only imperfectly, so that general rules or conditions cannot yet be formulated.

With these problems in mind, we nevertheless try to show that many of the meaning properties of the example discourses that follow can be accounted for. It should finally be added that the aim and function of our analysis is didactic, that is, to show how the theory fragments do or do not fit the data. Each semantic analysis used in practice, for example, in the social sciences, will select the semantic aspects that may provide data for a more embracing aim of description or explanation (e.g., in psychotherapy or mass communication research).

Example 1

> WOMAN DROWNS IN RIVER PLUNGE—A young woman was drowned when a car plunged 15 feet down an embankment into the rain-swollen River Severn at Shewsbury yesterday. Her husband and the other occupants of the car, a married couple, managed to scramble to safety as the vehicle floated for a few seconds before disappearing under 10 feet of water. It had failed to negotiate a bend at a spot where the river bank is unfenced. (The *Times*, Nov. 23, 1981)

This rather stereotypical newspaper text about a car accident has a number of specific semantic properties that do not characterize everyday stories about such an accident (van Dijk, 1985). Newspaper stories respect what may be called a relevance structure: What is most important or interesting comes first and details, such as causes or other conditions and backgrounds, come later, so that the editor may eventually cut these to obtain the wanted size (which is an organizational constraint). The reader thus gets the most relevant information first before going (or not) to the details. This is a cognitive and communicative constraint on newspaper ordering of information. From this text we see that the temporal ordering of (presumed or reported) facts is not parallel with the ordering of clauses in the text that denote these facts: The cause of the accident comes last, and the ultimate consequence (which makes the accident newsworthy), the death of a woman, comes first. The various propositions of this text together define, on the basis of our world knowledge about accidents and what happens with cars in rivers, the overall theme, that is, the macrostructure as it is partially expressed in the title.

The first sentence, composed of an initial main clause and a subordinate clause stating the cause of death and the place and time of the accident (which typically come last, unlike in other story types), can be taken as the fuller expression of this underlying macrostructure. Such a thematic sentence has a rather independent nature. It cannot simply be connected with connectives such as *and* and *so* to the following sentence. Rather, the following sentence (*The husband . . .*) is linked functionally with the first sentence because it is a specification of the car plunge into the river; it introduces further participants and their fate. Yet, at the same time, with respect to the proposition 'a car plunged 15 feet down an embankment into the river', this second sentence expresses a possible consequence of the previous proposition. The local coherence between the sentences is further marked by the definite noun phrase *the car* and by the possessive pronoun *her* relating woman and husband (also by world knowledge about such a relation). That a car is 'floating' is a specific consequence of the special circumstance of a car being in the water, and the same holds for 'disappearing under water'; the action of the participants, 'to scramble to safety', is also part of the specific car accident script. The final sentence, mentioning the cause of the accident, provides the stereotypical information about the causes of cars plunging in a river (bend in the road, no fence). Although the ordering of the expressed propositions is specific for the news text, they do respect the normal criteria for conditional connection. The respective propositions, according to the accident script, allow the derivation of a macrostructure, as it is expressed in title and lead sentence, so the text is also globally coherent. The relatedness of the facts is further indicated by the identity of individuals, namely, the woman and the car as expressed by pronouns (*her, it*), definite articles (*the car*), and synonyms (*the vehicle*). That the concepts of 'husband' and 'occupants' are expressed in definite noun phrases is due to presuppositions derived from world knowledge, namely, that a woman may have a husband and that cars may have other occupants. The use of *other* is also a cohesion marker implying that the woman and her husband were also occupants.

Note that the informational structure of the text follows the usual rules. The concept of 'woman' and of 'car' are introduced as topics in the first two clauses by indefinite articles (which means that the title is not to be considered as a previous sentence). The same holds for 'husband' and other 'occupants' in the next sentence. This means that the criteria for the topic–comment articulation for sentences require a specific analysis for topic introduction. Indefinite noun phrases in initial position, especially those denoting human individuals as experiencers or agents, are interpreted as new topics, an interpretation strategy that may of course be falsified by further interpretation of the sentence and the text. Strictly speaking, the only entities known in the first sentence are the locations (Severn and Shewsbury), which formally speaking would make the rest of the sentence the new information, and hence comment.

Example 2

> and the little kid came by, and he si . . . and he . . . hesitated, but then he stole,
> . . . one of the baskets of pears . . . and put it on his . . . bicycle and rode off.
> . . . And as he was . . . riding down the r . . . this . . . this uh . . . dirt road,
> . . . /it/ was full of rocks, . . . you could hear the . . . the rocks creak underneath,
> . . . u—m . . . this other little girl in pigtails, . . . black pigtails, . . . rode by,
> . . . and he tipped his hat to her, . . . and as he did that, . . . lost his hat, . . .
> and ran into a b—ig rock, and the . . . pears spilled all over. (Data and transcript
> from Tannen, 1980).

Again a story about a (more mundane) accident, this time given in the course of an oral retelling of an experimental movie. As we observed above, such a more natural everyday story (though it is a retelling of movie events rather than of real events), more or less follows the ordering of the denoted facts. The beginning of the embedded story of the accident is linked up with the end of a previous story about a kid on a bike who stole a basket of pears. The first story perfectly respects the conditional ordering of the propositions and facts: a boy comes by on a bike, hesitates, steals pears, puts them on his bike and rides off. Note, that coming by on a bike is the initial setting (which is a narrative category) of the first story, after which the subsequent sentences specify the complication (the theft). Hesitation is a normal condition for stealing (world knowledge), and 'putting something stolen on your bike' is a normal component of the stealing action, whereas 'riding off' is the normal final consequence.

In a wider narrative context this little story functions again as the background, and hence as the setting, of the next story about the bike accident: The main participant and the fact that he is riding a bike with a basket of pears have been introduced. This setting is expressed explicitly in *And he was riding down the . . . road,* which semantically speaking is a specification of 'riding off', and at the same time a condition for the following events. Interpolated we have a typical functionally coherent sentence, *(the road) was full of rocks, you could hear the rocks creak underneath,* which is not a consequence of the previous sentence, but rather a specification of the kind of road (a gravel road) and a specification of the storyteller's observations. That is, in the linear account of events, a storyteller may interpolate specific perceptions, interpretations, or evaluations to explain what was going on. At the same time, though, this functional sentence serves as the introduction of the information that is the condition for the later event (ran into a big rock). The introduction of the other participant follows (with the narrative demonstrative for new participants, *this*), and the action in which she is involved (riding by), which enable the action of tipping one's hat, losing one's hat, running into a big rock, and spilling the pears, which is a possible conditional (causal) sequence. Note that the action of tipping one's hat is repeated in *and as he did that,* which perhaps should be interpreted causally, not temporally, with respect to the next sentences. The repetition may, among other conversational and narrative functions, be motivated by the production strategy of marking the special cause of some event. Another observation that is necessary for the semantic analysis is the fact that the causal sequence is not strictly complete (van Dijk, 1977). Although the states and actions reported are fairly detailed, the storyteller normally leaves out many intermediary components of events and actions, which are supposed to be derivable from world knowledge by the hearer. Thus it is not stated that the boy went to the basket of pears, nor that he got off his bike to do so, nor that he looked at the girl, nor that he was actually falling with his bike and basket. In other words, even crucial main actions may sometimes be omitted if the conditions and the consequences are given. Given our world knowledge, then, textual sequences need not be complete in order to be conditionally coherent: The coherence links may be formally or cognitively reconstructed from propositions in our memory.

So at the local level we obtain semantic coherence by (1) propositions denoting conditionally related facts, (2) functional specifications of objects, and (3) expressed or implied propositions that actualize general script knowledge about landscapes, roads, rocks, bikes, and the causes of falling off a bike, whereas the ordering of the sentences expressing these propositions is a rather direct linear rendering of the conditional links between the facts (there are no lookbacks, no backward explanations, no previews, which may occur in stories), with the exception of an interpolated perception statement (*you could hear . . .*). The topic–comment articulation of the respective sentences is also straightforward: *little kid, he . . . he* express the topical agent as subject and in initial positions, which is the canonical case. Halfway, a new topic is introduced in the usual way (see above), but the next sentence again puts *he* in initial position, in the agent role and as primary topic. Since *her* is a pronoun, the individual is known and hence formally also a topic function: It is the pair (*he, her*) that expresses the complex topic. That *he* is nevertheless in initial position, and not *she* (which was last named), may be explained by the sequential and textual prominence of 'the boy': he is the sequential topic and agent of the macroproposition, hence part of the discourse topic. Main actors have topical precedence over minor actors in sentence structure, especially when involved as agents in an action (here the action cannot even be put in passive sentence form).

Note also that a number of noun phrases are in definite form although the individuals they refer to are not previously introduced. We already mentioned the indefinite use of narrative *this*. *Baskets* has been introduced in the story before, whereas *road* has a definite article because there is just one in the scene of the movie.

One of the specific features of this story is its relative semantic completeness. It has information that in normal everyday stories would perhaps not be mentioned, for example, the fact that the road was a dirt road, that the girl had pigtails, and that these were black. The special context, retelling a movie story, not only requires that the storyteller be relevant, but also that details in the movie be reproduced. In fact, most other stories in this experiment do not mention these details but pick out the most relevant events: riding on a bike with a basket of pears, a girl coming by, looking at the girl, hitting a rock, falling, spilling the pears.[4]

The overall coherence of this passage may be construed as two macropropositions, 'The boy stole a basket of pears' for the first story and 'The boy looked at a girl, hit a rock with his bike, and fell' for the second. Since stories have several major narrative categories such as setting, complication, and resolution each of these categories should be connected with a macroproposition (Chafe, 1980) so that a full macrostructure of a story, as well as an appropriate summary, should at least have as many macropropositions as narrative categories. On the basis of world knowledge about stealing and about bike accidents, we are able to delete irrelevant details (e.g., the color of the girl's hair) and to construct conditions (hesitating) and components (losing his hat) into a more overall action proposition. In general then, the semantic analysis of a macrostructure in a story should be specified relative to the narrative functions of certain discourse units, such as paragraphs. That is, actions

---

[4] For the role of world knowledge and its possible integration into the representation of the discourse in memory, see Schank and Abelson (1977), Kintsch and van Dijk (1978), Bower, Black, and Turner (1979), and den Uyl and van Oostendorp (1980). In this last study it is shown that the various proposals vary as to the amount of knowledge needed and the necessity of integrating it into the memory representation of discourse: Do we need fully coherent representations for understanding, or is a more sloppy understanding, with partial coherence, also a viable strategy (see van Dijk & Kintsch, 1983).

may be more important than descriptive details, at least in everyday stories.

Example 3

A LITTLE PLUG FOR BRITISH TELECOM'S NEW SOCKET

At British Telecom, we're rather proud of ourselves.

Our new plug and socket is going to revolutionise the way you use the phone.

No longer will it be fixed in one place. Thanks to our little device, you'll be able to make and take calls wherever you want.

From now on, it'll be the standard fitting with all new extensions we install in the home.

While they're doing that job, our engineers will convert any existing instruments free.

And they'll be happy to put extra sockets in any other rooms you like for a small charge.

Apart from making it possible to move phones around, the new plug and socket makes it easier and cheaper to replace one phone with another.

Eventually, all new phones will use the system, which has been developed exclusively by British Telecom.

It's the beginning of our great plan for the 80's.

A semantic analysis of this advertisement (*Times*, Nov. 23, 1981) for British Telecom follows the principles explained and applied above. At the local coherence level, we have the following connections. A functional relation of explanation between the first sentence and the second sentence (and the rest of the text): A reason why BT is proud is given. Between the third and second sentence we also have a functional relation: The overall predicate 'to revolutionise the way you use your phone' is specified by the information that the new plug and socket is no longer fixed in one place so that mobile phoning in several places of the home is possible. The fourth sentence is a consequence of this third sentence. The next sentence gives a functional generalization for this particular use: It will be installed in all homes. There follows a general specification that conversion will be free and that extra sockets will be installed for a small charge. Another reason (repeating the previous one as a presupposition) is given in the next explanation (easier and cheaper to replace phones). The next generalization extends to all phone connections and adds the qualification for the plug: exclusive for BT. Finally we have another generalization, this time from the action of installing a new plug and socket to a more general *plan for the 80's*. At the global level the coherence is established by the headline for the ad: *a little plug for British Telecom's new socket*. The text of the ad gives details, such as reasons and consequences of the general action of installing a new device, and at the

same time explains that this is one of the revolutionary plans of BT.
Rhetorically interesting is the (apparent?) contrast between 'great plans'
and 'revolutionary' on the one hand and the size and simplicity of the
new device (a plug). This contrast is also expressed in a picture, in which
the tiny plug is contrasted with a much larger human hand.

The local coherence between the respective sentences is not signaled
by connectives—most connections are functional—but by juxtaposition
alone. It is marked by the various cohesion devices mentioned earlier,
for example, *we–our* in sentences 1 and 2, *new plug and socket* and *it*
in sentences 2 and 3, and *little device* as a paraphrase in sentence 4.
Interesting is the *it* in the last sentence, It's the beginning . . ., which
does not strictly corefer with the new 'plug and socket', but rather with
the macroproposition 'we will install a new system for all phones'. Another
coherence chain is the addressed *you,* the reader or the telephone sub-
scriber, which makes the message more personal. The coherence should
also be construed relative to our knowledge of the world, namely, our
knowledge of telephones, telephone companies, and technology. This
knowledge allows us to link such concepts as 'phone', 'plug and socket',
'extension', 'in the home', 'little device', 'instruments', and 'engineers'.
The general pragmatic function of advertisement discourse is to recommend
or suggest the use of new articles or services (Dyer, 1982). This means
that an advertisement should specify (1) what the (superior) qualities of
the article or service are, (2) comparison with other or previous articles,
and (3) reasons to use the article, and optionally or implicitly make a
generalization about the quality of the products of a specific business.
In the example, the positive evalutions of the product and the action for
introducing it can be generalized (by a macrorule) from the predicates
'proud', 'new', 'revolutionise', 'thanks to', the respective predicates
about the 'ease of use', and 'great plan for the 80's'. The comparison
is expressed by *no longer will it be fixed in one place,* and the reason
by *you'll be able to . . .* and *makes it easier and cheaper to replace one
phone with another.* A possible counterargument (costs money) is met
with the information that installment is free for existing instruments and
only a small charge will cover additional extensions. We see that, apart
from the semantic coherence at the local and global levels, there is a
general argumentative structure, a kind of superstructure like the narrative
structure of our earlier examples, implied by the text (see van Dijk, 1978,
1980; and Gülich and Quasthoff in Chapter 10 of this Volume). The
general macroconclusions for the argument may be 'use our new plug',
'Telecom is a good company', and so 'have a phone installed in your
home'. The general premise (a fact) is that Telecom is planning a tech-

nological revolution: the mobile use of phones in the home. Several grounds are given for this general fact: a specific fact (a new plug) and reasons for using it (handy, cheap), an implicit general backing for the argument (if a plug is mobile then it is easier to use the phone), and the extended backing (mobile use is one additional reason to have a phone). We see, therefore, that the semantics of the ad is organized not only by the local and global coherence of related facts but also by the superordinate organization of an argumentative schema. It is also typical for this kind of discourse (see, e.g., Dyer, 1982, for details) that the propositions denote not only existing facts, such as 'we're proud of ourselves', but also future possibilities, such as possible actions of users (most of the sentences have future tenses).

Example 4

1 yes is a pleasant country:
2 if's wintry
3 (my lovely)
4 let's open the year

5 both is the very weather
6 (not either)
7 my treasure,
8 when violets appear

9 love is a deeper season
10 than reason;
11 my sweet one
12 (and april's where we're) (Cummings, 1963, p. 64)

The semantic structure of this modern poem is more complicated and does not follow the rules mentioned in this chapter, at least not in a straightforward manner (see van Dijk, 1972; and Gutwinski, 1976, for the semantic analysis of literary discourse). We do not have complete sentences with a recognizable syntactic structure, some of the phrases do not seem well-formed, and the propositions and fragments are not literally meaningful (*yes is a pleasant country*). Semantic analysis, therefore, requires some additional principles in this case. The surface structure, apart from being semigrammatical, is not necessarily a linear expression of propositions or facts. It may also express prosodic, metric, or spatial structures (rhymes, verse organization, strophic organization, etc.). As for the semantics, there are not straightforward full propositions nor a specific ordering, conditional or functional. That is, the local and global coherence may be reduced to mere conceptual coherence, that is, relations between individual concepts, for instance by the associative links mentioned in the beginning of this chapter. This may mean that the referential basis (often fictional or at least not intentionally or retrievably realistic) is also fragmentary and limited to some associated individuals and some of their properties. According to our world knowledge (scripts), we can find links among 'country', 'wintry', 'year', 'weather', 'violets appear', 'season' and 'april'. This conceptual series, as we might call it, suggests a higher order concept contrast between 'winter' and 'spring'. Parallel to this is the "love" series composed of the concepts 'my lovely', 'my treasure', 'us', 'love' and 'my sweet one'. Both series are fundamentally stereotypic: There is a presupposed general knowledge about traditional love poems in which seasons or landscapes are compared to the moods of people in love (as in lines 9–10). Although it is possible to provide further interpretations of the phrases or clauses and the propositions they express, a superficial analysis does not yield more than this kind of conceptual coherence, at both the local and global levels.

CONCLUSIONS

Our analyses of four discourses, though very informal and incomplete, have illustrated that the major principles outlined in the theoretical section are followed in these discourses but that additional semantic properties for specific contexts and text genres must be worked out. Thus the newspaper text showed that semantic ordering is not primarily determined by a conditional structure of the facts but rather by the functional coherence based on relevance: Important information comes first and details, such as causes, components, or consequences, are mentioned later. The relations between the facts are construed on the basis of our world knowledge about accidents, whereas the cohesive surface structure is characterized by coreferential pronouns, paraphrases, or possessives. The natural story, on the other hand, is organized by conditional links denoting causing or enabling relations between the facts. Again, component actions are not mentioned but are left to the reader for inference from world knowledge, although specific tasks may induce the storyteller to be overcomplete, that is, to specify details that normally would be irrelevant for natural storytelling. The newspaper ad also has an overall structure, that of argumentation, and a local coherence structure that is predominantly functional: Specifications are given of new products brought on the market with explanations why the use of such products is beneficial. Typically the overall semantic meaning is in the global speech act of recommendation or advice, which is also marked by the continuous future tenses predicated of the reader (addressed as *you*). Finally, there is an overall positive predicate being generated for the recommended product. The modern poem, finally, does not have a clear propositional coherence, either conditional or functional. Rather there is the establishment of what may simply be called "conceptual" coherence, manifesting itself by series of contrastive concepts from the same script or semantic range. These series may be organized by macrorules, providing the overall themes of the poem (seasonal change, love), although such a macrostructure is also fragmentary, consisting of isolated concepts, instead of propositional. Except for some lexical cohesion and some pronouns, there are no surface cues that exhibit propositional coherence.

A number of conclusions can be drawn about the nature of semantic discourse analysis:

1. Discourses are in principle characterized by an overall meaning or macrostructure that formalizes the theme or topic of the discourse as a whole. Such a macrostructure may often be expressed by titles or headlines, or by initial thematic or final summarizing sentences. The macrostructure propositions are derived by macrorules (such as deletion, generalization, and construction) from the propositions expressed by the text and from activated world knowledge. Without a semantic macrostructure, even a fragmentary one, there is no overall coherence and hence no point to the discourse. Macrostructures may be further organized by general ordering principles (a kind of specific discourse syntax), which also specify the schematic functions or categories of the sections (e.g., paragraphs) of the text, such as setting, complication and resolution in a story, or premises and conclusion in an argument (or advertisement or scholarly paper); newspaper discourse first gives the main facts, mostly conclusions or consequences, followed by causes, previous events, explanation, and background or context. In other words, the overall meaning of the discourse has a double function: It provides the semantic content for schematic categories that are typical for a specific discourse genre and at the same time provides the basis for the establishment of local coherence. That is, the macroproposition contains the concepts by which the associated world knowledge (scripts) is activated to interpret the sentences and words of the discourse.

2. The local coherence of discourse is to be formulated in terms of propositional relationships denoting relations between facts in some possible world. These relationships may be conditional (denoting conditional relations between the facts) or functional (showing relations between the information provided relative to previous information).

3. There are general ordering constraints on propositions and sentences expressing them. These constraints take into account the conditional,

spatial, or temporal ordering of the facts and perceptions, and the cognitive and pragmatic relevance of the facts.

4. The global and local coherence of discourse is expressed by surface properties of discourse, such as clause organization, clause ordering, sentence ordering, connectives, pronouns, adverbs, verb tenses, lexical identity, paraphrases, and definite articles.

5. Local coherence may also serve various pragmatic, stylistic and rhetorical functions, such as linking speech acts, establishing functions for speech acts (such as concluding, exemplifying, contrasting), marking didactic functions of the discourse, marking esthetic functions (by the lack of propositional coherence in a modern poem), or emphasizing the rhetorical, persuasive function of an advertisement.

6. Each clause and each sentence is marked for its function within the communicative sequence of information distribution: Some semantic information is already known, or is inferrable, whereas other information is presented as new. Thus a topic–comment schema is imposed on the semantic representation of sentences and expressed, depending on language and context, by word order, morphological devices, stress, intonation, fixed syntactic phrases, left or right dislocation of phrases, and pronouns or other pro- elements at the syntactic level, and by participant roles (e.g., agent) at the semantic level. For each stage in the unfolding of the textual sequence, the reader is presented with the information that, cognitively, should be kept in short term memory or (re-)activated for predication. It was observed that although permanent topic change is possible, there is often a strategy for the maintenance of sentence-topic providing what may be called "topical coherence" through the discourse. Thus, maintenance of sentential topics may result in sequential topics, which may be candidates for a participant position, often agent, in the macro-proposition of the discourse.

7. This kind of semantic analysis is highly abstract, restricted, and general. It abstracts from actual cognitive processing, does not explicate the knowledge, beliefs, or other cognitive systems involved, and disregards personal or subjective information (memories, goals, interests, tasks); it studies meaning and reference in isolation from pragmatic speech acts, superstructural schemata, and rhetorical effectiveness, and thereby in isolation from the whole sociocultural context. It has been shown for some examples, though, that these multiple links exist between the meanings of the discourse and its actual uses in communication.

To summarize the various aspects of discourse meaning we could account for in this (linguistic) semantics, we provide the following schema of the major components of a semantic discourse analysis:

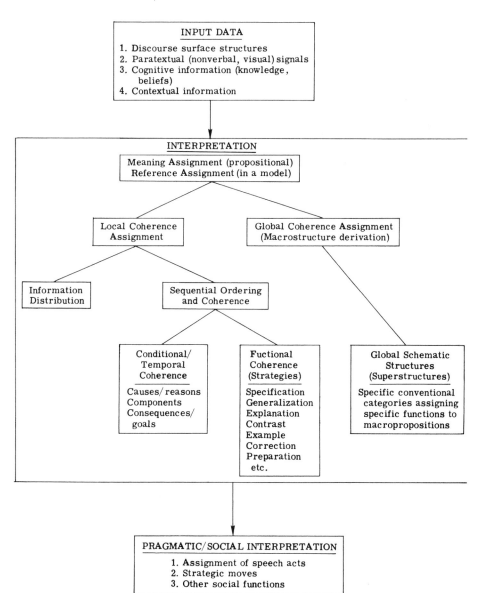

INPUT DATA

1. Discourse surface structures
2. Paratextual (nonverbal, visual) signals
3. Cognitive information (knowledge, beliefs)
4. Contextual information

INTERPRETATION

Meaning Assignment (propositional)
Reference Assignment (in a model)

Local Coherence Assignment

Global Coherence Assignment (Macrostructure derivation)

Information Distribution

Sequential Ordering and Coherence

Conditional/ Temporal Coherence

Causes/reasons
Components
Consequences/ goals

Fuctional Coherence (Strategies)

Specification
Generalization
Explanation
Contrast
Example
Correction
Preparation
etc.

Global Schematic Structures (Superstructures)

Specific conventional categories assigning specific functions to macropropositions

PRAGMATIC/SOCIAL INTERPRETATION

1. Assignment of speech acts
2. Strategic moves
3. Other social functions

REFERENCES

Beaugrande, R. de. (1980). *Text, discourse and process.* Norwood, NJ: Ablex.
Beaugrande, R. de, & Dressler, W. U. (1981). *Introduction to text linguistics.* London: Longman.
Bower, G. H., Black, J. B., & Turner, T. J. (1979). Scripts in memory for texts. *Cognitive Psychology, 11,* 177–220.
Carnap, R. (1956). *Meaning and necessity.* Chicago: University of Chicago Press.
Chafe, W. L. (1980). *The pear stories.* Norwood, NJ: Ablex.
Clark, H. H. (1976). *Semantics and comprehension.* The Hague: Mouton.
Clark, H. H., & Clark, Eve. (1977). *Psychology and language.* New York: Harcourt Brace.
Clark, H. H., & Haviland, S. E. (1977). Comprehension and the given-new contract. In R. O. Freedle (Ed.). (1977). *Discourse Production and Comprehension* (pp. 1–40). Norwood, NJ: Ablex.
Cotton, J. W., & Klatzky, R. L. (Eds.). (1978). *Semantic factors in cognition.* Hillsdale, NJ: Erlbaum.
Cresswell, M. J. (1973). *Logics and languages.* London: Methuen.
Cummings, E. E. (1963). *Selected poems.* Harmondsworth: Penguin.
den Uyl, M., & van Oostendorp, H. (1980). The use of scripts in text comprehension. In T. A. van Dijk (Ed.), Story comprehension [special issue]. *Poetics, 9,* 1–3, 275–294.
Dik, S. C. (1978). *Functional grammar.* Amsterdam: North Holland.
Ducrot, O. (1980). *Les mots du discours.* Paris: Minuit.
Dyer, G. (1982) *Advertising as communication.* London: Methuen.
Freedle, R. O. (Ed.). (1977). *Discourse production and comprehension.* Norwood, NJ: Ablex.
Freedle, R. O. (Ed.). (1979). *New directions in discourse processing.* Norwood, NJ: Ablex.
Givón, T. (1979a). From discourse to syntax: Grammar as a processing strategy. In T. Givón (Ed.), *Syntax and Semantics* (Vol. 12). *Syntax and discourse* (pp. 81–112). New York: Academic Press.
Givón, T. (Ed.). (1979b). *Syntax and semantics* (Vol. 12). *Syntax and discourse.* New York: Academic Press.
Grice, H. P. (1967). *Logic and conversation.* William James Lectures, unpublished.
Grice, H. P. (1975). Logic and conversation. In P. Cole & J. L. Morgan (Eds.), *Syntax and semantics (Vol. 3)—Speech Acts* (pp. 41–50). New York: Academic Press.
Grimes, J. E. (1975). *The thread of discourse.* The Hague: Mouton.
Gutwinski, W. (1976). *Cohesion in literary texts.* The Hague: Mouton.
Halliday, M. A. K., & Hasan, R. (1976). *Cohesion in English.* London: Longman.
Jones, L. K. (1977). *Theme in English expository discourse.* Lake Bluff, IL: Jupiter Press.
Just, M., & Carpenter, P. (Eds.). (1977). *Cognitive processes in comprehension.* Hillsdale, NJ: Erlbaum.
Kempson, R. M. (1975). *Presupposition and the delimitation of semantics.* London: Cambridge University Press.
Kintsch, W. (1974). *The representation of meaning in memory.* Hillsdale, NJ: Erlbaum.
Kintsch, W. (1977). *Memory and cognition.* New York: Wiley.
Kintsch, W., & van Dijk, T. A. (1978). Toward a model of text comprehension and production. *Psychological Review, 85,* 363–394.
Kreckel, M. (1981). *Communicative acts and shared knowledge in natural discourse.* London: Academic Press.
Lehrer, A., & Lehrer, K. (Eds.). (1970). *Theory of meaning.* Englewood Cliffs, NJ: Prentice Hall.

Levelt, W. J. M. (1981). The speaker's linearization problem. *Philosophical Transactions of the Royal Society of London,* B 295, 305–315.

Lindsay, P. H., & Norman, D. A. (1972). *Human information processing.* New York: Academic Press.

Linsky, L. (Ed.). (1952). *Semantics and the philosophy of language.* Urbana, IL: University of Illinois Press.

Linsky, L. (1967). *Referring.* London: Routledge & Kegan Paul.

Linsky, L. (Ed.). (1971). *Reference and modality.* London: Oxford University Press.

Li, C. N. (Ed.). (1976). *Subject and topic.* New York: Academic Press.

Lyons, J. (1977). *Semantics* (Vols. 1 & 2). London: Cambridge University Press.

Marslen-Wilson, W., Levy, E., & Komisarjevsky-Tyler, L. (1981). Producing interpretable discourse: The establishment and maintenance of reference. In R. J. Jarvella & W. Klein (Eds.), *Language, place and action* (pp. 339–378). Chichester: Wiley.

Meyer, B. F. (1976). *The organization of discourse and its effect on memory.* Amsterdam: North Holland.

Meyer, P. G. (1975). *Satzverknüpfungsrelationen.* Tübingen: Verlag Gunter Narr.

Montague, R. (1974). *Formal philosophy.* New Haven: Yale University Press.

Norman, D. A., & Rumelhart, D. (Eds.). (1975). *Explorations in cognition.* San Francisco: Freeman.

Östman, J. O. (Ed.). (1978). *Cohesion and semantics* (Rep. No. 41). Åbo: Publications of the Research Institute of the Åbo Akademi Foundation.

Petöfi, J. S. (Ed.). (1979). *Text vs. sentence* (Vols. 1 & 2). Hamburg: Buske Verlag.

Petöfi, J. S., & Franck, D. (Eds.). (1973). *Presuppositions in linguistics and philosophy.* Frankfurt: Athenaeum.

Petöfi, J. S., & Rieser, H. (Eds.). (1973). *Studies in text grammar.* Dordrecht: Reidel.

Petöfi, J. S., & Rieser, H. (1974). *Probleme der modelltheoretischen Interpretation von Texten.* Hamburg: Buske Verlag.

Reder, L., & Anderson, J. R. (1980). A comparison of texts and their summaries. *Journal of Verbal Learning and Verbal Behavior, 19,* 121–134.

Reichman, R. (1981). *Plain speaking: A theory and grammar of spontaneous discourse.* Cambridge, MA: Bolt, Beranek & Newman.

Schank, R. C., & Abelson, R. P. (1977). *Scripts, plans, goals and understanding.* Hillsdale, NJ: Erlbaum.

Sgall, P., Hajičová, E., & Benešová, E. (1973). *Topic, focus and generative semantics.* Kronberg: Scriptor.

Tannen, D. (1980). A comparative analysis of oral narrative strategies: Athenian Greek and American English. In W. Chafe (Ed.). *The pear stories* (pp. 51–87). Norwood, NJ: Ablex.

Tulving, E., & Donaldson, W. (Eds.). (1972). *Organization of memory.* New York: Academic Press.

van Dijk, T. A. (1972). *Some aspects of text grammars.* The Hague: Mouton.

van Dijk, T. A. (1977). *Text and context.* London: Longman.

van Dijk, T. A. (1978). *Tekstwetenschap* (Discourse studies). Utrecht: Spectrum. German translation: (1980) *Textwissenschaft,* Tübingen: Niemeyer.

van Dijk, T. A. (1980). *Macrostructures.* Hillsdale, NJ: Erlbaum.

van Dijk, T. A. (1981). *Studies in the pragmatics of discourse.* The Hague: Mouton.

van Dijk, T. A. (1983). Cognitive and conversational strategies in the expression of ethnic prejudice. *Text, 3,* 375–404.

van Dijk, T. A. (1984). *Prejudice in discourse.* Amsterdam: Benjamins.

van Dijk, T. A. (1985). *News as discourse*. New York: Longman (in press).

van Dijk, T. A., and Kintsch, W. (1983). *Strategies of discourse comprehension*. New York: Academic Press.

Wilson, D. (1975). *Presuppositions and non-truth conditional semantics*. New York: Academic Press.

CHAPTER **8**

Pragmatics

Alessandro Ferrara

INTRODUCTION

Suppose you and a friend are walking down the street in a foreign city, among people whose language you can neither speak nor understand. A stranger comes up to you and very decidedly, but with a courteous tone of voice, utters a mercilessly obscure sentence. You could wonder how the seemingly continuous stream of sounds is in reality made out of more basic, elementary sounds. Or you could ask yourself how the sentence breaks down into words and how these words are related to one another. In this case you might even get into an argument with your friend over how you could possibly discover a pattern of relations within the sentence before you know the meaning of its elements. And your friend might convince you that the right thing to ask is what the conditions are under which what the stranger said would be true. But maybe what you would really want to know is something else: What on earth does he want from me? Well, this is pragmatics. If you wonder: Is he pointing out something wrong that I have done? Does he want me to do something? Does he want some information? Is he insulting me? Is he offering something? Is he warning me of some danger? All these questions belong to what in this chapter I take to be pragmatics.

Pragmatics is not a new term. It was coined in 1938 by Morris. In a famous work on the foundations of the theory of signs, he defined it as "the science of the relation of signs to their interpreters" (Morris, 1938, p. 30; see also Morris, 1946). The concept has undergone thorough shifts since then, but it can still be taken as a point of reference for sorting out where the different conceptions of pragmatics stand.

The first great divide is between those who contend, against Morris' underlying assumption, that no sharp distinction can be drawn between

HANDBOOK OF DISCOURSE ANALYSIS, Vol. 2
Dimensions of Discourse

Copyright © 1985 by Academic Press London.
All rights of reproduction in any form reserved.
ISBN 0-12-712002-5

pragmatics and either the study of the relations of signs to signs (syntax) or the study of the relations of signs to the world (semantics)[1] and those who more or less go along with Morris on that score. Within the first group, we could still distinguish those who believe such a distinction to be impossible in principle and those who only question its fruitfulness. But those who believe in at least a polarity between syntactic or semantic and pragmatic questions—our second group—still disagree as to what the "relation of signs to their interpreters" is. Among them, we can identify at least three basic positions, ordered along the continuum of an increasing broadness of the boundaries of pragmatics. The first, a highly reductionist approach to pragmatics, perhaps an over-reductionist one, held sway coextensively with the fortunes of the most syntax-oriented brand of generativism. This approach centered around Montague's (1974) notion of pragmatics as concerned with the truth of expressions where there happened to be elements referring to the time and place of utterance or to the participants to the interaction. Pragmatics in this sense was more a truth-functional semantics extended to deictics than a distinguishably autonomous endeavor. A second sense of pragmatics that also has enjoyed some popularity, especially as a target for polemics, is as a sort of residual category into which is lumped all that cannot be labeled as phonological, syntactic, or semantic in a straightforward manner. In the pragmatic hodgepodge would be found such diverse phenomena as some types of presuppositions, presupposition failure, conversational implicatures, speech acts, cross-cultural misunderstanding, performative analysis, anaphoric and indexical terms, politeness and argumentative strategies, and code switching. In this chapter I follow a different approach, designed to steer a course between reducing pragmatics to a substanceless, technical attempt to meet formalization problems, on one hand, and making of it an umbrella concept covering the most disparate kinds of interests on the other. This third approach occupies the middle point of the continuum. I take pragmatics to refer to the systematic study of the relations between the linguistic properties of utterances and their properties as social action.

Every utterance is both a string of symbols, somehow connected and standing in a signifying relation to some mental construct, and a full–fledged social action, oriented to the normative expectations of a community. The theory of speech acts has spelled out some aspects of this

---

[1] Many contemporary linguists and philosophers of language fall into this category. Scholars as diverse as G. Lakoff, Searle, Fillmore, R. Lakoff, Ross, Sadock, and Wunderlich would probably converge on the impossibility of drawing sharp distinctions between some or all of these three fields.

normative background underlying the use of linguistic forms and has accounted for it in terms of constitutive rules (Austin, 1962; Searle, 1969, 1975a, 1975b). These rules work as culturally deposited guarantees that, if certain conditions obtain, uttering a certain sentence (e.g., *I am sorry for being late*) will amount to appropriately accomplishing a certain action (e.g., to apologize). The theory investigates these conditions and describes what has to be the case—in terms of both the linguistic features of the sentence and the context in which it is used—in order for given utterances to count as assertions, orders, promises, questions, or requests. Typically, the theory would claim, for instance, that in order for my saying *Take that chair over there* to count as an order, the addressee of my utterance must indeed be able to take the chair, and I must believe he or she is able. It must not be the case that he or she was going to take the chair anyway, I must want to have him or her take the chair, and, finally, I must be in a position of authority over him or her. If any of these conditions is not satisfied in the context of the interaction, then the order is defective to various possible degrees, ranging from being insincere, motivated by a manipulatory intent, to being illegitimate, issued by an impostor. Let us take another example: In order for my utterance to count as a promise, it must contain reference to a future act of mine, it must not be the case that I was going to do this action anyway, I must believe that my hearer would rather have me do the action than refrain from it, I must have the intention to perform the action, and I must intend to place myself under the obligation to do so. These conditions help us to understand why *I promise to give you $100* can be readily accepted as a promise, while to see a promise in *I promise to steal $100 from you* requires a more imaginative and unusual context. By this approach it becomes possible to explain the properties of certain sentences that are commonly used in order to convey a given type of speech act, as well as to investigate how the constraints on social action that are institutionalized into roles translate into constraints on the usage of linguistic forms.

Pragmatics, however, is not to be taken as exactly synonymous with a philosophical speech act theory, although it is rooted in it. In contrast to classical speech act theory, it tries to study speech acts as part of the sequential environment to which they are tied, and it pays attention to their contribution to the local and global coherence of a text (Ferrara, 1980b). Also, ideally, pragmatics would want to base its claims about appropriateness conditions on a firm empirical basis and to link its description of abstract act types to their roots in concrete social and cultural groups. Finally pragmatics, because of its effort to study speech acts and their appropriateness in a more realistic context of usage, that is, as they appear in sequences embedded in larger texts, cannot afford to leave out of its scope (as classical speech act theory did) an account of perlocutionary intent.

The pragmatics of discourse studies how the speech acts performed in uttering a text are linked to one another, their appropriateness, and their relation to the overall coherence of the text. It studies the way in which entire sequences of speech acts can enter into relations with one another, how they can be perceived as appropriate or inappropriate as a whole, how they are evaluated on the basis of higher-order expectations about the structure of a text, and how they, being themselves coherent microtexts, contribute to the global coherence of a larger text (Ferrara, 1980a). Insofar as its empirical basis is concerned, the pragmatics of discourse is grounded on the notion of macrostructure, elaborated initially by van Dijk and by others in the fields of text grammar, artificial intelligence and psycholinguistics as a tool for the investigation of semantic coherence (van Dijk, 1977a, 1977b, 1980; van Dijk & Kintsch, 1977). By and large, van Dijk's idea of a text as the enrichment and articulation of a semantic core, an articulation that has to follow paths laid out by the constraints (partly traditional and partly rational) of a discourse genre, can be carried over to the action aspect of a text. We can see a text, from a pragmatic point of view, as the articulation and implementation of a central core of intentions, an articulation that also is bound by considerations of tradition and rationality. Insofar as the theoretical presuppositions of the pragmatics of discourse are concerned, one common misunderstanding should be cleared away. It has been maintained that, because any sentence carries some indication of what speech act the speaker intends to convey, the study of linguistic forms as social actions is really part of a "semantics broadly conceived" (Searle, 1980, p. 19). Others have added another objection to this, claiming that because there is no way of drawing clearcut boundaries between syntactic, semantic, and pragmatic aspects of linguistic description, the aspiration of pragmatics to receive its proper place within grammar is also misconceived. Both these objections attribute to the present approach to pragmatics an implicit commitment to a particular form of grammar, subdivided in the sacred trinity of a syntactic, a semantic, and a pragmatic component. To the contrary, no such conclusion as to the form of grammars is embedded in the pragmatics of discourse. In fact, whether in the end it will prove more useful to build pragmatic components of grammars along with syntactic, semantic, or syntactic-semantic ones, or whether it will appear more convenient to dissolve pragmatics into something else, cannot be judged a priori. The only claim that the pragmatics of discourse takes for granted is the specificity and legitimacy of new types of questions hitherto ignored in all linguistic theories; these questions regard the relation of linguistic forms to their valences and effects as social actions.

FUNDAMENTALS OF THE PRAGMATIC ANALYSIS OF LOCAL COHERENCE

If we are to reconstruct and assess the pragmatic coherence of a text, we need (1) a concept of pragmatic coherence and (2) a procedure for assessing whether a given text is in fact pragmatically coherent or not. Concerning the former, let us go back very briefly to van Dijk's characterization of the global semantic coherence of a text. To understand a text semantically means, from a cognitive–psychological point of view, to be able to identify, under the series of the logicosemantic structures of its component sentences, a macrosemantic representation (i.e., one or more macropropositions) of which that series represents an expansion. A text is semantically coherent to the extent that it allows for such an operation. Similarly, the pragmatic coherence of a text depends on our ability to identify, under the linear chain of speech acts conveyed by the single sentences of the text, a macropragmatic content (i.e., one or more macro–speech acts). Under this basic similarity, however, there lies a crucial difference. The relation of the macropropositions to the micro ones is a relation of condensation, consisting of the systematic, selective reduction of information. With this in mind, it becomes possible, from the point of view of production, to speak of the surface of the text as an expansion of its semantic global core. This is not so at the pragmatic level. The relation of the macro–speech acts to the micro ones is also hierarchic, but in a different way. Surface speech acts are linked to superordinate ones on a means/ends dimension. The macro–speech act of a text, for example, "to prove the innocence of my client", is not expanded through the thousands of speech acts performed in my defense speech, rather it is implemented through them. Thus, in such a case, if I want to prove my case and convince you that my client is innocent, it might help if I can prove to you that he was not in town when the crime was committed, and, in order to prove and convince you of this, it might help if I remind you that on the day of the crime two witnesses have seen him at a meeting a thousand miles away, and it might also help if I suggest that the one witness who claims to have seen him on his way from the airport that same day is not reliable, given his record of drunkenness. All these speech acts, which could dominate long and complex sequences of other acts, help me in achieving subgoals that are instrumental to my being able to realize the overarching goal of the text, 'to prove to you that my client is innocent'. It is the presence and the tightness of this network of relations between its constituent speech acts that makes up the pragmatic coherence of a text.[2]

Given this view of pragmatic coherence, how can we analyze a text in order to see whether it meets this criterion? How do we come to identify its pragmatic core, its macro–speech acts? A number of problems will have to be solved along the way. Let us begin by looking at simple cases, pairs of connected speech acts or otherwise straightforward sequences.

From Surface Manifestation to Hierarchic Organization

In analyzing a text, the first problem is how we go from the unbroken linearity of its surface manifestation to the identification of clusters of hierarchically organized speech acts. We can recognize sentence boundaries and proposition boundaries, but, given that speech acts may well have more than one proposition as their propositional content, according to which criterion shall we distinguish between sentence boundaries and speech act boundaries? Let us take as an example two excerpts from a therapeutic situation. In the first, Jack, a nine-year-old child, has just resolved to start painting and is at a loss about what to paint. The following dialogue is exchanged:

(1) (Rogers, 1951; p. 240)

        Jack: What do you want me to paint? You tell me.

        Therapist: Jack, I know you want me to decide for you, but I really can't, because I don't want you to paint any particular thing.

In the second excerpt the eleven-year-old Henry, who began therapy with a view of his problems as coming only from without, from the

---

[2] It is unfortunate, however, that pragmatic research has so far unduly confined itself to a one-sided conception of the rationality embedded in the chain of speech acts constituting a text. In fact, speakers make their choices and construct their plans not only on purposive-rational grounds, but also on value–rational and affective ones. One of the most telling theoretical biases of pragmatic studies has been the underlying assumption that people link certain speech acts only because they see the linking as useful, never because they believe it is morally right for them to do so. As a consequence, the implicit image of the language user conveyed by pragmatics has also suffered from the same restriction, which has brought the language user to resemble more the mythical rational actor of economic theory than the more complex concept of the actor in a social context. I see this as one of the areas where pragmatics is in need of a major conceptual realignment.

actions of other people, confronts the therapist at a turning point in the therapeutic dialogue with a direct question:

(2) (Rogers, 1951; p. 248)

> Henry: What good does it do to feel better about things if they still go on?
>
> Therapist: Sometimes boys and girls can understand the way they really feel about things, and it helps them to know what they really want to do about their situations.

How many speech acts are performed by the therapist in his replies to Jack and Henry? Again we can draw on our general concept of action coherence. If it is sensible to say that when one produces a text one implements a plan (a mental hierarchy of goals) by performing a certain number of speech acts realized in the sentences that constitute the text, then an equally sensible method for segmenting the surface into simple speech acts is to look at the goal structure of this plan, to determine how many goals and subgoals are therein represented, and finally to map the linear manifestation onto an equal number of speech acts. This mapping is based on the following principle:

Principle 1: For each hypothetically identified speech act to be confirmed as a single and distinct act, we must find at least one goal, besides its illocutionary point,[3] that can conceivably motivate its performance.

Going back to our examples, notice how the plans underlying the therapist's responses differ in structure. To his response to Henry we can attribute the unique goal of describing the good inherent in talking things over and feeling better about them even if they do not go away. This "good" happens to be described with the help of a complex sentence, embedding many propositions, but since the goal underlying this whole utterance is

---

[3] By "illocutionary point" we understand the intention necessarily inherent in the performance of a certain type of speech act, as distinct from other intentions and goals that may or may not be present. Thus, when I ask a question appropriately I must want to know something, whatever the reason(s) I want to know it, and when I promise something I must intend to commit myself to some future action, whatever the reason(s) I might want to do so. We must go beyond these illocutionary intentions when we study sequences of speech acts or when we interpret them, because they are analytically built into the concept of the speech act being performed and thus are trivial and uninformative. Rather, we need to frame the already-identified actions of asserting, promising, requesting, ordering, and so on into a more comprehensive action structure, with respect to which we can evaluate the usefulness of a given speech act as a means of achieving any type of goal. For a classical treatment of the notion of illocutionary act, as well as for a distinction between locutionary, illocutionary and perlocutionary acts, see Searle (1969) and Austin (1962).

just one, we assign to it one assertion. In a different way, the therapist's reply to Jack is underlain by three distinct goals: to let Jack know that the therapist is aware of Jack's request to be told what to paint, to reject the request, and finally to provide a reason for this refusal. Consequently we segment the manifestation of this small text into three speech acts: an assertion, an indirect refusal, and another assertion. Notice that in neither of these examples of speech act assignment has the number of sentences or propositions in the text played any significant role.

Relations among Speech Acts

Our second problem, after sorting out all the speech acts of a text and determining their illocutionary force and propositional contents, is how to find what relations connect these speech acts with one another. How do we decide which speech acts dominate which others? This decision is important for assessing the appropriateness of the speech acts that compose each sequence and of entire sequences, and also for sorting out the macro–speech acts of the text. The hierarchic position of each act in the speaker's plan can be identified by looking at the hierarchic position of the corresponding goal that motivated the performance of the act in the first place. This operation is based on

Principle 2:   The hierarchic status of a speech act in a sequence corresponds to the hierarchic status of the extra-illocutionary goal that it is meant to achieve.

To decide that the achievement of a certain goal is considered by a speaker as a preliminary step or a subsidiary aid toward the achievement of another one is at the same time to determine the respective statuses of the speech acts performed in order to realize these goals. By definition it cannot ever be the case that the main act in the sequence is motivated by a secondary goal. This only shifts our problem, but it shifts it onto a plane that makes its solution easier. In fact, the relative status of goals in the speaker's plan can be accounted for in terms of

Principle 3:   The goals that, relative to a given context, require fewer other goals to be intended for the speaker's plan to be acceptable or simply understandable rank highest.

Let us look at another excerpt from a therapy session. A group of high school problem children in a group therapy session is instructed to get together and talk about whatever they want, but the group finds it difficult to break the ice. Nobody seems to be able to break out of the circle of tension and impotence. Finally one of the participants addresses the therapist directly:

(3) (Rogers, 1951, p. 341)
      B: Trouble is, you should give us something definite to talk on.
          This way we will get all mixed up. Nobody wants no—nobody
          knows what to talk about. Give us a definite point.

If we break down this sequence into its component speech acts, we can
see the speaker requesting twice that some precise topic be offered by
the therapist, supporting his request with the assertion that by continuing
on the same track the group *will get all mixed up,* and supporting this
assertion with the other assertion that *nobody knows what to talk about.*
Laying aside for the time being the issue of repeated speech acts, we
can connect these three speech acts with their respective goals of (probably)
relieving the group from the embarrassment of the present situation (by
obtaining a definite subject to discuss), increasing the chances of the
request to be fulfilled (by justifying it with a sensible assertion), and
strengthening the justification for the request (by explaining why the
situation that justifies the request came into being in the first place). On
the basis of Principle 3, we can now see how these goals are hierarchically
related to one another. The speaker would not want to back up his
justification (and therefore assert *Nobody knows what to talk about*) if
he also did not want to provide a justification, particularly a strong one
(which he does by asserting *This way we will get all mixed up*). In turn,
he would not want to provide a justification, strong or otherwise, unless
he also wanted something else, that for which justification is being provided,
namely, if he did not want to have the therapist propose a topic for
discussion (an attempt that he makes with his request *Give us a definite
point*). By mirroring back these hierarchic relations between goals onto
the speech acts that were supposed, in the speaker's plan, to implement
them, we can see how B's request is indeed the dominant speech act in
the sequence and how the first assertion (*This way we will get all mixed
up*) is a subordinate act with respect to the request but a dominant one
with respect to the second assertion (*Nobody knows what to talk about*).
This distinction between the main speech act and the subordinate ones
in a sequence is important in two ways: to evaluate their appropriateness
and to identify the pragmatic macrostructure of the text. In fact, whereas
the appropriateness of the topmost, main speech act in a sequence is
assessed in terms of the standard conditions of appropriateness that apply
to it, the appropriateness of a subordinate one is defined not only in
terms of standard conditions but also in terms of its context-bound potential
for entering a certain kind of relation (we have already seen examples
of relations of justification and explanation) with the main speech act in
the sequence. The macro–speech acts that hold together a text from a
pragmatic point of view are usually among the main speech acts in the

various sequences. For example, in the sequence uttered by B, it is his request, not the two assertions, that is most likely to be part of the pragmatic macrostructure of the whole therapeutic session.

Types of Relations among Speech Acts

Let us move on to our third problem on the way to the assessment of the pragmatic coherence of a text. If, as we have seen, subordinate speech acts are performed mainly because of their capability to contribute to the success of the dominant ones, and if this contributing to the chances of success of another act depends on the potential for the subordinate act to enter successfully a certain type of relation with the main one (e.g., to be a good justification or a good explanation for it), then we should be able to specify what defines several types of relations and what counts as entering them successfully. How many types of relations is it possible to have between two speech acts in a sequence? Very little research on this exists, and, given that it is not the primary aim of this chapter to provide a detailed or exhaustive list of such relation types, I confine myself to a few words about some of the most common ones (and see van Dijk, 1981, pp. 265–284).

We have already seen relations of justification and of explanation. In order for a subordinate speech act to enter successfully a justificatory relation with the main act in the sequence, it must be able to relate (in its own way) to a state of the world and be capable of inducing a favorable attitude toward the class of actions to which the main act belongs. Assertions, as in (3), do this by describing such states of affairs, but other types of speech acts can obtain the same effect in different ways. A promise, for instance, may be said to justify a question, as in *I'll buy you an ice cream. Do you like bittersweet chocolate?* The promise commits the speaker to a course of action, for which he needs to know whether the hearer likes a particular type of ice cream. We have also seen explanatory relations: A speech act enters an explanatory relation with another if it represents an answer to the question "why p?" (where p is the propositional content of the dominant act). Notice also that these relations attach to different objects: In an explanatory relation what is explained is the propositional content of the main act, whereas in a justificatory relation what is justified is not the content but the entire dominant act.

There exist other types of relations. One or more subordinate speech acts can expand or elaborate on a central one. Sometimes this relation of expansion goes in the direction of making the dominant speech act more specific in some respect, at other times of making it more general. Expansion in the direction of specification is what Richard Nixon does while he reviews for his collaborators one of the alternative ways to deal with Watergate:

(4) (Presidential Transcripts, p. 127)
> Nixon: Another way to do it then . . . is to continue to try to cut our losses. Now we have to take a look at that course of action. First it is going to require approximately a million dollars to take care of the jackasses who are in jail. That can be arranged. That could be arranged. But you realize that after we are gone, and assuming we can expend that money, then they are going to crack and it would be an unseemly story.

If I say *John will be late today, too. He is always late on Mondays*, for at least one reading of the sequence I may be said to have expanded the main speech act by generalization. To put it more precisely, in order for a subordinate speech act to enter successfully an expansion relation with another speech act, it must relate (in its own way) to a state of the world that includes, or is included by, the state of affairs pointed to by the main speech act.

Nixon can also give us a good example of repetition, a type of relation where a speech act points (in its own way) to the same state of affairs conveyed by another immediately preceding act:

(5) (Presidential Transcripts, p. 129)
> Nixon: Now, let me tell you. We could get the money. There is no problem in that. We can't provide the clemency. Money could be provided. Mitchell could provide the way to deliver it. That could be done. See what I mean?

Furthermore, and with this we can finally leave Mr. Nixon in peace, one speech act may constitute a comment on another if by its performance the speaker intends to express his attitude, feeling, or opinion with respect to the propositional content of this other speech act. Comment relations do not involve a fixed hierarchic ordering: sometimes the commented speech act is also the main one, at other times it merely functions as pretext for introducing the comment. For example,

(6) (Presidential Transcripts, p. 129)
> Nixon: It's about $120,000. That's what, Bob. That would be easy. It is not easy to deliver, but it is easy to get.

Answers and replies are not specific types of speech acts, rather they are relations between acts. One can reply to somebody else's question with many types of speech acts, all constituting a perfect answer to it.

In order for a speech act to enter an answer–reply relation with a previous speech act, it must have been somehow elicited, in an intentional way, by that previous act. Typical instances of this relation are provided in dialogues by the so-called adjacency pairs, that is, pairs of speech acts such as request–grant, excuse–acceptance of excuse, congratulations–thanks.

Another very common type of relation between speech acts is correction. In order for a speech act to enter successfully such a relation with another speech act, it must be able to relate (in its own way) to a state of affairs that can conceivably disengage or suspend the commitments embedded in the corrected speech act. In this type of relation no act is subordinated to the other. A good example of correction, actually a double correction, is contained in the last two utterances of speaker A in the following telephone conversation (A, who is visiting the city, and B, who lives there, have been engaged for some time in making arrangements to see each other):

(7) (Schegloff & Sacks, 1973, p. 259)

B: Well, even if you get here et abayout eh ten thirty, or eleven uh'clock, we still have en hour en a hahf,

A: **O.K., Al**right.

B: Fine. We'd have a bite, en//(talk),

A: Yeh. Weh- **No!** No, **don't** prepare any//thing,

B: And uh - I'm not gunnah **prepare,** we'll juz whatever it'll// be, we'll ( ).

A: **NO!** No. I don't mean that, I min—because uh, **she** en I'll prob'bly be spending the day togethuh, so uh:::we'll go out tuh lunch, or something like that. hh So I mean if you::have a cuppa cawfee or something, I mean//thatuh that'll be fine.

Finally, sometimes speech acts are performed in order to prepare the ground for another speech act and enhance its chances of success. Typically the act that prepares the terrain for another tries to obtain some of the conditions of appropriateness for the dominant act, as in the following sequence:

(8)   *Do you have five minutes time? I would like to talk with you.*

In addition to those mentioned, other types of functional relations may link speech acts in sequence, for example, conclusion, protest, addition, objection, agreement, approval, and announcement relations. But clearly, more research is needed in this area, which hopefully will generate more complete and structured inventories of types of relations among speech acts and will derive for each type the special conditions of appropriateness that it imposes on the subordinate speech acts.

FUNDAMENTALS OF THE PRAGMATIC ANALYSIS OF GLOBAL COHERENCE

Let me sum up, before moving on to this new level, some of the points underlying the analysis. From a conceptual point of view, we know that speech acts, although necessarily performed in a linear temporal sequence, are hierarchically interrelated; we also know that in a text there are local hierarchies of speech acts and more extended ones, stretching across sequences; finally, we take the global pragmatic coherence of a text to be defined by the possibility of relating its single speech acts to a set of overarching macro–speech acts. From the point of view of a technique of analysis, we know how to segment an unbroken sequence into its constituent speech acts and how to detect the nature and the direction of the various relations that link speech acts with one another. Our next step is to reconstruct, out of the series of these already identified local hierarchies of speech acts, the set of macro–speech acts that underlies the entire text and insures its pragmatic coherence. In particular, I focus on how the application of three pragmatic macrorules can help in identifying the macro–speech acts. Just as the macrorules of deletion, construction and generalization (see van Dijk, Chap. 7, this volume) help in reducing the semantic information conveyed by the surface manifestation of a text to a restricted number of macropropositions, similar rules can be devised for the pragmatic aspects of textual coherence. A deletion rule suggests that all speech acts that are subordinate and do not dominate any other be discarded from the pragmatic macrostructure of the text. This holds, however, only for those speech acts that are not selected through one of the other macrorules. Secondly, a generalization rule suggests that those speech acts that are repetitions of the same action be regrouped whenever possible. Finally, a construction rule suggests that speech acts that, taken together, amount to a higher-order action be regrouped whenever possible under the heading of that action.

As a sample text I have taken a sufficiently complex passage from the transcript of a class on conversation studies. Mark is a young instructor and Paul is one of the students, who happens to be older than Mark. Mark has been talking about various types of disruption of the turntaking system in conversation. He now introduces a distinction:

(9) Mark 1: Now notice that's how an interrupter is different from an overlapper.

    Other: um

    Mark 1: 'cause an overlapper is someone who is trying to orient the a an overlapper is trying to orient to the right spot for ⌈starting to speak

    Paul 1: ⌊the conversation or continue the conversation, and

		the
Mark:		yeah
Paul	1:	interrupter is trying to guide it to his advantage
Mark	2:	well we can't say what they're trying to do but they aren't following the rules for ⌞the cooperation uh ⌞for
Paul	2:	⌞the cooperation uh
Mark	3:	⌞for

speaker selection

Paul   3: Are you uh I have found myself in um in cases where uh I've been in a conversation and there has been an interrupter but he would be an interrupter of ego I call him a person that has such a strong ego that he has to monopolize the conversation he has to you know be the speaker all the time if possible and if by any chance you are able to put your foot in the door he would try his best to you know interrupt you to try to gain the uh the floor again how would you handle something like that

Mark   4: Well notice you're there are two different things in what you're saying one you're saying that there are certain people who regularly and repeatedly interrupt and in addition you're mak- you're putting a psychological interpretation onto that that you're saying that this has to do with ego and a compulsion to be the speaker.

Paul   4: Well I have known the person for a long ⎪time and you know it ⎪

Mark: ⎣ yeah

Paul   4: was not a you know just a hasty you know it's a matter of many years of observing that phenomenon

Mark   5: So notice this is the kind of thing that I was talking about in class today that one of the ways that you may get punished for violating the rules of conversa- for violating norms is that people may say nasty things about you you know you know you've just said you know this person is you know has an ego such that he has to ⌈always be speaking.

Paul   5:   ⌊You you have never observed that phenomenon

Mark   6: Ahm ⌈I've observed the phenomenon of people inter-

Paul   6:   ⌊I'm sure that

Mark   6: rupting all the time and I may even have put that inter- pretation on it but it's impossi- the the it's impossible to observe that a person has an ego that's not an observable thing that's an inference that you draw from observation

Paul   7:   But then you have to make this sort of inferences every time you are looking at data after all that's what a hypothesis is

Mark   7:   Well you may or may not have to make that kind of inference it's not it's not obvious to me that making that kind of inference helps us with the kind of analysis with analyzing this kind of data and th⌈at's what

Paul   8:   ⌊not this kind of data no I don't think so but still there is a possibility that this type of interruptions might play a role someplace else

Mark   8:   Oh sure the fact that people make psychological judgments about them if that's a re⌈al fact

Paul   9:   ⌊are you trying to be an overlapper or an interrupter I don't quite get you (general sound of voiceless laughter)

Mark   9:   The feeling is mutual wait you know what did you say (more laughter)

Paul   10:   That's all right you are successful that's all right (more laughter) no recycling possible (more laughter, slightly voiced) please go ahead I was just trying to make all right I apparently this is the feeling I'm getting now ⌈that all these things give me dif-

Mark: ⌊yeah

Paul   10:   ferent you know different insights whether you know relevant or not relevant according to your judgment might be because you are focusing more narrower or narrowing or narrower than I am

Mark: yeah

Paul   10:   and therefore you know there would be this discrepancy between focusing and I notice sometimes when I have an insight and I come out with it you have a tendency to say that it is irrelevant and what you are really trying to say is that this is not really you know my focus please ⌈don't misunderstand me I'm only ⌈

Mark: ⌊yeah   ⌊yeah

Paul   10:   you know trying to contribute an insight but if ⌈it is you know

Mark: ⌊sure

Paul   10:   if it is not relevant or something like that you know you don't have to get upset about it

Mark 10:   Ok le le le let me explain to you how I'm conflicted

> because ok I'll start off by telling a technique that Sacks
> would use in classes

This text is interesting for several reasons. It is more complex than the ones examined above; the speakers' plans are dense with different types of goals, and these goals are implemented through a large number of conversational moves and speech acts. Sometimes these plans interweave in a cooperative way, but at other times they stand opposite one another in a more antagonistic way. The text is discontinuous in another sense, too. Sometimes the speakers' plans appear to have been worked out a few sentences in advance, but most of the time they appear to be constructed, elaborated, changed, or simply dropped as the necessity of the moment dictates and as the other participant's utterance requires. And yet even a text produced in such a piecemeal, turn-to-turn manner, with no preformed structure, in the context of a speech activity (an academic seminar) that is relatively unstructured, may exhibit a large degree of pragmatic coherence. What specific properties make us perceive it as a coherent whole?

Let us begin by looking at some local aspects of the pragmatic coherence of this text. In his third turn Paul does basically two things. He performs a number of assertions, which are used in order to introduce a question, and eventually asks his question. The preface to the question *How would you handle something like that?* is internally structured as well. The assertion *He would be an interrupter of ego* and its repetition *I call him a person that has such a strong ego that he has to monopolize the conversation* dominate other speech acts performed by Paul in this turn. In fact, the opening assertion of Paul's third turn, *I have found myself um in cases where I've been in a conversation and there has been an interrupter,* is performed in order to prepare the ground for the first assertion in the pair mentioned above. And the last assertion in the turn unit, *He has to you know be the speaker all the time if possible and if by any chance you are able to put your foot in the door he would try his best to you know interrupt you to try to gain uh the floor again,* appears to be performed by Paul mainly in order to justify the second assertion in our dominant pair. The pragmatic macrorules can now help us to identify the specific way in which this sequence of speech acts contributes to the global coherence of the text. By applying the rule of deletion we can eliminate the two subordinate assertions from the set of possible macro–speech acts. At the same time notice that the two dominant assertions in the sequence share a very similar propositional content and underlying goal. Both of them were intended by Paul to make the point that there exist people who interrupt others all the time as a way of asserting power and of aggrandizing their self-image. The rule of generalization can be used in order to simplify the dominant pair into a unique assertion, conveying precisely this propositional content. This reconstructed macroassertion is part of the pragmatic macrostructure of the text.

Moving on to the next utterance by Paul (Paul 4), we can see a similar hierarchic structure. The first assertion in this turn unit, *I have known the person for a long time,* prepares the ground for what Paul wants to stress more: the fact that his remark was not a hasty one and furthermore that he has been observing the phenomenon in question for many years. The two assertions that Paul performs in order to convey this emphasis can be reduced, through the generalization rule again, to one dominant assertion. But this assertion dominating turn unit 4 is also connected to the dominant speech act found in Paul's preceding utterance. More specifically, the main assertion in Paul 4, to the effect that the phenomenon of 'ego interrupters' has been observed by Paul over a long period of time, serves the purpose of lending more credibility and support to his earlier introduction of this new concept. (As it happens in a context where an asymmetry of power exists, such as classroom interaction, Paul's contribution had to be legitimated as valid, appropriate, and insightful, by the authority present, in this case Mark. And this legitimation is what Paul indirectly asks for with his question in 3.) In turn, the assertion which dominates 3 expands and justifies the assertion offered by Paul in his second utterance as a possible completion for the distinction, that Mark has just begun to draw, between overlappers and interrupters in conversation. We begin to see how there can be functional relations among speech acts not only within sequences of speech acts performed during the same turn unit but also across turn units. These ties, spanning broader portions of the text, are the primary factor contributing to pragmatic coherence, for they integrate local goals and the higher-order ones that underlie and unify the whole of a text.

So far, however, reasons of simplicity have led us to examine only Paul's speech acts, as though they were part of a monological text. In such a case only one plan needs to be identified, but in the case of a dialogue the very nature of the interchange forces the participants to continuously review and modify their plans in view of what the other person is doing. Let us now go back to our text and focus more on the functional ties between the sequences performed by both speakers. Mark, the instructor, opens the exchange by trying to draw a distinction between overlapping and interrupting in conversation. Paul offers a completion to Mark's sentence. With a minimal *yeah,* Mark accepts the first part of Paul's completion but then, in his second turn, he rejects it quite explicitly: To Paul's suggestion that what an interrupter does is guide the conversation to his advantage he objects that *we can't say what they're trying to do*. One more such completion offer and rejection takes place in the two following units, and then we begin to see a major shift in the interaction. Paul initiates the complex attempt to back up his completion offers, which we have examined in some detail above. The effect of this sequence is to put Mark under pressure to come to terms more thoroughly with Paul's suggestions. This Mark does in his fourth utterance, where he continues not to accept Paul's definition of an interrupter; this utterance also prepares a way of integrating what Paul has said within the broader context of the seminar session. In the subsequent turn unit this integration is carried out. Sequence Mark 5 as a whole, in fact, and especially its main assertion, provides Mark's answer to the question raised before by Paul, *How would you handle something like that?*. The answer is indirect, yet precise. The way Mark would handle the whole matter of ego interruption is to call it an instance of the negative attitude that rule breakers elicit in their hearers. What Paul suggested can have a place in the record of that day of class (*notice this is the kind of thing I was talking about in class today*), but the substance of it is dismissed as yet another instance of the illegitimate psychological imputations that people impose on linguistic material. The new question that Paul raises in his turn 5 ties up with the one he asked previously. *You have never observed that phenomenon*, that is, people who must always have the floor, is a way to revive the former question about ego interruption by repeating it in an indirect way. This new question increases the pressure for Mark to come up with a more conclusive response to Paul's point. This reponse is what we see in Mark's sixth turn. The first two assertions—*I have observed the phenomenon of people interrupting all the time* and *I may even have put that interpretation on it*—are intended as a preparation for the main one—*It's impossible to observe that a person has an ego*. And this main assertion, together with the following one, constitutes the answer to Paul's question. Mark here relies again on a distinction between naive, lay observation of interaction and the kind of controlled study he is illustrating. Within the frame of the first he recognizes the plausibility of Paul's remarks and also admits to having indulged in similar speculations. But still he insists on denying scholarly legitimacy to the notion of ego interrupter.

Another important cross-unit tie can be found between Mark's last assertion in this turn—*that's not an observable thing that's an inference that you draw from observation*—and the next assertion in Paul's turn 7—*But then you have to make this sort of inferences every time you are looking at data*. What is this exchange really about? By calling Paul's claim that some people are compelled by hidden motives to interrupt others all the time an inference, Mark implicitly presents it as less real, less objective than the data. The data are closer to reality than any inference you draw from them. It is at this idea that Paul's assertion aims: If it is an inference, then it is an inference you have to make all the time. Therefore, runs the implication, it is as important, objective, and real as the data. At this point the interaction between Mark and Paul has ceased to be just a plain discussion of the fruitfulness of a notion of ego interrupter. It has taken on the character of a struggle in which Paul is determined to win at least a share of legitimacy for his claim and Mark is trying to delimit and qualify more and more this legitimacy, up to the point of actually emptying it. In fact Mark, in turn-unit 7, denies precisely, although indirectly, what Paul had asserted. Against Paul's contention that one makes these inferences (on motives for interruptions) all the time, he maintains that *you may or may not have to make that kind of inference*. Furthermore he qualifies this assertion by specifying that, at least as far as the data at hand are concerned, *that kind of inference* would not help. This is now a stiffer kind of rejection of Paul's idea, for its relevance to the material treated in the seminar session is now thrown into discussion. How does Paul react to this? He reduces the scope of his claim and at the same time offers a way out to Mark. He admits that the idea of ego interrupter is not that important after all for the problem under discussion in class, but he still demands from Mark recognition of the fact that it might be important for analyzing other sets of data. But Mark's reply offers nothing different from the move we have seen already. In his eighth unit Mark conditionally (*if*) agrees to recognize as real and common the imposition of psychological interpretations on people who infringe conversational expectations, something on which he has offered agreement since his fifth utterance, but he still refuses to agree on the fruitfulness of drawing those inferences about ego interrupters that Paul has been emphasizing all along. Against an appearance of agreement and positive reception of Paul's remarks, the overall rejection of their substance stands out all the more conspicuously. Paul reacts to this by starting a joking insulting sequence—*Are you trying to be an overlapper or interrupter?*—to which Mark replies in kind—*The feeling is mutual*. Laughter and a marked increase in false starts all point to the embarrassment created by this short piece of interaction gone out of hand along an aggressive path. Finally, Paul's last turn unit has a complex internal structure. His first assertion—*This is the feeling I'm getting now that all these things give me different you know different insights whether you know relevant or not relevant according to your judgment*—dominates the second—*[It] might be because you are focusing more narrower or narrowing or narrower than I am*—which stands in an explanatory relationship to the former and in turn dominates the third—*therefore you know there would be this discrepancy between focusing.* The subsequent two assertions specify this general point of view and exemplify it with reference to Mark's way of handling the class. If we apply the construction macrorule to the sequence we can see how these assertions, taken together, constitute an explanation, an account offered by Paul about how this situation came into being. They are Paul's version of the controversy. Notice how the account cleverly shifts the emphasis from the substantive issue of the merit of Paul's claims to the metacommunicative side of the interaction. With his last unit Paul manages to shift general attention from the relevance of his remarks to Mark's way of handling the interaction in class. This amounts to a sharp escalation of hostility, for at least two reasons. First, this way of directly and publicly questioning the communicative style of somebody is very threatening and potentially offensive (especially if the target person is in a position of authority). Second, Paul also turns his comment into an explicit reproach which casts the entire responsibility for the tension on Mark: *if [my insight] is not relevant or something like that you know you don't have to get upset about it.* The suddenness of this move apparently throws Mark off balance, as can be seen from his hesitating and defensive posture in the next utterance.

We are finally in a position to obtain an accurate picture of the pragmatic macrostructure underlying the text, by bringing together the main speech acts performed in the turn units or reconstructed through the macrorules. Here is a discursive, nonformalized version of it (the macro–speech acts are boldface):

> Mark **introduced a distinction** between overlappers and interrupters, Paul **contributed** the notion of ego interrupter as a valid, relevant analytical category, Mark **acknowledged** the existence of the phenomenon described by the concept but at the same time **discounted** it as a naive, lay, and ultimately irrelevant concept. Paul **defended** his point. More specifically then Mark **objected** that ego interrupting cannot be observed but only inferred. Paul **countered** that such inferences must be made all the time, which was denied by Mark. He then **claimed** such inferences to be relevant in at least some cases, which Mark still denied. At this point Paul jokingly **insulted** Mark, who **reciprocated**. Finally, Paul **gave his account of** the whole exchange, and **attributed the responsibility** for it to Mark's getting upset every time Paul contributed some idea that would not fit with his.

This set of macro–speech acts captures the essential core of the actions accomplished by the participants in the utterance of the text and implemented through the execution of all the single speech acts contained in the manifestation of the text. It captures the essential core of the text in yet another sense: to be able to identify these macro–speech acts is a necessary condition for understanding the text itself. Finally, in addition to the appropriateness of its dominant and subordinate speech acts, to the appropriateness of its component sequences, and to the frequent and tight intersequential ties, it is the possibility of abstracting from the text this set of macro–speech acts that makes us perceive this text as pragmatically coherent, in spite of all the improvisation it contains.

REFERENCES

Austin, J. L. (1962). *How to do things with words.* London: Oxford University Press.

Ferrara, A. (1980a). Appropriateness conditions for entire sequences of speech acts. *Journal of Pragmatics, 4,* 321–340.

Ferrara, A. (1980b). An extended theory of speech acts: Appropriateness conditions for subordinate speech acts in sequences. *Journal of Pragmatics, 4,* 233–252.

Montague, R. (1974). *Formal philosophy.* New Haven: Yale University Press.

Morris, C. W. (1938). *Foundations of the theory of signs.* Chicago: International Encyclopaedia of Unified Science.

Morris, C. W. (1946). *Signs, language and behavior.* New York: Prentice Hall.

The presidential transcripts. (1974). New York: Dell.

Rogers, C. R. (1951). *Client-centered therapy.* Boston: Houghton Mifflin.

Schegloff, E. A., & Sacks, H. (1973). Opening up closings. *Semiotica, 8,* 289–327.

Searle, J. R. (1969). *Speech acts.* London: Cambridge University Press.

Searle, J. R. (1975a). Indirect speech acts. In P. Cole & J. L. Morgan (Eds.), *Syntax and semantics: Speech acts* (pp. 59–82). New York: Academic Press.

Searle, J. R. (1975b). A taxonomy of illocutionary acts. In K. Gunderson (Ed.), *Language, mind and knowledge.* (pp. 344–369). Minneapolis: University of Minnesota Press.

Searle, J. R. (1980). An interview. In J. Boyd & A. Ferrara (Eds.), Speech act theory: Ten years later. [Special issue]. *Versus, 26/27.* (pp. 17–27).

van Dijk, T. A. (1977a). Semantic macro-structures and knowledge frames in discourse comprehension. In P. Carpenter & M. Just (Eds.), *Cognitive processes in comprehension.* (pp. 3–32). Hillsdale, NJ: Erlbaum.

van Dijk, T. A. (1977b). *Text and context. Explorations in the semantics and pragmatics of discourse.* London: Longman.

van Dijk, T. A. (1980). *Macrostructures. An interdisciplinary study of global structures in discourse, interaction and cognition.* Hillsdale, NJ: Erlbaum.

van Dijk, T. A. (1981). *Studies in the pragmatics of discourse.* The Hague: Mouton.

van Dijk, T. A., & Kintsch, W. (1977). Cognitive psychology and discourse. In W. U. Dressler (Ed.), *Current trends in text linguistics* (pp. 61–80). New York: De Gruyter.

CHAPTER 9

An Analysis of Argumentation

Josef Kopperschmidt

AN EXPLANATION OF THE
TERM 'ARGUMENT'

In this chapter the term 'argument' is understood to mean the use of a statement in a logical process of argumentation to support or weaken another statement whose validity is questionable or contentious. The system of rules according to which a statement (p) functions as an argument for or against the validity of another statement (q) and on which an evaluation of the argumentative success of a statement is oriented is called the logic of argumentation (Klein, 1980, 1981). The reconstruction of this logic is one of the tasks of a general theory of argumentation.

In contrast to the causal explanation of fact or of the motivational factors in actions, this argumentative support is concerned with the validity of statements that, by means of an assertion or an evaluation, enable one to judge facts or actions. The explicit exposure of the validity of the claim implicitly raised by such statements is achieved through the reconstruction of the bases by which such validities justify themselves and is the broadest function of any argumentation.

Such a functional understanding of argument or argumentation presumes that the constantly motivating force of the situational problematic of the validity belongs to the pragmatic requirements of the argumentation, through which the understanding between communicating subjects or groups (X, Y) will be hindered or their chances for cooperative interaction lessened or eliminated. Argumentation is, nonetheless, not just an indication of a breakdown in communication but becomes as well, through its use, a sign of the willingness to solve problems and conflicts without the use of force.

HANDBOOK OF DISCOURSE ANALYSIS, Vol. 2
Dimensions of Discourse

Copyright © 1985 by Academic Press London.
All rights of reproduction in any form reserved.
ISBN 0-12-712002-5

The specific feature of the argumentative support of problematic validity is found in the rationality of a speech process or, more precisely, a dialogue, that is oriented on the cognitive character of the validity and consequently recognizes the validity as a proof of its justification, a justification that is methodologically capable of being reconstructed and intersubjectively able to be in agreement.

The principle of such methodological reconstructions is based on the attempt by X to relate the problematic validity of q to an unproblematic validity of p by Y, the immanent logic of which is needed by Y so that he can accept q on grounds of the acceptability of p: q is valid because p is valid. The ability of argument to convince proves itself in the success of a rationally motivated necessity of acceptance.

Despite the influential work of, among others, Toulmin (1958, 1976), Perelman & Obrechts-Tyteca (1958), and Habermas (1973, 1976, 1981), there are still no general theories of argumentation employing a consistent terminology and binding paradigm. At present there are, however, in the most varied fields—linguistics (Öhlschläger, 1979), literature (Kindt & Schmidt, 1976), philosophy (Scwemmer, 1971), law (Alexy, 1978), philosophy of science (Gethmann, 1980), logic (Gethmann, 1979), and rhetoric (Brandt, 1970; Kopperschmidt, 1976)—intensive efforts to explore at least discipline-specific aspects of this procedure, using the title "argumentation" as one that can be easily integrated in a variety of fields.

Because no general theory of argumentation has been propounded, there is also no methodologically recognized analysis of argumentation (Metzing, 1975, 1976). Consequently, the methodology of argumentation analysis described in the following section is to be understood only as a proposal that provides for a systematic reconstruction of the logical structure of communicative processes in which statements function as argument for or against the validity of other statements. A justification of the analytical categories used must await the publication of a theory of argumentation, since their explanation is, for reasons of space, not possible here.

THE METHODOLOGY
OF ARGUMENTATION ANALYSIS

The most general task of analysis is the reconstruction of the logical structure of concrete processes of argumentation as well as a critical evaluation of them according to the standards rationally set by understanding. Only the first aspect is discussed in this chapter. Concrete examples of argumentation processes appear in texts where they are classified linguistically as argumentative text types (Kummer, 1972;

Schnelle, 1975) or as argumentative discourse types (Wunderlich, 1976) and where they can be interpreted as belonging to a sequence of speech acts with functional specifications through which, according to a theory of action, a pattern of interaction can be found (Kallmeyer & Schütze, 1976; Metzing, 1976). Argumentation analysis is a method that reconstructs the specific and logical structure of argumentative texts and, as such, is capable of being supplemented by other methods of discourse analysis; indeed, it needs to be so aided.

According to their level of complexity, concrete processes of argumentation are formed from parts of argumentative processes that provide the boundaries within which the individual arguments function, although arguments often are only made use of by implication. In this connection, we speak of strands of argumentation and understand by this partial argumentations that are incorporated within a functionally integrating global argumentation. As a result of this, it is useful to differentiate between microstructural and macrostructural argumentation analysis.

The aim of macrostructural analysis is the reconstruction of the global structure of a more or less complex process of argumentation. By global structure is meant the widest boundaries within which logic processes argumentatively functioning statements. The realization of this macrostructural analytical aim proceeds through the following five analytical steps:

1. The Definition of the Problem. The establishment of the problem leads to the difference between two types of problems arising from the differing problem fields of which they may be representative according to whether the problem is based on the reliability of the information offered (How do you know that p . . . ?) or on the acceptance of obligation (Why should x be done?) or evaluation (Why is y good?), we speak about theoretical or practical problems. Accordingly one can differentiate between the strategies for solving the problem argumentatively: Do we seek our solution in implicit theoretical validity resulting from a presentation of knowledge, which we call truth, or in a validity arising from obligations and evaluations, which we call correctness. In the first case we speak of a theoretical argumentation, in the second of a practical argumentation.

Whether atomic power plants should be built—which is, in Germany, a hotly debated issue (Strohm, 1981; Véron, 1981)—is a practical problem that might be formulated in writing as follows:

(1)   *Should atomic power plants be built?*

2. Formulation of the Contentious Thesis. Each argumentation, insofar as it tries functionally to solve the contentious demands of truth or correctness in a statement, assumes that the communicating subjects or

groups have a prejudiced point of view or have taken a stand on the question that can, however, be modified in the process of argumentation. Any point of view has its own validity that is contentious, but its intersubjective acceptance is the aim of the argumentative support. This explicit or implicit prejudice is formulated within the basic thesis (T) or, by a number of points of view finding themselves in conflict, as competing theses $(T_1 \ldots n)$. Referring to the problem in (1), the point of view could be formulated at T as follows:

(2)   *Atomic power plants should be built!*

3. Segmentation of the Arguments.   The segmentation of identification of individual argumentatively functionalizing statements in a text of the argumentative type is a clearly interpretive act. As such, it can only be aided by linguistic signals of argumentation (*because, then, therefore, yes, from,* etc.) (Lenders, 1975, pp. 201 ff.). In the same way, the standard formula of argumentation already mentioned, q, because p, is of heuristic value, since with this formula every possible argumentative relation between statements can be clearly expressed. Thus, the statement

(3)   *Only the building of atomic power plants can eliminate energy shortages in the 1980s,*

is, with the help of the standard formula, clearly identifiable as an argument for the thesis:

(4)   *Atomic power plants should be built, because only in this way can energy shortages in the 1980s be eliminated.*

Nonetheless, the argumentatively functioning statement (3) can be more accurately determined in two different ways. The first is in regard to its specifically argumentative function for the thesis; according to whether an argument supports or weakens a thesis, we speak of a pro-argument (P) or a contra-argument (C). The (dialogue) reformulation of the differentiation of the argumentative function leads to a corresponding differentiation between the proponent role (P_r) and the opponent role (O) within the communicative relationship between X and Y. According to this, (3) would be more accurately described a pro-argument (P) for the thesis or, with more pro-arguments $(P_1 \ldots n)$, as pro-argument 1 (P_1). An analogous situation would, of course, apply for possible contra-arguments $(C_1 \ldots n)$. The second way in which an argumentatively functioning statement can be even more definite in regard to its position to the thesis is as follows: According to whether an argument directly supports or weakens a thesis, or the thesis indirectly is supported or weakened, so that an argument supporting or weakening a thesis itself is either supported or weakened, we speak, as did Naess (Naess, 1975), of an argument first class or of an argument second . . . n class. It would thus be still more precise to designate (3) as P_1 first class, which could be attacked by the following argument second class:

(5)   *The energy shortage can also be eliminated by using other energy sources.*

According to the proposal of Naess, this indirect C could be symbolized as C_1P_1, and would be read from left to right as first C second class, as contrasted to first P first class for T.

4. Reconstruction of the Argumentation Strands.   Together with the indirect arguments that either support or weaken it, each direct argument forms a strand of argumentation. The strand of argumentation serves to disclose and evaluate the argumentative potential that can be achieved with an argument. Aside from pragmatic factors (like time), the complexity of length of a strand of argumentation is determined by the intensity of the conflict between X and Y as well as by the exhaustion level of the respective argumentative potential. Within such a strand of argumentation, a direct C, for example, being used in a discussion about atomic power plants, can, together with its indirect and partially supporting–partially weakening arguments, be reconstructed as follows:

(6)   T: *Atomic power plants should be built!*
             C_1:   *Atomic power plants are much too dangerous.*
         C_1C_1:   *There are adequate safety regulations.*
     $C_1C_1C_1$:   *Nevertheless, Harrisburg was possible.*

If or whether an individual argument is able to be convincing depends on whether it can effectively hold its own within a strand of argumentation.

5. Reconstruction of an Argumentative Global Structure.   After the individual arguments have been indentified with the help of the standard formula, differentiated according to their specific functions for the thesis (such as position to the thesis), and reconstructed in the appropriate strand of argumentation (see 4 above), they can be arranged in a table that enables the complex network of argumentative relationships within a global structure of argumentation to be visualized. In such a table, the arguments present in statements (3), (5), and (6), for example, could be tabulated and the corresponding roles (O or P_r) in the argumentative situation be positioned:

(7)   O P_r

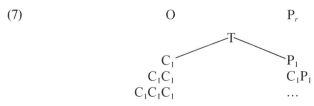

Other systems of symbolization or visualization have been proposed by, among others, Klein (1980); von Savigny (1976) and Grewendorf (1975).

Whereas macrostructural analysis discloses the global structure of an argumentation, microstructural analysis reconstructs the detailed structure of the individual partial argumentations. Microstructural analysis proceeds in three steps:

1. Role Analysis. With the help of this analytical step we are able to determine more precisely the varying roles of the argumentatively functioning statement within a strand of argument, something not possible in the symbolization system of Naess. Thus, for example,

(6) $C_1C_1C_1$: *Nevertheless, Harrisburg was possible.*

is, indeed, triply determinable as first C third class; nevertheless, what is not definable is the precise role of this contradictory statement within the strand of argumentation of which it is a part. It evidently lies in the fact that with only one assumption of a fact, a general presupposition (that is implicated in C_1C_1) is contradicted: the presupposition, namely, that the unarguable existence of safety regulations could effectively minimize the danger of atomic power plants.

In the symbolization system of Naess, the difference in role between the singular indication of a fact in $C_1C_1C_1$ (*Nevertheless, Harrisburg was possible*) and the likewise singular assumption in C_1C_1 (*There are adequate safety regulations*) is also unable to be distinguished. This time, in contrast to $C_1C_1C_1$, no implicit general assumption, but, instead, the validity of one other statement (C_1) is contradicted: the statement that atomic power plants are very dangerous. The variegations in these differing argumentative roles of statements can only be adequately described with the help of a system of categories that permits not only the explicit statements but also the assumptions that are implicitly formed to be taken into account. Such a differentiated analytical system of categories is offered by the Toulmin model of argumentation (Toulmin 1958), in that it visualizes the ideal type of full structuring of an argumentative network as a differentiating framework of invariable roles that can place statements in concrete processes of argumentation.

If one attempts to reformulate the prior reconstruction of the strand of argumentation of example (6), the result is approximately as in the following diagram (8), in which W (warrant) represents the general assumption that justifies the transition from a singular D (datum) to K (conclusion). (For other analytical categories see Toulmin, 1958, Chap. 3; for the model see also Heringer, 1977, pp. 251 ff.)

It is clear from example (6) that, in contrast to (8), only language is dealt with in explaining the data (D), whereas the functional role of the

(8)

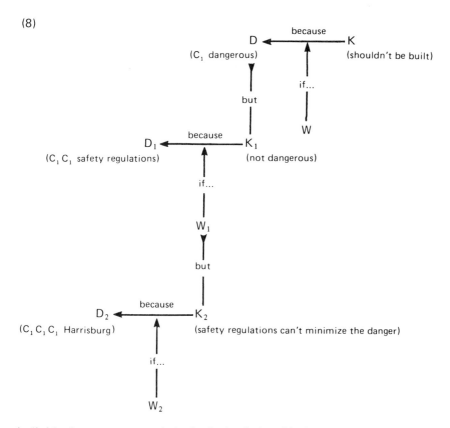

individual statements and the logical relationship between them remains latent. In this diagram one can also see that the strand of argumentation does not evince the smallest functional unity but instead is itself once again a differing sequence of individual argumentation features. For the reconstruction of these as the smallest analytical unit of argumentation analysis, the Toulmin (1958) model of argumentation provides the most appropriate categories.

2. An Analysis of the Argumentative Potential. Statements used argumentatively are not only defined by the role that they play at times in argumentation structure, but also materially through the nature of their argumentative potential that is made use of to support or weaken a given validity. This argumentative potential is predetermined by the choice of a problem perspective from which, on the basis of the respective definition of the problem, a theoretical or a practical problem is to be discussed.

Seen in this way, the examples shown in the section on macrostructural argumentation analysis define the problem of atomic power plants as a combination of safety (in a technical sense) and politics (the politics of energy) and discuss the problem according to these perspectives, although naturally these could be joined with or confronted by other perspectives (foreign, military, economic, and political–economic, for example). A decision can be made about the suitability and relevance of the properties of problem perspectives or, in the case of a number of possible perspectives, over their compatibility and hierarchic arrangement—only, again, on the basis of their argumentative effectiveness. Such an argumentation can, nonetheless, function on another level of logic (Habermas, 1973) as long as the validity of an argumentative functionalizing statement is not involved, but, instead, the validity of the prior step of understanding the properties of a problem and thereby the validity of argumentative potentials, which can be linked categorically with the understanding of the respective problem. Because the criteria of a possible argument are defined at the same time as those of the argumentative potentials, the choice of a particular argumentative potential also determines the conditions under which statements come into consideration at all as possible arguments. (Architectural and aesthetic arguments would hardly be relevant in the atomic power plant debate sketched here.) Toulmin calls this the field dependency of validity criteria in contrast to the field invariance of roles.

Arguments that actualize a common argumentative potential on the basis of a corresponding understanding of a problem together form a so-called argument-type. For possible classification proposals for such types compare von Savigny (1976), Grewendorf (1975), and Schroth (1980).

If one does not classify the various material argumentative potentials according to the problem perspectives with which they might be identified but instead places them in various groups from which they can be actualized in the solution of the respective problems, one is then enabled to develop a model with a group-specific thought and judgment pattern, rather than one which is a field-specific argumentation type. Following an already conventionalized term, one calls such thought and judgment patterns "social topoi" (Bornscheuer, 1976, pp. 129 ff.; Negt, 1971).

3. Formal Analysis.   Arguments cannot only be analyzed functionally from the aspect of their field-dependency role within a unit feature of argumentation or materially from the aspect of the actualization of their field-specific argumentative potential. Arguments can also be formally analyzed from the viewpoint of both field-invariant and role-indifferent abstract patterns, according to which concrete argumentation patterns can be formed. Such abstract patterns or strategies of possible argu-mentations might be, for example, a reference to public-oriented or group-directed authority, the citing of pertinent examples, and recourse to

precedents. Using the argumentation pattern, an *a simili* example based on the atomic power plant discussion might be formed as follows:

(9)   *Anyone who is willing to put up with 12,000 deaths on the road each year must also accept the dangers of atomic power plants.*

Following Aristotle's first attempts to systematize (in his Topic and Rhetoric; compare Lausberg, 1960, pp. 190 ff.), the systematization of such patterns of possible argumentation has been attempted again, particularly in the efforts of Perelman & Olbrechts-Tyteca (1958) in an article entitled "Schèmes Argumentatifs" (cf. Bornscheuer, 1976).

BIBLIOGRAPHY

Alexy, R. (1978). *Theorie der juristischen Argumentation*. Frankfurt: Suhrkamp.
Bar-Hillel, Y. (1970). *Aspects of language*. Jerusalem: Magnes Press.
Berk, U. (1979). *Konstruktive Argumentationstheorie*. Stuttgart: Frommann-Holzboog.
Bornscheuer, L. (1976). *Topik*. Frankfurt: Suhrkamp.
Brandt, W. J. (1970). *The rhetoric of argumentation*. New York: Irvington Public.
Espersen, J. (1969). *Logik og argumenter*. Kopenhagen: Reitzel.
Geach, P. T. (1976). *Reason and argument*. Oxford: Oxford University Press.
Gethmann, C. F. (1979). *Protologik*. Frankfurt: Suhrkamp.
Gethmann, C. F. (1980). *Theorie des wissenschaftlichen Argumentierens*. Frankfurt: Suhrkamp.
Göttert, K.-H. (1978). *Argumentation*. Tübingen: Niemeyer.
Grewendorf, G. (1975). *Argumentation und Interpretation*. Kronberg: Scriptor.
Habermas, J. (1973). Wahrheitstheorien. In H. Fahrenbach (Ed.), *Wirklichkeit und Reflexion* (pp. 211ff.). Pfullingen: Neske.
Habermas, J. (1976). Was heißt Universalpragmatik? In K.-O. Apel. (Ed.), *Sprachpragmatik und Philosophie* (pp. 174ff.). Frankfurt: Suhrkamp.
Habermas, J. (1981). *Theorie des kommunikativen Handelns* (2 vol.). Frankfurt: Suhrkamp.
Heringer, H. J. *et al.* (1977). *Einführung in die praktische Semantik*. Heidelberg: Quelle u. Meyer.
Johnstone, H. W. (1959). *Philosophy and argument*. Philadelphia: University of Pennsylvania Press.
Kallmeyer, W., & Schütze, F. (1976). Konversationsanalyse. *Studium Linguistik, 1*, 1ff.
Kindt, W., & Schmidt, S. J. (Eds.). (1976). *Argumentationsstrukturen in literaturwissenschaftlichen Arbeiten*. München: Fink.
Klein, W. (1980). Argumentation und Argument. *Zeitschrift für Linguistik und Literaturwissenschaft. 38/39*, 9ff.
Klein, W. (1981). Logik der Argumentation. In P. Schröder & H. Steger (Eds.), *Dialogforschung* (pp. 226ff.). Düsseldorf: Schwann.
Kopperschmidt, J. (1976). *Allgemeine Rhetorik*. (2nd ed.), Stuttgart: Kohlhammer.
Kopperschmidt, J. (1978). *Das Prinzip vernünftiger Rede*. Stuttgart: Kohlhammer.
Kopperschmidt, J. (1980). *Argumentation*. Stuttgart: Kohlhammer.
Kummer, W. (1972). Aspects of a theory of argumentation. In E. Gülich & W. Raible (Eds.), *Textsorten* (pp. 25ff.). Frankfurt: Akademische V. G.
Lausberg, H. (1960). *Handbuch der literarischen Rhetorik*. München: Hueber.

Lenders, W. (1975). *Semantische und argumentative Textdeskription*. Hamburg: Buske.

Metzing, D. W. (1975). *Formen kommunikationswissenschaftlicher Argumentationsanalyse*. Hamburg: Buske.

Metzing, D. W. (1976). Argumentationsanalyse. *Studium Linguistik, 1/2*, 1ff.

Naess, A. (1975). *Communication and argument*. Oslo: Universitets-Forlaget.

Natanson, M., & Johnstone, H. W. (1965). *Philosophy, rhetoric and argumentation*. Philadelphia: University of Pennsylvania Press.

Negt, O. (1971). *Soziologische Phantasie und exemplarisches Lernen*. Frankfurt: Europäische Verlagsanstalt.

Öhlschläger, G. (1979). *Linguistische Überlegungen zu einer Theorie der Argumentation*. Tübingen: Niemeyer.

Perelman, C., & Olbrechts-Tyteca, L. (1958). *La nouvelle rhétorique. Traité de l' argumentation*. Paris: Presses Universitaires de France.

Schnelle, H. (1975). Zur Explikation des Begriffs "argumentativer Text". In *Linguistische Probleme der Textanalyse. Jahrbuch des Instituts für Deutsche Sprache* (pp. 54ff.). Düsseldorf: Schwann.

Schwemmer, O. (1971). *Philosophie der Praxis*. Frankfurt: Suhrkamp.

Schroth, U. (1980). Eine Methode der formalen Rekonstruktion von Gerichtsurteilen. In W. Hassemer, A. Kaufmann, & U. Neumann (Eds.), Argumentation und Recht. *Archiv für Rechts- und Sozialphilosophie*. Beiheft N.F. 14 (pp. 197ff.). Wiesbaden: Steiner.

Strohm, H. (1981). *Friedlich in die Katastrophe. Eine Dokumentation über Atomkraftwerke*. Frankfurt: Zweitausendeins.

Toulmin, S. (1958). *The uses of argument*. Cambridge: Cambridge University Press.

Toulmin, S. (1976). *Knowing and acting*. New York: MacMillan.

Toulmin, S., Rieke, R., & Janik, A. (1979). *An introduction to reasoning*. New York: Macmillan.

Véron, E. (1981). *Construire l' evénement*. Paris: Minuit.

Völzing, P. (1979). *Begründen, erklären, argumentieren*. Heidelberg: Quelle und Meyer.

von Savigny, E. (1976). *Argumentation in der Literaturwissenschaft*. München: Beck.

Wunderlich, D. (1976). *Studien zur Sprechakttheorie*. Frankfurt: Suhrkamp.

Wunderlich, D. (1980). *Arbeitsbuch semantik*. Frankfurt: Athenäum.

CHAPTER 10

Narrative Analysis

Elisabeth Gülich and Uta M. Quasthoff

LIMITATION OF TOPIC

Storytelling is seen as a general human semiotic skill that is not confined to a particular historical epoch, a particular situational or communicative context, or a particular medium. As a result, the objects of narrative analysis can be traditional or modern, literary or everyday conversational texts, written as well as oral texts, and, at least under the demands of an all-encompassing semiotic approach, even stories without language, such as those using visual symbols or pictures. In order to cover all of these research interests an independent discipline, narratology, has been proposed (Pavel, 1973, pp. 6–7, 1976, pp. 2–3; Ryan, 1979; Todorov, 1969, p. 10, 1973, p. 139; van Dijk, 1973, p. 191). Although narrative analysis is an area with a long tradition, it has been primarily concerned with linguistic narration. This chapter also restricts itself to linguistic narratives.

Traditionally, the areas that have been most closely associated with narrative analysis have been the literary sciences, anthropology, psychology, theology, and history. Linguists did not begin to do research on narratives until the development of text analysis, and later, discourse analysis. There are, of course, some early linguistically relevant studies done on the literary narratives (see e.g., Hamburger, 1953; Lämmert, 1955). This holds especially for structural or semiotic studies (e.g., Greimas, 1967). The focus of this chapter is the linguistic analysis of narratives. However, sociological and psychological aspects as influencing factors are necessarily integrated into the presentation.

There are two different lines of interest in early text linguistic approaches to narrative analysis: On the one hand, singular structural phenomena

HANDBOOK OF DISCOURSE ANALYSIS, Vol. 2
Dimensions of Discourse

Copyright © 1985 by Academic Press London.
All rights of reproduction in any form reserved.
ISBN 0-12-712002-5

like tenses (Weinrich, 1971), connectives and discourse markers (Gülich, 1970; Rychner, 1970, 1971; Stempel, 1964, 1971), or beginning sentences of texts (Harweg, 1968) are studied. On the other hand there are more global attempts toward theories and methodologies including structural models designed to analyze entire narratives (Labov & Waletzky, 1967) within a textgrammatical framework (van Dijk, 1972; van Dijk, Ihwe, Petöfi, & Rieser, 1974). Under the influence of pragmatics and conversational analysis with its ethnomethodological origin, narrative analysis became more and more communicatively or interactively oriented, and consequently, storytelling as a communicative act or as an interactive process attracted interest.

The remainder of this article does not deal with the historical development of narrative analysis. Instead, a systematic presentation dealing with this extremely complex area from the perspective of an interactively based discourse analysis is attempted.

In the next section we present several definitional criteria for narratives. In the following section the major theoretical problems confronting narrative analysis are outlined and alternative solutions are discussed. Finally, an analysis of a conversational narrative serves as an illustration of the foregoing discussion.

WHAT IS A NARRATIVE?

As yet there seems to be no consensus among linguistic studies on narration as to what exactly the concept 'narrative' means. The most frequently used definitional criteria are outlined below.

1. A narrative refers to a series of real or fictional actions or events that take place in the past relative to the time of the narration (or are told as if occurring in the past). In more succinct terms, a narrative is based on a story (Schütze, 1976).

As early as Propp's analysis of the Russian folk tales (1928/58); for precursors of Propp see Jason, 1977), this criterion played a central role in his definition of 'function' (Gülich & Raible, 1977, Chap. 3, p. 2; Ryan, 1979, pp. 128 ff.), which is actually a unit of action. This analysis of functions forms the basis of many of the later narrative analyses, especially those of a structural nature (Ducrot & Todorov, 1972, p. 378; Gülich, 1976, p. 225; Labov, 1972, pp. 359–360; Quasthoff, 1980a, p. 27; van Dijk, 1980c, p. 140).

This criterion allows for the differentiation between narratives and descriptions, on the one hand, and on-the-spot-reporting, on the other hand.

However, fictional texts still fall under the category of narrative, including novels set in the future and works of science fiction. Even though they refer to imaginary futuristic actions and events, these are presented as having taken place in the past.

This criterion can be further specified in that the story is a unique event that can be specified as to a particular time and place. This restriction, used by Quasthoff (1980a, p. 27) for the conversational narrative, is also valid for a large number of literary narrative texts, especially for shorter narratives such as exempla, novellas, fables, and short stories. This restriction, however, excludes biographies, chronicles, or novels (see Genette's [1972] analysis of Proust's novel *A la recherche du temps perdu*). It also excludes everyday depictions of series of habitual actions.

2. The course of action or events that makes up the story contains some kind of transformation or change (van Dijk, 1972, p. 292).

This criterion also plays a role in Propp's analysis in which he points out that, in contrast to the introduction functions of the folk tale, there are functions that bring the action into motion. In later structural narrative analysis, this criterion appears, for example, in the work of Bremond, as a threefold division of the elementary narrative sequence. An initial state, for example, a lack, is followed by action to remove this lack. The result is the final state, in which the action taken has proven to be either successful or unsuccessful (Bremond, 1973, p. 131).

What all this amounts to is that the story must contain some element that makes it reportable (Labov, 1972, pp. 370–371; van Dijk, 1974–1975, pp. 286–287). In other words, the story has to fulfil a minimum of conditions concerning the quality of being out-of-the-ordinary relative to general norms and to the expectations of the participants (Quasthoff, 1980a, p. 27). These expectations and therefore the reportability of an event are, however, culturally specific (Polanyi, 1979).

It appears to us that an adequate description of 'unexpected' or 'out of the ordinary' is best approached using a theory based on the logic of action and cognitive psychology. The cognitive psychological concept of plan (Miller, Galanter, & Pribram, 1960, pp. 25 ff.; Quasthoff, 1980a, pp. 48 ff.) seems to fulfil this need as it allows the conceptualization of out of the ordinary as a disruption of a plan (see below).

3. The participants involved in the actions and events related are animate, usually humans (Schütze, 1976b, p. 11; van Dijk, 1972, pp. 294 ff.). If the participants are not humans, as, for example, in fables or fairy tales, they still possess human qualities and act like humans.

Quasthoff (1980a) makes the restriction that the narrator be identical with one of the participants involved in the story. However, she refers explicitly only to conversational narratives. For the majority of narrative literature this restriction does not apply.

4. Narratives are specified by certain formal characteristics. Among

these formal characteristics is a specifically narrative macrostructure that manifests itself linguistically in a special way (Gülich & Raible, 1979; Labov, 1972; Labov & Waletzky, 1967). Other typically formal characteristics include narrative tenses (Weinrich, 1971) and particular connective devices (Gülich, 1970, 1976; Stempel, 1964). Quasthoff (1980, p. 27) lists four formal restrictions, which, however, only apply to conversational narratives: evaluative and expressive speech devices, direct speech, historical present, and a high degree of detail.

All of these definitional criteria retain their validity only so long as they are couched in relatively vague terms. An attempt at precision results in criteria that apply only to specific types of narratives.

The question thus arises as to whether or not criteria applicable to all narrative forms should continue to be developed, since criteria formulated in very general terms do not provide a satisfactory basis for narrative analysis. If, however, the definition of narrative in general is abandoned altogether, the concept of general narratology becomes questionable.

DESCRIPTIVE ALTERNATIVES OF NARRATIVE THEORIES AND POSSIBLE SOLUTIONS

What Is the Object of Narrative Analysis: A Materialized Text or the Act of Telling a Story?

A question aiming at the object of narrative description appears trivial; the majority of the studies on the subject takes for granted that the object of narrative analysis is the narrative or the narrative text. In most of the structural analyses (starting with Propp and continuing through Bremond, Todorov, and Greimas) as well as in literature on text linguistics (e.g., Gülich & Raible, 1979; Pavel, 1976; van Dijk, 1972; Weinrich, 1971) the narrative text is taken as a given, that is, as a finished product.

However, from the point of view of pragmatics and ethnomethodological conversational analysis, the focus changes to the process of narration itself. The analytic interest is extended in the following two ways:

1. The narrative is seen as being an integral part of the communicative or interactional process. From the pragmatic–linguistic perspective this means that all factors relevant to the process must be taken into consideration. These include narrator and listener and their relation to one another, the situation in which the narration takes place, and the further

verbal and nonverbal context (prerequisites, interactive goals, processing of the narrative, etc.).

Ethnomethodologists describe how a storytelling situation is established, what sequential positions narratives have within the conversational framework, how narratives are elicited and possibly told one after the other, and how the narrator and listener negotiate for their roles (Sacks, 1971a, 1971b).

2. The focus is on the process of storytelling itself, on narration as a complex verbal activity, that is, on the speaker's verbalization process and the interaction between speaker and listener. Procedural and cognitive psycholinguistics describe how the narrator materializes his verbalization plan (Quasthoff, 1980a, pp. 84 ff.) and how he linguistically organizes the underlying series of actions and events.

The ethnomethodological approach places emphasis on the role of the listener as an active interactional partner; intervention by the listener, even the way in which the listener signals his attention, guides the narrative process (Quasthoff, 1980b; Schütze, 1976b, pp. 9–10). It can be argued that even written narrative texts should be analyzed processually in that textual structures are established through the reader's active (re-)structuring of information (Bock, 1980; Schenkein, 1979; Wienold, 1972a, 1972b, Chap. 2, 1977; Wienold & Rieser, 1979).

What Has To Be Described: The Narrative Structure or the Function(s) of Telling a Story?

Description of Narrative Structures

For a long time narrative analysis was synonymous with the description of narrative structures. This is true (with only a few exceptions) for the approaches of the French structuralists and for the first text-linguistic approaches (van Dijk, 1972).

In light of the definitional criteria discussed above, the question must be raised as to whether the structure of the narrative should be analyzed in terms of content or in terms of more formal criteria. The distinction is made in most of the structural or semiological analyses for example, Bremond's 'raconté' and 'racontant', Todorov's 'histoire' and 'discours', and Greimas' 'niveau immanent' and 'niveau apparant' (Genot, 1979; Grosse, 1977, 1979, pp. 596–597; Gülich & Raible, 1977, pp. 216–217; Rimmon, 1976, pp. 34–35). All the structuralist approaches give first priority to the underlying structure of the story itself (e.g., Bremond, 1973, p. 323). Even van Dijk (1972) attempts to describe narrative structure in terms of semantic macrostructure using text-grammatical categories.

If one reduces the concept of 'narrative structure' to the underlying
narrated actions, the following problems result: First of all, the problems
of how this structure is related to the narrative text itself and how the
deep structure is transferred to the surface structure must be solved
(Brooke-Rose, 1977, pp. 517–521).

The second question is whether or not it is sufficient to distinguish
between the underlying actions and events, and the narrative text. Brooke-
Rose (1977, p. 519), for instance, introduces two surface structures in
addition to the deep structure: the structure or the presentation of events,
and the texture or the sequence of words.

Quasthoff (1980, pp. 46 ff.) advocates the distinction between the actual
and, if possible, objectively verifiable course of events and actions and
the information that is subjectively perceived and processed. She proposes
a three-way distinction: (1) the actions at the time of occurrence of the
story, (2) the cognitive story (the cognitive construction or reconstruction
of the part of real world events that constitute the story), and (3) the
storytelling activities.

Limitation of the concept 'narrative structure' to only the underlying
structure almost necessarily leads to neglect of the narrative text. With
the exception of Genette (1972) concerning Proust (see Rimmon, 1976)
and Greimas (1976) concerning Maupassant, the majority of the French
structuralists concern themselves with their own résumé of narratives
rather than with the narratives themselves.

On the whole, there have been relatively few attempts to describe the
surface structures of narrative texts. This is surprising since one of the
most influential (at least most-often quoted) narrative models is that of
Labov & Waletzky (1967) and Labov (1972), which can be classified as
surface oriented (Quasthoff, 1980a).

Another surface structure-oriented approach is that of Gülich & Raible
(1979). They attempt to describe the macrostructure specific to narrative
texts by using a hierarchy of discourse markers. These markers allow
the delimitation of an ordered set of sub-texts (see also Hellholm, 1980;
Hoek, 1975; Wienold, 1982). Quasthoff's (1980) formal criteria of conversational narratives (see above) are also oriented toward the narrative
text.

In our opinion, a useful concept of narrative structure must include
at least the narrative text structure and the underlying series of actions
and events as related to the cognitive story. This calls for a much more
differentiated concept of structure than has been developed.

If one is not willing to exclude the interactive aspect from the analysis
and instead chooses to focus on the process of narrating, the narrative
text itself naturally takes on added importance. Of greatest interest in

this connection are the linguistic devices that allow the linguist to recognize how the narrator gradually comes to materialize his verbalization plan, how the cognitive story is organized linguistically, and how the listener contributes to the structuring of the narrative as an interactive product. Speech devices used in this connection include discourse markers (Gülich, 1970; Wald, 1978), sentential connectives and hesitation phenomena (Quasthoff, 1979a, 1979b, 1980a, pp. 198, 209–223). This subject is taken up again in more detail in the text analysis below.

The Functions of Telling a Story

Naturally, a description of the narrative process remains incomplete as long as only the text and content of the narrative are the objects of analysis. The functions that the narrative fulfills in the interaction or the functions that the participants attribute to the narrative also deserve attention. According to the terminology of Labov & Waletzky (1967), storytelling has at least a twofold function: referential (reference to 'event constellation'), and evaluative, a "function of personal interest determined by a stimulus in the social context in which the narrative occurs" (p. 13). According to Malinowski (1923, p. 149), this second function—he calls it a "social and emotive function"—dominates the referential function. Van Dijk proposes a distinction between practical functions (e.g., advice or warning) and emotional functions (e.g., impressing the listener) (1974–1975, p. 286).

It is doubtful whether the numerous and manifold functions of narratives in concrete interactions can be anywhere near adequately described using only two categories. Kallmeyer & Schütze (1977) propose three levels of orderedness for the description of communicative interaction: discourse organization, constitution of action, and the presentation of information. Narratives are informational schemata to the extent that they contain—as do descriptions—complex, interrelated subject matter. Narrative functions can be derived from the dominant action schema. (For a critical review of Kallmeyer & Schütze, see Quasthoff, 1980a, pp. 28 ff; for narratives without schematic functions see Gülich, 1980.)

Another possibility for dealing with this vast array of functions is starting with relatively general distinctions and differentiating within these categories. Quasthoff (1980a, pp. 146 ff.) makes two distinctions based on the fundamental functions of language, namely the representation of contents (communicative functions) and the constitution of social relations through linguistic forms (interactive functions). Communicative functions are subdivided into (1) primarily speaker-oriented functions, such as psychological and communicative unburdening and self-aggrandizement, and (2) primarily listener-oriented functions, such as making the other person laugh, entertainment, and information, and (3) primarily context-oriented functions, such as evidence and explanation. Interactive functions—performed through the use of the discourse pattern of a story instead of a report, for instance—include the phatic function, that of guiding the interaction, and that of defining the situational frame (Goffman, 1974).

These functions have been developed through the analysis of conversational narratives in everyday and in institutional communication settings. They therefore pertain specifically to narratives in these settings, just as do the considerations of Kallmeyer & Schütze. One can assume, however, that these functions could be applied to written everyday narratives such as those found in letters and to a certain extent to literary narratives (this holds especially for the entertainment function). Of course, attention must be paid to the stylized contexts and conventionalized determination of function of literary genres.

If narrative analysts choose to view the narrative not as a finished product or a narrative structure but rather as an integral part of the narrative process, the following two considerations take on added importance: First, in line with the principles of ethnomethodological conversation analysis, a narrative does not have an intrinsic function based on semantic information. Instead, in the interactive situation the narrator and listener attribute one or more functions to the narrative; storytelling also means that the listener has the responsibility of showing his having understood the functions of the narrative (see the concept of appreciation in Sacks, 1971b). Second, structure and function should not be seen as mutually exclusive descriptive categories. Instead, the interconnectedness between structure and function should be made explicit (Quasthoff, 1980a, pp. 191 ff.).

What Is a Functionally Based Structure: A Static System of Categories or the Dynamic Flow of Processes?

We have argued for a description of narratives as the interactional procedure of storytelling, including structural and functional aspects. We now have to raise the question as to whether narrative theory can add a functional description to any of the structural approaches. If not, the notion of structure in itself must be delimited in order to be compatible with an integrative description.

If the organization of the process of storytelling is to be described, it follows that 'structure' cannot mean a static set of elements. In other words, structural descriptions insofar as they simply divide a narrative text into an ordered set of elements are not processual in the sense of our basic assumptions. This holds even if the structural elements are explicitly functional in nature as in the classical narrative analysis of Labov and Waletzky (1967) and Labov (1972).

The theory of subtexts (Gülich & Raible, 1979) is in one respect more in line with a dynamic concept of structure: The structuring into subtexts is established at the surface level of the narrative text by hierarchically ordered discourse markers. Thus it is the process of comprehension, that is, the listener's activity of reconstructing the narrative structure, that serves as an argument for the functional explanation of surface-level markers.

Narrative structure, as described by the structuralists, is to be understood as constraints on the meanings of narrative texts, meaning—and thus structure—being a static concept. Structural categories are also used by different approaches in cognitive psychology and artificial intelligence to conceptualize invariant semantic elements of stories. There is one main difference, however, in comparison to the structuralists' approach. The concept of meaning presupposed by the cognitive approaches is operationalized as text processing and is thus a dynamic one. Meaning is comprehension.

The basic cognitive activity that underlies both comprehension and (re)production of textual information is memory. Since Bartlett (1932), memory and information processing in general have been viewed as the organism's active integration of incoming information with knowledge structures that are already available. Schemata are defined as the organizing principles of this cognitive activity.

This basic idea of an organizing principle that governs information processing according to structural patterns or expectations specific to the different domains of human experience has become crucial to cognitive approaches in narrative analysis. Note, however, that in these approaches narratives are not the objectives of theorizing but are taken heuristically as prototypic for discourse (processing) in general. This prototypical status is, of course, due to their relatively simple and highly regular structure.

Cognitively based research on narrative structure can be divided into those approaches that describe narrative schemata and those that explicate implicit nonlinguistic knowledge elements necessary for story processing. Within the framework of the latter approach the notion of 'script' (Schank, 1980; Schank & Abelson, 1977) has become the most well-known conceptualization. The notion was developed in artificial intelligence to enable a formal description of the different domains of knowledge of the world that human text processors automatically use to reconstruct the meaning in the structure of an input text. Automatic systems, on the other hand must be provided with this information in order to process natural language. (For examples see Schank & Abelson, 1977, pp. 38–39.)

Two main lines of research stand out among the attempts to describe story schemata and thus to predict and explain processing regularities: the theory of macrostructure, associated with van Dijk and Kintsch, and story grammar, associated with Rumelhart and others.

In contrast to earlier work (van Dijk, 1976, 1979), van Dijk's macrostructure model now assigns two different structures to a (narrative) discourse: semantic micro- and macrostructure express the information of a specific text on a local and global level, while the schematic superstructure provides the general pattern for the entire type of discourse. This distinction seems to be analogous to the differentiation between informational structure and relational structure developed independently by Quasthoff (1980b).

Macrorules such as generalization, deletion, and construction generate the global semantic macrostructure from the semantic microstructure of a text. A summary of the text is the expression of the macrostructure. (For an example of the informal generation of a macrostructure of a narrative discourse by the use of macrorules see van Dijk, 1980a, Sec. 2.5).

These few remarks about some of the most basic ideas of the macrostructure model are of course far from an adequate presentation of the theory. More detailed surveys may be found in van Dijk (1977, 1980a, 1980b), Kintsch (1977a), and Kintsch & van Dijk (1978). For critical remarks on earlier versions of the theory see Gülich & Raible (1977) and Quasthoff (1980b, pp. 39–44).

Story grammar models (Johnson & Mandler, 1980; Mandler & Johnson, 1977; Rumelhart, 1975, 1977; Stein & Glenn, 1979; Thorndyke, 1977) are comparable to the macrostructure approach in the following respects:

1. They are also based on cognitive reality in that they claim to predict (and thus explain) processing regularities: Their empirical foundations are the recall and summarizing of data from textual information.

2. The descriptive framework is that of a grammar, that is, the explication of rules that underlie comprehending, (re-)producing, and summarizing a narrative text. Van Dijk's concept of text structuring was first based on a very close analogy to the standard and generative semantic models of sentence grammar (van Dijk, 1972), but was later expanded into a considerably broader framework including pragmatic aspects (van Dijk, 1977b). Rumelhart's early grammar (1975) strictly separated syntactic and semantic components. Rumelhart (1977) later proposed a semantically based description using relations as structural nodes. For a discussion of the

grammatic format of story grammars see the controversy in *Cognitive Science* (Black & Wilensky, 1979; Mandler & Johnson, 1980; Rumelhart, 1980).

In contrast to the macrostructural approach, story grammar models

1. restrict their schematic descriptions to stories of the problem-solving type:

> First, something happens to a protagonist which sets up a goal that must be satisfied. Then the remainder of the story is a description of the protagonist's problem solving behavior in seeking the goal coupled with the results of the behavior. (Rumelhart, 1980, p. 313);

2. make no distinction between microstructural and macrostructural levels. Summarizing regularities are explained by summarizing rules and the identification of different levels in the hierarchic structural description of the entire narrative text to which these rules apply (Rumelhart, 1977);

3. make no distinction between informational content structures of the particular text and the schematic superstructure that determines text type.

For a more detailed review of story grammar models, including critical aspects, see van Dijk (1980b) and Beaugrande (1982). Further very interesting research activities on the developmental aspects of the formation of story schemata in children are reported in Stein and Glenn (1979), Mandler (1978), McClure, Mason, and Barnitz (1979), and Stein and Trabasso (1982).

The decisive difference between the structuralists' and the psychologists' approach to narrative description does not necessarily lie in the structural categories but in the empirical dimensions of the different theories. The empirical basis of the structuralists' theories is in principle a large corpus of narrative texts. Empirical adequacy is achieved if the described structure is systematic and covers the instances of the corpus exhaustively. The theory is proven false if there are narrative texts of the described kind that do not fit the description.

The psychological notion of 'schema' derives its theoretic value from a theory of information processing. Consequently, empirical adequacy of a schematic structural description of a narrative must be shown in terms of its explanatory power for the processes of comprehending, storing, retrieving, reproducing, and summarizing narrative discourse. The theory is proven false if it does not properly predict the processing regularities found in the experimental results.

As in the surface-oriented theory of subtexts, here again it is the process of comprehending a narrative that adds a dynamic dimension to an otherwise static structural description. What is needed in addition to the postulated functionally based concept of structure, however, is a description of the structure of the process of producing a narrative.

After all, it is in the process of planning and uttering a narrative that intended interactive and communicative functions are turned into communicative reality. Quasthoff (1980a; see also Rehbein, 1977) represents the processual structuredness and the interactive boundedness of planning and producing a narrative by mapping these processes in a diagram that includes steps such as situation, communicative–interactive goal, and relational structure (narrative schema) (see Figure 10.1).

The application of this model to a sample narrative is discussed below; a more detailed description is found in Quasthoff and Nikolaus (1982) and Quasthoff (1983).

A somewhat different approach is to treat the course of the interactional structure, that is, the mutual activity of storytelling, as a structural system in itself. This work has mostly been done by conversational analysts (Jefferson, 1978; Kallmeyer & Schütze, 1977; Ryave, 1978; Sacks, 1971a, 1971b, 1972). It deals with the working machinery of interactional moves performed by the participants in conversation.

One of the answers to the question of how this machinery works is that interactants mark their moves and their more global activities in order to make them unambiguous. Among the means by which interactive clarity is achieved are the sequential placement of particular activities and the use of lexical and other devices to indicate which types of activities are to follow. It is therefore not surprising that conversational analysts have focused on the sequential embedding of stories in conversation. Sacks (1971b, Lectures 1 & 2), Jefferson (1978), and Quasthoff (1981) deal with the listener's "appreciations" that obligatorily follow stories in conversation. Wald (1978) and Jefferson (1978) describe announcements as well as local occasioning of stories and other "pre's" of stories in conversation. Ryave (1978) analyzes series of stories in conversation. Kallmeyer and Schütze (1977) focus on the sequential obligations presented by the internal structure of the storytelling interaction.

The metaphor of working machinery makes clear that a dynamic concept of structure is assumed. The concept of function, of course, is different from the communicative and interactive functions associated with the planning model mentioned above. Functions here are realized in connection with the different structural units in the machinery of the interactive process. They underlie the organization—the structure—of this process. For instance, the announcement (Wald), preface (Sacks), or the abstract (Labov & Waletzky) preceding a story in conversation establishes the initiator of the narrative as the principal speaker (Wald) and gives him special rights to the floor during the course of the narrative. The abstract

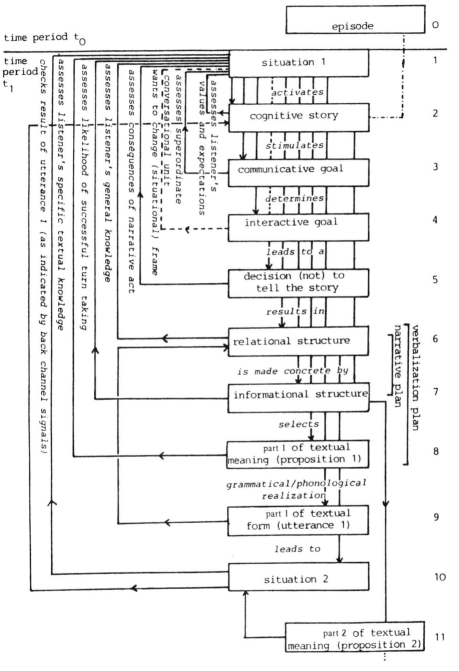

Figure 10.1 Production schema for conversational narratives: (– – –), variable processes;
(———), necessary processes; (– · – · –), processes not included in narrative production.

also marks the point of the story (*I just saw a car accident at the corner!*) and orients the listener to the evaluative (Labov & Waletzky, 1967) nucleus of the story that is to be appreciated (Sacks) by the listener.

In this chapter we do not specifically focus on the methodology of narrative analysis. Methodological alternatives and empirical procedures in narrative analysis must be inferred from the general methodological foundations of the approaches to narratives described above.

DESCRIPTIVE DECISIONS TESTED THROUGH EMPIRICAL ANALYSIS

The decisions made in the discussion of descriptive alternatives above have now to stand the test of empirical applicability and analytic success. A general and exemplary presentation of the way in which the favored descriptive alternatives are applicable to the analysis of a sample narrative follows: We do not apply all of the descriptive devices discussed, nor is it possible to give a thorough analysis of the whole narrative using all of the analytic procedures presented.

Description of the Data

The descriptive power of the different approaches is tested in the following analysis of a conversational narrative. The narrative selected for analysis is taken from a counseling session on November 14, 1975 in a Berlin welfare institution. (The recordings were made by the psychological research project Bürgernahes Verhalten in der Sozialhilfe. We are grateful to Rainer K. Silbereisen for offering us the data for linguistic analysis. We present only the English translation of the transcript.) The participants are a female social worker (B) and a female client (K) approximately 40 years of age, who has just found an apartment for her family after two years of living in welfare housing.

```
1   B   /ya Mrs. X that's fine
2       how long have you lived on the Katzbachstraße/
        [rapidly]
3 ⌈ K   it'll be 2 years on December 6
4 ⌊ B                well
5       the way it all worked out really because of your taking
6       the initiative—
7   K              yeah
8   B   and now you're
```

9	K	I sure spent a lot of time running around—
10	B	you ran around
11	K	Boy—I ran all over creation
12		you wouldn't believe how much money I spent on transportation—telephone calls
13		6 o'clock in the morning 6 o'clock in the ((stutters)) bought the paper
14	B	mhm
15	K	Wednesdays
16	K	n then Sundays the "Morgenpost"——
17		[L] in everything fell through every time they found out
18	⌈K	welfare housing you know
19	⌊B	yeah

20	⌈K	n—then they turned me d＿some of 'em didn't come out an say it＿
21	⌊B	hm
22	K	then they just asked for my birth date—un uh—address
23		n then they said call us tomorrow
24		n then they turned me down
25	⌈K	n then they found out somehow ye know—where we all li＿
26	⌊B	uh huh
27	K	except for this one guy he was the one we went to— Paris Street—
28	K	this——[L] Association of Berlin Apartment Managers ye know
29	B	yeah
30	⌈K	I go why not try there ye know—
31	⌊B	uh—huh
32	K	I went there
33		yeah n then we had to pay 61 marks to be in the
34		Association of A Berlin Apartment Managers so that we could be insured right away
35	B	uh - huh
36	⌈K	ye know? ye get insurance for ah legal protection—
37	⌊B	yeah yeah
38	K	(. . .) we'd already tried ye know w＿worked out great
39		we'd already gone to the lawyer's
40	⌈K	we didn't need to pay ye know cause of the apartment
41	⌊B	great
42	K	Yeah = then——we paid the 61 marks—
43		n then it was s'pposed it was on a Friday or a Thursday

44   n Tuesday we were s'pposed to go in the morning n
      then——
45   he'd be able to let us know
46   n then (he) could we went there
47   n then he says good God he says I've been waiting for
      you he says—ye know—
48   I've got a nice apartment manager job just between you
      and me uh—((stutters))
49 ⎡ K   It's really a good deal ye know—
50 ⎣ B   yeah
51   K   then we had t'go to Kurfürstendamm——
52   there was this realty office
53   n then he told us
54   that wh__ at five o'clock the—the man
55 ⎡ K   he lives in Ulm ye know—
56 ⎣ B   mhm
57   K   he's in Berlin right now—
58   n then you can meet him in person
59   yeah n then ((stutters)) he really—liked us
60   and we liked him too and all that
61   they were pretty nice—and everything and they——
62   (ye know) then I go after that I go Up til now I haven't
63   done anything but run around I said
64   "if I only knew if you're on the level or not
65   then ye always get a no just because we live in welfare
      housing I said—
66 ⎡ K   but nobody ever asks how come"
67 ⎣ B   yes that's why I was going to ask you—
68   if did they in fact ask you where you live
69 ⎡ K   no he didn't even ask pay any attention to it—ye know
70 ⎣ B   (. . .)
71   K   he had to fill out the form
72   he just read through it
73 ⎡ K   anyway didn't even notice it ye know?
   ⎣ B   yeah
74 ⎡ K   an = ah I didn't even know that he didn't notice
75 ⎣ B   it ye know—
         yeah
76   K   n then I go by the way—um—we live in welfare housing
77   I go people always look down look d__ at ye ye know
78 ⎡K   'cause nobody asks why you're there ye know what the
   ⎢   reasons are
79 ⎣B   mhm mhm mhm

80 K an everything ye know——
81 K an then he goes I see he goes and like that
       ((stutters))
82 ⌈K um we'll let you know
83 ⌊   uh—huh
84 K n then we went home
85   n then one day Mr. Krüger from downstairs—said—
86   somebody's been here asking questions about you—ye
       know
87 ⌈   n we figured it had to be him didn't it
88 ⌊B   (. . .)   uh—huh
89 K n then I decided to call him 'cause we hadn't
90 ⌈K heard anything for a long time
91 ⌊B   yeah
92 K we were supposed to / oh yeah we got a letter / [change
       of voice]
93 ⌈K we were supposed to get a certificate of good conduct
94 ⌊B from the police—and
                    yeah
95 K forms for an apartment manager's contract and
96   and everything—and my I.D. papers and everything ye
       know—
97   and then we were supposed to look at the apartment
98   then we went there—
99   an then the woman says the apartment she says / it's
       already
100   rented out [imitates uppity voice] / she says—
101   that's the
102   it's not worth getting your hopes up it's been
103   Mr. Sch. (. . .) already gave it to somebody. / [still imitating]
104   they live on Kottbusser Damm—
105   you can ask them if you want
106   you can go there and ask them
107   they're a young married couple
108   I go / that sounds funny to me / [voice changes]—
109   he wrote us we're supposed to get a police certificate
110 ⌈ we even had to pay for it came to 8 Marks a piece ye know
111 ⌊B   uh-huh   uh-huh uh-huh
112 K n then we got all the forms together
113   n went all over the place——
114   n I thought to myself I'm not going to let I'm going to
       have a talk with him
115   I'm not going to let him get away with it

116 ⎡K   I'll give 'im a piece of my mind
117 ⎣B   right
118 K   then I called him in uh—in uh Ulm
119   n told him about it—
120   [L] I go/Mr. Sch. I go I don't think that's very nice I go—
121 ⎡K   (uh you send us) we went out and got the forms
122 ⎣B   and everything
            uh-huh
123 K   I go—
124 B   uh-huh
125 K   an now the apartment's rented out/—[imitates]
126   /who told you that? [imitates the other person's astonished voice]/
127   ——ye know——I explained it to him—
128   n he goes I don't know anything about it I've never even seen the people
129 K   he goes how could they say a thing like that
130 B   you mean it wasn't true?
131 K   yeah no it wasn't true at all—
132   he says /for goodness sakes he says Mrs. P. I'm
133   really happy that I've found you ye know—
134   send me your papers
135   and fill out the form
136   and then you'll get—I'll send you your contract/ [imitates]
137   I go you mean it's really all right?
138   yeah sure he says you can move in as soon as you want he says—
139 ⎡K   as soon as the apartment's vacant
140 ⎣B   but that wasn't true because the apartment the
141   apartment wasn't vacant
142 K   no it wasn't they had one of their friends—
143 ⎡   ready to pay uh a thousand marks extra——see what I mean
144 ⎣B   oh I get you
145 K   that's what they wanted
146   n he told us we shouldn't pay anything extra
147   that we didn't have to pay—
148   except maybe for the ceiling in the hall—
149   they lowered it and put in a new one with lamps and things a couple a' hundred marks
150   n he'd deduct it from our salary——ye know
151   n this he didn't say anything more about it

```
152 ⎡ K   he even offered them 800 marks so that they'd
153 ⎣ B                                          to move
154 ⎡ K   move out—ye know—
155 ⎣ B   out
156   K   and then they didn't move when they were supposed to
157       so he told—he told anyway they're
158       not going to get the money ye know——
159   B   well—Mrs. P. that sounds just wonderful
160       'll keep my fingers crossed for you
161       now we just have to worry about—oh what are
162       we going to do about the move. . .
```

Explanation of notation used in transcriptions

—	caesura
——	short pause (about 2 seconds)
———	medium-length pause (about 3 seconds)
[L]	takes a breath
(. . .)	short, unintelligible
(xyz)	probably as transcribed, but somewhat difficult to understand
xyz__	interruption, self-correction in a word; anacoluthons are subsumed under this category and not separately marked
⎡zyz xyz ⎣xyz xyz	simultaneous utterances of two speakers, first speaker's utterance appears above second speaker's utterance
[xyz]	transcriber's commentary
/xyz xyz/	probable range of commentary
=	ligature (joining of words at boundaries)
?	interrogatory intonation
xyz=eh⎫ xyz=ah⎭	prolongation of sound at the end of a word

As mentioned above, the sample narrative is a conversational narrative, that is, it corresponds to the semantic and formal restrictions formulated in Quasthoff (1980a, pp. 27–28) and mentioned above. For instance, it is reportable because it goes against normal expectations; ''Anyone who's ever lived in a welfare home, that is, who has sunk to the bottom of the social ladder, has a hard time getting back on his feet.'' The formal speech devices include:

1. Evaluative and expressive speech forms, for example, repetitions of the same form or different form, but same content (e.g., 65–66 and 76–78, 115 and 116), especially to indicate direct speech (e.g., 62–63) and exclamation (e.g., 11, 47).
2. Direct speech appears in the text extremely often: The narrator gives an extensive replay of her own utterances (e.g., 62–66, 76–

80, 108–113, 114–116, 120–125) as well as those of her interlocutors (e.g., 47–49, 53–58, 81–82, 85–86). The way in which she occasionally imitates the intonation or manner of speech of the person quoted is quite noticeable (e.g., 99–107, 126, 128–129).

3. Certain phases of the narrative show a high degree of detail. The event continuum is atomized (e.g., 43–45, 51–53, 109–113).

4. In these passages the preferred narrative tense is historical present, e.g., 99, 108, 120.

Structural–Functional Analysis

Earlier in this chapter, a structural model of the production process was seen as the compensatory descriptive device needed for the integration of the functional aspects in narrative analysis. Let us now turn to a descriptive proposal in an attempt to map the process of situationally bound, goal-oriented narrative production.

To give hints as to the applicability of the production schema (see Figure 10.1), we contextualize parts of the schema relating to the storytelling process of the above narrative, concentrating on the situational, functional, and semantic aspects. Let us first look at the different feedback loops that can be read as the relevant factors constituting the social setting of storytelling from the perspective of the narrator. In retrieving the cognitive story, that is, the cognitive representations of the past event at the time of narration, the narrator checks the situation by trying to assess the listener's values and expectations. In other words, the narrator knows her listener shares the value of self-initiative as being a prerequisite for success (B, line 6). (This is especially true since the German social welfare law defines social aid as "help to help oneself"!) If finding an apartment had been due to pure chance without any effort on the part of the narrator, the story would either not have been told, or the cognitive story would have been transformed into a narrative by adding activity and initiative to the role of the narrator according to the assumed expectations of the listener. (Since in our analysis we have access only to the meaning of the text, and not to the cognitive story or the real event, we can, of course, not decide to what extent this transformation process has taken place in the case of our narrative.)

Turning to the next step of the production schema, the situationally adequate recall of a past event (cognitive story) stimulates a communicative and an interactive goal of the storytelling activity. This is where the intended communicative and interactive functions of the narrative process are planned. In the case of our narrative, a careful discourse analysis of the conversational activities (too detailed to be reproduced here) reveals the communicative function of self-aggrandizement. The way in which the narrator presents herself as a character in the story is designed to establish her interactively as the kind of personality she wants to be in the view of her listener.

The communicative goal of a storytelling activity, achieved by means of the story content, has of course to be situationally adequate, that is, it must conform to the topical context of the conversation. For this reason the feedback loop associated with the communicative goal in the production schema (Figure 10.1) is named "assesses superordinate conversational unit."

The situational check as to the contextual adequacy of a conversational narrative is a good example of the relation between the storytelling process and its social setting. This relation is not conceptualized as a correlation of two independent factors but as integrative in the sense that the narrative activity not only reacts to a certain context but also creates and changes this context. In the case of the sample narrative, the general topic 'apartment has been found' is first established (lines 1–5). This topic allows for a narrative about the circumstances surrounding this event. But the narrative itself still presents a self-initiated deviation from the topical progression on the part of the narrator. The context actually focuses on the result of the event (lines 5, 8). It is the social worker's remark concerning the client's initiative (line 6) that activates (see Figure 10.1) the narrator to initiate her story. She does this by interrupting the social worker (lines 8–9) and thus changing the topical progression from focusing on the results to the circumstances of the finding of a new apartment. That the narrative is treated as a topical digression by the social worker is made entirely clear by the way in which the social worker immediately shifts the topic after appreciating the narrative (lines 159–161).

Just as a communicative function of a narrative can be activated by changing an established topic and thus creating a new one, an interactive function is typically put into effect by changing the social frame (Goffman, 1974) of a conversation instead of reacting to one already established. Presenting a past event conversationally, in the discourse pattern of a story (as opposed to a report), with its formal characteristics such as direct speech, imitation, evaluation, and historical present, establishes a certain kind of social setting. This social frame is specified by a certain degree of intimacy, informality, and personalness. Telling a story in an institutional setting such as a welfare institution very often serves an interactive function in that it attempts to change the setting from professional, decision-oriented counseling, to chatting with a friend. (For a detailed analysis of an interactive function see Quasthoff, 1980a).

Skipping the step of the decision (not) to tell the story in the production schema, we now turn to the structural nucleus of the processual narrative description. The relational structure and the informational structure are largely comparable to the cognitively based story grammar model. They differ, however, in three ways:

1. There are different structures for the schema of stories in general (relational structure) and the structured information of a particular story (informational structure).
2. The concepts of relational and informational structure include the situational boundedness by means of pragmatically oriented structural elements (see below).
3. These concepts are embedded in a descriptive modeling of the entire planning process for the realization of a situationally bound, goal-oriented narrative production (see Figure 10.1).

Figure 10.2 gives the relational structure of the sample narrative. The diagram is to be read in the following way: Each node names the relation over its subordinate nodes, which again are relations. The principle holds unless relations are instantiated by informational units of the narrative discourse. Instantiations are represented by the right most lines.

The relations dominated by the goal relation integrate the aspects of the communicative–interactive goal and the setting of the storytelling process into the relational net of the narrative schema. Thus we follow the assumption that the semantic structure of discourse is influenced by these pragmatically oriented structural elements. We also indicate the fusing of the schematic structure of the story with the production schema of the storytelling process. What is still lacking in this semantic description is the processing aspect. The relational net is seen as part of the production schema that is processed step by step. However, since it is itself semantic in nature it is not sequentially ordered. This remains one of the numerous unsolved problems with which further research in a processual approach to narrative analysis will have to deal.

One of the objections one might have against the analysis presented here is an assumed arbitrariness of the structural units as suggested by the structural description (see Figure 10.2). Why not define the argument with the present tenants and the telephone conversation with the landlord

Figure 10.2   Relational structure of the conversational narrative: O, owner; N, narrator; T, present tenant.

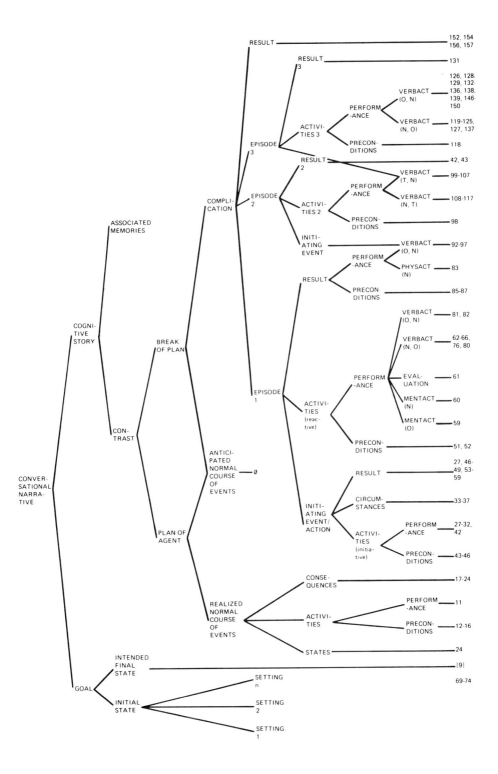

as part of one episode? Why define the important border between the initiating event and the reacting activities of the first episode between lines 49 and 51 and lines 53 and 58 as being a violation of the temporal order? A close analysis of the discourse shows that these are the structural units that the interactants establish between themselves; one of the methods (in the ethnomethodological sense of the word) by which interactants mark structural units is the use of discourse markers (Gülich, 1970) like the episodic markers discussed above. The narrator uses change of location as one of the structuring principles: *to Paris Street* (27), *Kurfürstendamm* (51), *went home* (84), *we went there* (to the apartment) (98) *called . . . Ulm* (118). Most of the structural units are marked cooperatively by both participants, for example, B's backchannel signals (lines 29 and 50) invited by a tag question (line 28) or by K's slot (line 49) and B's backchannel signals following K's falling intonation (lines 82–83). One is even marked only by the listener: B's evaluative reinforcement in line 117.

Of course these few analytic remarks cannot replace a complete sequential analysis of our sample discourse. What should have become clear, however, is that in the light of a processual interactive concept of storytelling, structural units cannot be arbitrary, any more than the formal and semantic characteristics of conversational narratives can be purely definitional features. In view of the interactants' task of making the quality and relevance of their activities mutually unambiguous, definitional characteristics have to be seen as structuring devices, too. These devices mark and thus interactively establish the specific activity of storytelling, opposed to other discourse forms such as turn-by-turn talk or giving a report.

BIBLIOGRAPHY

Bartlett, F. C. (1932). Remembering: A study in experimental and social psychology. Cambridge: Cambridge University Press.
Beaugrande, R. A. de. (1982). The story of grammars and the grammar of stories. *Journal of Pragmatics, 6,* 383–422.
Black, J. B., & Wilensky, R. (1979). An evaluation of story grammars. *Cognitive Science, 3,* 213–229.
Bock, M. (1980). Some effects of titles on building and recalling text structures. *Discourse Processes, 4,* 301–312.
Bremond, C. (1973). *Logique du récit.* Paris: Seuil.
Brooke-Rose, C. (1977). Surface structure in narrative. The squirm of the true, Part III. *PTL, 3,* 517–562.
Chabrol, C. (1973a). De quelques problèmes de grammaire narrative et textuelle. In C. Chabrol (Ed.), *Sémiotique narrative et textuelle* (pp. 7–28). Paris: Larousse.
Chabrol, C. (Ed.) (1973b). *Sémiotique narrative et textuelle.* Paris: Larousse.

Dressler, W. U. (Ed.) (1977). *Current trends in textlinguistics*. Berlin: de Gruyter.
Ducrot, O., & Todorov, T. (1972). *Dictionnaire encyclopédique des sciences du langage*. Paris: Seuil.
Ehlich, K. (Ed.) (1980). *Erzählen im Alltag*. Frankfurt: Suhrkamp.
Genette, G. (1972). Discours du récit. Essai de méthode. In G. Genette (Ed.), *Figures III* (pp. 67–273). Paris: Seuil.
Genot, G. (1979). Narrativity and text grammar. In J. S. Petöfi (Ed.), *Text vs. sentence. Basic questions of textlinguistics* (Vol. 2) (pp. 524–539). Hamburg: Buske.
Goffman, E. (1974). *Frame analysis: An essay on the organization of experience*. Harmondsworth: Penguin.
Greimas, A. J. (1967). La structure des actants du récit. Essai d'approche générative. In Linguistic studies presented to André Martinet. *Word, 23*. Reprinted in Greimas (1970), pp. 249–270.
Greimas, A. J. (1970). *Du sens. Essais sémiotiques*. Paris: Seuil.
Greimas, A. J. (1976). *Maupassant. La sémiotique du texte. Exercices pratiques*. Paris: Seuil.
Grosse, E. U. (1977). French structuralist views on narrative grammar. In W. U. Dressler (Ed.), *Current trends in textlinguistics* (pp. 155–173). Berlin: de Gruyter.
Grosse, E. U. (1979). Von der Satzgrammatik zum Erzähltextmodell. Linguistische Grundlagen und Defizienzen bei Greimas und Bremond. In J. S. Petöfi (Ed.), *Text vs. sentence: Basic questions of textlinguistics* (Vol. 2) (pp. 595–617). Hamburg: Buske.
Gülich, E. (1970). *Makrosyntax der Gliederungssignale im gesprochenen Französisch*. München: Fink.
Gülich, E. (1976). Ansätze zu einer kommunikationsorientierten Erzählanalyse (am Beispiel mündlicher und schriftlicher Erzähltexte). In W. Haubrichs (Ed.), *Erzählforschung 1. Theorien, Modelle und Methoden der Narrativik* (pp. 224–256). Göttingen: Vandenhoeck & Rupprecht.
Gülich, E. (1980). Konventionelle Muster und kommunikative Funktionen von Alltagserzählungen. In K. Ehlich (Ed.), *Erzählen im Alltag* (pp. 335–384). Frankfurt: Suhrkamp.
Gülich, E., & Raible, W. (1977). *Linguistische Textmodelle. Grundlagen und Möglichkeiten*. München: Fink.
Gülich, E., & Raible, W. (1979). Überlegungen zu einer makrostrukturellen Textanalyse. J. Thurber, *The lover and his lass*. In E. Gülich, K. Heger, & W. Raible (Eds.), *Linguistische Textanalyse. Überlegungen zur Gliederung von Texten* (pp. 73–147) (2nd ed.) Hamburg: Buske.
Hamburger, K. (1953). Das epische Präteritum. *Deutsche Vierteljahrsschrift für Literaturwissenschaft und Geistesgeschichte, 27*, 329–357.
Harweg, R. (1968). Textanfänge in geschriebener und in gesprochener Sprache. *Orbis, 17*, 343–388.
Hellholm, D. (1980). *Das Visionenbuch des Hermas als Apokalypse. Formgeschichtliche und texttheoretische Studien zu einer literarischen Gattung*. Lund: CWK Gleerup.
Hoek, L. H. (1975). Contribution à une délimination séquentielle du texte: l'exemple du chevalier au lion (Yvain). In *Mélanges de linguistique et de littérature offerts à Lein Geschiere par ses amis . . .* (pp. 181–208). Amsterdam: Rodopi.
Hurrelmann, B. (1980). Erzähltextverarbeitung im schulischen Handlungskontext. In K. Ehlich (Ed.), *Erzählen im Alltag* (pp. 296–334). Frankfurt: Suhrkamp.
Jason, H. (1977). Precursors of Propp: Formalist theories of narrative in early Russian ethnopoetics. *PTL, 3*, 471–516.
Jefferson, G. (1978). Sequential aspects of storytelling in conversation. In J. Schenkein (Ed.), *Studies in the organization of conversational interaction* (pp. 219–248).

Johnson, N. S., & Mandler, J. M. (1980). A tale of two structures: Underlying and surface forms in stories. *Poetics, 9,* 51–86.
Just, M., & Carpenter, P. A. (Eds.) (1977). *Cognitive Processes in comprehension.* Hillsdale, NJ: Erlbaum.
Kallmeyer, W., & Schütze, F. (1977). Zur Konstitution von Kommunikationsschemata der Sachverhaltsdarstellung. In D. Wegner (Ed.), *Gesprächsanalysen* (pp. 159–274). Hamburg: Buske.
Kintsch, W. (1977a) On comprehending stories. In M. Just & P. A. Carpenter (Eds.), *Cognitive Processes in Comprehension* (pp. 33–62). Hillsdale, NJ: Erlbaum.
Kintsch, W. (1977b). *Memory and cognition.* New York: Wiley.
Kintsch, W., & Greene, E. (1978). The role of culture-specific schemata in the comprehension and recall of stories. *Discourse Processes, 1,* 1–13.
Kintsch, W., & van Dijk, T. A. (1978). Toward a model of text comprehension and production. *Psychological Review, 85*(5), 363–394.
Klein, K. P. (1980). Erzählen im Unterricht. Erzähltheoretische Aspekte einer Erzähldidaktik. In K. Ehlich (Ed.), *Erzählen im Alltag* (pp. 263–295). Frankfurt: Suhrkamp.
Labov, W. (1972). The transformation of experience in narrative syntax. In W. Labov (Ed.), *Language in the inner city. Studies in the Black English Vernacular* (pp. 354–396). Philadelphia, PA: University of Pennsylvania Press.
Labov, W., & Waletzky, J. (1967). Narrative analysis: Oral versions of personal experience. In J. Helm (Ed.), *Essays on the Verbal and Visual Arts* (pp. 12–44). Seattle and London: University of Washington Press.
Lämmert, E. (1955/1980). *Bauformen des Erzählens* (7th ed.). Stuttgart: Metzler.
Lämmert, E. (Ed.) (1982). *Erzählforschung. Ein Symposium.* Stuttgart: Metzler.
Malinowski, B. (1923). Phatic communion. Reprinted. In J. Laver & F. Hutcheson (Eds.) (1972), *Communication in face-to-face-interaction* (pp.146–152). Harmondsworth: Penguin.
Mandler, J. M. (1978). A code in the node: The use of a story schema in retrieval. *Discourse Processes, 1,* 14–35.
Mandler, J. M., & Johnson, N. S. (1977). Remembrance of things parsed: Story structure and recall. *Cognitive Psychology, 9,* 111–151.
Mandler, J. M., & Johnson, N. S. (1980). On throwing out the baby with the bathwater: A reply to Black and Wilensky's evaluation of story grammars. *Cognitive Science, 4,* 305–312.
McClure, E., Mason, J. & Barnitz, J. (1979). An exploratory study of story structure and age effects on children's ability to sequence stories. *Discourse Processes, 2,* 213–249.
Miller, G. A., Galanter, E. & Pribram, K. H. (1960). *Plans and the structure of behavior.* New York: Holt, Rinehart and Winston.
Pavel, T. G. (1973). Some remarks on narrative grammars. *Poetics, 8,* 5–30.
Pavel, T. G. (1976). *La syntaxe narrative des tragédies de Corneille. Recherches et propositions.* Paris: Klincksieck.
Petöfi, J. S. (Ed.) (1979). *Text vs. sentence. Basic questions of textlinguistics* (2 Vols.). Hamburg: Buske.
Polanyi, L. (1979). So what's the point? *Semiotica, 25,* 207–241.
Propp, V. J. (1958). *Morphology of the folktale.* Bloomington: Indiana University Press. (Original work published 1928).
Quasthoff, U. M. (1979a). *Gliederungs- und Verknüpfungssignale als Kontextualisierungshinweise: Ihre Formen und Verwendungsweisen zur Markierung von Expansionen in deutschen und amerikanischen konversationellen Erzählungen.* Trier: Linguistic Agency University of Trier. (Series A, Paper No. 62).

Quasthoff, U. M. (1979b). Verzögerungsphänomene, Verknüpfungs- und Gliederungssignale in Alltagsargumentationen und Alltagserzählungen. In H. Weydt (Ed.), *Die Partikeln der deutschen Sprache* (pp. 39–57). Berlin: de Gruyter.

Quasthoff, U. M. (1980a). *Erzählen in Gesprächen. Linguistische Untersuchungen zu Strukturen und Funktionen am Beispiel einer Kommunikationsform des Alltags.* Tübingen: Narr.

Quasthoff, U. M. (1980b). Gemeinsames Erzählen als Form und Mittel im sozialen Konflikt oder: Ein Ehepaar erzählt eine Geschichte. In K. Ehlich (Ed.), *Erzählen im Alltag* (pp. 109–141). Frankfurt: Suhrkamp.

Quasthoff, U. M. (1981). Zuhöreraktivitäten beim konversationellen Erzählen. In *Dialogforschung*, Jahrbuch 1980 des Instituts für deutsche Sprache (pp. 287–313). Düsseldorf: Schwann.

Quasthoff, U. M. (1983). Text connection as mental plan and interactional structure. In *Proceedings of the symposium "Connectedness in Sentence, Text, and Discourse"* (pp. 237–254). Tilburg: Tilburg University.

Quasthoff, U. M. (1984). On the ontogenesis of doing personal reference: Syntactic, semantic, and interactional aspects. *Folia Linguistica, 18,* (3–4), 168–195.

Quasthoff, U. M., & Nikolaus, K. (1982). What makes a good story? Towards the production of conversational narratives. In A. Flammer & W. Kintsch (Eds.), *Discourse processing* (pp. 16–28). Amsterdam: North Holland.

Rehbein, J. (1977). *Komplexes Handeln. Elemente zur Handlungstheorie der Sprache.* Stuttgart: Metzler.

Rimmon, S. (1976). A comprehensive theory of narrative. Genette's Figures III and the structuralist study of fiction. *PTL, 2,* 33–62.

Rumelhart, D. E. (1975). Notes on a schema for stories. In D. Bobrow & A. Collins (Eds.), *Representation and understanding. Studies in cognitive science* (pp. 211–236). New York: Academic Press.

Rumelhart, D. E. (1977). Understanding and summarizing brief stories. In D. La Berge & J. Samuels (Eds.), *Basic processes in reading comprehension* (pp. 265–303). Hillsdale, NJ: Lawrence Erlbaum.

Rumelhart, D. E. (1980). On evaluating story grammars. *Cognitive Science, 4,* 313–316.

Ryan, M.-L. (1979). Linguistic models in narratology: From structuralism to generative semantics. *Semiotica, 28,* 127–155.

Ryave, A. L. (1978). On the achievement of a series of stories. In J. Schenkein (Ed.), *Studies in the organization of conversational interaction* (pp. 113–132). New York: Academic Press.

Rychner, J. (1970). L'articulation des phrases narratives dans la "Mort Artu." Neuchâtel and Genève: Université de Neuchâtel, Recueil des travaux publiés par la Faculté des Lettres, 32.

Rychner, J. (1971). Analyse d'une unité transphrastique. La séquence narrative de même sujet dans la "Mort Artu." In W. D. Stempel (Ed.), *Beiträge zur Textlinguistik* (pp. 79–122). München: Fink.

Sacks, H. (1971a). Das Erzählen von Geschichten innerhalb von Unterhaltungen. In R. Kjolseth & F. Sack (Eds.), *Zur Soziologie der Sprache* (pp. 307–314). Opladen: Westdeutscher Verlag.

Sacks, H. (1971b). *Lectures, Oct. 8–Dec. 3, 1971.* Typescript.

Sacks, H. (1972). On the analyzability of stories by children. In J. J. Gumperz & D. Hymes, (Eds.), *Directions in sociolinguistics* (pp. 325–345). New York: Holt, Rinehart, and Winston.

Schank, R. C. (1980). Language and memory. *Cognitive Science, 4,* 243–284.

Schank, R. C., & Abelson, R. P. (1977). *Scripts, plans, goals and understanding*. Hillsdale, NJ: Erlbaum.

Schenkein, J. (Ed.) (1978). *Studies in the organization of conversational interaction*. New York: Academic Press.

Schenkein, J. (1979). The Radio Raiders story. In G. Psathas (Ed.), *Everyday language—Studies in ethnomethodology* (pp. 187–201. New York: Irvington.

Schütze, F. (1976a). Zur Hervorlockung und Analyse von Erzählungen thematisch relevanter Geschichten im Rahmen soziologischer Feldforschung—dargestellt an einem Projekt zur Erforschung von kommunalen Machtstrukturen. In Arbeitsgruppe Bielefelder Soziologen (Eds.), *Kommunikative Sozialforschung* (pp. 159–260). München: Fink.

Schütze, F. (1976b). Zur soziologischen und linguistischen Analyse von Erzählungen. In *Internationales Jahrbuch für Wissens- und Religionssoziologie, 10* (pp. 7–41).

Stein, N. L., & Glenn, C. G. (1979). An analysis of story comprehension in elementary school children. In Roy O. Freedle (Ed.), *New directions in discourse processing II* (pp. 53–120). Norwood, NJ: Ablex.

Stein, N. L., & Nezworski, T. (1978). The effects of organization and instructional set on story memory. *Discourse Processes, 1,* 177–193.

Stein, N. L., & Policastro, M. (1984). The concept of a story: A comparison between children's and teacher's viewpoints. In H. Mandl, N. L. Stein, & T. Trabasso (Eds.), *Learning and comprehension of text* (pp. 113–155). Hillsdale, NJ: Erlbaum.

Stein, N. L., & Trabasso, T. (1982). What's in a story: An approach to comprehension and instruction. In R. Glaser (Ed.), *Advances in instructional psychology* (Vol. 2) (pp. 213–267). Hillsdale, NJ: Erlbaum.

Stempel, W.-D. (1964). *Untersuchungen zur Satzverknüpfung im Altfranzösischen*. Braunschweig: Westermann.

Stempel, W.-D. (1971). Möglichkeiten einer Darstellung der Diachronie in narrativen Texten. In W.-D. Stempel (Ed.), *Beiträge zur Textlinguistik* (pp. 53–78). München: Fink.

Thorndyke, P. W. (1977). Cognitive structures in comprehension and memory of narrative discourse. *Cognitive Psychology, 9,* 77–110.

Todorov, T. (1969). *Grammaire du Décaméron*. Den Haag: Mouton.

Todorov, T. (1973). Die zwei Prinzipien des Erzählens. *Neue Hefte für Philosophie, 4,* 123–139.

van Dijk, T. A. (1972). *Some aspects of text grammars. A study in theoretical linguistics and poetics*. The Hague: Mouton.

van Dijk, T. A. (1973). Grammaires textuelles et structures narratives. In C. Chabrol (Ed.), *Semiotique narrative et textuelle* (pp. 177–207).

van Dijk, T. A. (1974–1975). Action, action description and narrative. *New Literary History, 6,* 273–294.

van Dijk, T. A. (1976). Philosophy of action and theory of narrative. *Poetics, 5,* 287–338.

van Dijk, T. A. (1977a). Semantic macrostructures and knowledge frames in discourse comprehension. In M. Just & P. A. Carpenter (Eds.), *Cognitive Processes in Comprehension* (pp. 3–32). Hillsdale, NJ: Erlbaum.

van Dijk, T. A. (1977b). *Text and Context. Explorations in the semantics and pragmatics of discourse*. London: Longman.

van Dijk, T. A. (1979). Recalling and summarizing complex discourse. In W. Burghardt & K. Hölker (Eds.), *Text Processing–Textverarbeitung* (pp. 49–118). Berlin: de Gruyter.

van Dijk, T. A. (1980a). *Macrostructures. An interdisciplinary study of global structures in discourse, interaction and cognition*. Hillsdale, NJ: Erlbaum.

van Dijk, T. A. (1980b). *Story comprehension: An introduction*. Poetics, 9, 1–21.

van Dijk, T. A. (1980c). *Textwissenschaft. Eine interdisziplinäre Einführung*. München: dtv.

van Dijk, T. A., Ihwe, J., Petöfi, J. S., & Rieser, H. (1974). *Zur Bestimmung narrativer Strukturen auf der Grundlage von Textgrammatiken* (2nd ed.). Hamburg: Buske.

Wald, B. (1978). Zur Einheitlichkeit und Einleitung von Diskurseinheiten. In U. Quasthoff (Ed.), *Sprachstruktur–Sozialstruktur. Zur linguistischen Theorienbildung* (pp. 128–149). Kronberg/Ts: Scriptor.

Weinrich, H. (1971). *Tempus. Besprochene und erzählte Welt* (2nd ed.). Stuttgart: Kohlhammer.

Wienold, G. (1972a). On deriving models of narrative analysis from models of discourse analysis. *Poetics, 3,* 15–28.

Wienold, G. (1972b). *Semiotik der Literatur.* Frankfurt/M: Athenäum.

Wienold, G. (1977). Textlinguistic approaches to written works of art. In W. U. Dressler (Ed.), *Current trends in textlinguistics* (pp. 133–153). Berlin: de Gruyter.

Wienold, G. (1982). Narrative texts and models of hierarchical and sequential structure. In M. Faust, R. Harweg, W. Lebfeldt, & G. Wienold (Eds.), *Allgemeine Sprachwissenschaft, Sprachtypologie Und Textlinguistic: Festschrift für Peter Hartmann* (pp. 417–430). Tübingen: Narr.

Wienold, G., & Rieser, H. (1979). Vorüberlegungen zur Rolle des Konzepts der Textverarbeitung beim Aufbau einer empirischen Sprachtheorie. In W. Burghardt & K. Hölker (Eds.), *Text Processing–Textverarbeitung* (pp. 20–49). Berlin: de Gruyter.

CHAPTER 11

Analysis of Nonverbal Behavior

Klaus R. Scherer and Harald G. Wallbott

INTRODUCTION

The social and behavioral sciences, and particularly the study of language and speech, have benefited greatly from the explosive development of discourse analysis in the 1970s. One of the major advantages of this tradition has been its focus on systematic empirical study of natural conversation, thereby correcting one of the major deficiencies of traditional linguistic methodology, namely the over-reliance on a few native informants and made-up examples to demonstrate linguistic rules. Unfortunately, discourse analysis has not yet succeeded in improving upon another major deficiency of traditional linguistics, namely the exclusive concern with words or verbal behavior to the neglect of the accompanying nonverbal or paralinguistic behavior. Many conversations in real-life settings cannot be adequately studied, at least in terms of pragmatics, unless both verbal and nonverbal behavior are studied jointly. While many students of conversation pay lip service to the necessity of a comprehensive approach, in practice purely verbal transcripts of conversation are still the rule rather than the exception. Consequently, the tape recorder rather than the video recorder is still the primary research tool in discourse analysis. In those rare cases where attempts are made to transcribe at least some of the nonverbal behavior in a conversation, the notational or coding systems often lack both validity and reliability.

Yet appropriate tools for the objective analysis of nonverbal behavior are currently available. Researchers from many different disciplines have developed techniques to study nonverbal communication that are well suited for the study of conversational processes. Unfortunately, the students of nonverbal communication have all too often been overly concerned

HANDBOOK OF DISCOURSE ANALYSIS, Vol. 2
Dimensions of Discourse

Copyright © 1985 by Academic Press London.
All rights of reproduction in any form reserved.
ISBN 0-12-712002-5

with just nonverbal behavior to the neglect of verbal behavior, which again has led to serious problems (Scherer, 1982b). There is an urgent need to combine the perspectives of conversation analysis and nonverbal communication to provide the foundation for a more comprehensive analysis of discourse processes.

This chapter provides a short overview of the methods available for the analysis of nonverbal behavior in conversation. Objective, empirical methods are stressed, in part because of the authors' bias in that direction, and also because hermeneutic techniques can be misleading in the study of nonverbal behavior. Nonverbal communicative behavior seems to be coded differently from verbal behavior. While verbal signs are coded arbitrarily, discretely, and invariantly, nonverbal signs are usually coded iconically, continuously, and probabilistically (Giles, Scherer, & Taylor, 1979; Scherer, 1977b). Because of the different nature of the code and the resulting differences in the inference processes used in decoding, the study of nonverbal signs requires a very different set of research strategies and paradigms (Scherer & Ekman, 1982).

THE FUNCTIONS OF NONVERBAL BEHAVIOR IN CONVERSATION

The research strategy and the type of measurement to be used depend not only on the type of behavior under observation but also on the particular function of a behavior in a social setting. We therefore first need to briefly review the major functions of nonverbal behavior in conversation (see Scherer, 1980, for a detailed discussion).

We distinguish between four functions: semantic, syntactic, pragmatic, and dialogic. Nonverbal signs function semantically by signifying referents directly or by amplifying, contradicting, or modifying meaning carried by verbal signs. The signification function is primarily served by facial, gestural, and vocal emblems, for example, the hitchhiker's thumb, the eyebrow flash as a greeting, or the *oh* indicating surprise (Ekman, 1976, 1979; Goffman, 1979; Scherer, 1977b). Often, nonverbal signs serve amplification functions, particularly in the form of emphasis, for example, energetic gestures or pitch and loudness accents. Nonverbal signs can also contradict the meaning that is simultaneously expressed verbally, as in collusive face work towards interaction partners while trying to gracefully end a lengthy telephone conversation. Similarly, verbal expression is often modified nonverbally, for example, by putting a humorous or ironic touch on an utterance or asking for something in an apologetic manner. Obviously, the total meaning of a speech act or another conversational unit cannot be properly understood unless the respective functions of accompanying nonverbal behavior have been thoroughly analyzed.

Nonverbal signs function syntactically in that they help to order the sequence and the occurrence of both verbal and nonverbal behavior. One of the major syntactic functions is the segmentation of the behavioral stream. This is true for both macroscopic segments of conversations, such as beginnings and endings (e.g., eye contact and smiling as signs to begin a conversation, leaning forward in one's chair to signal readiness to end a meeting) or topic changes (often signaled through gross changes in body posture [Scheflen, 1964]) as well as microscopic segments, such as shifts of attention during a speaker's utterance or signals indicating a paraphrase.

The second syntactic function is synchronization. Birdwhistell (1968, 1970), Condon and Ogston (1966), Kendon (1972), and others have provided some evidence for intrapersonal and interpersonal synchronization of both verbal behavior and various modalities of nonverbal behavior. In other words, both verbal and nonverbal behavior seem to be very carefully orchestrated in terms of rhythmic patterning of distinctive features of the respective behaviors. This type of synchronization may serve two functions: the coordinated production of a wide variety of motor movements and the impression produced on the interaction partner, for example, in giving emphasis to a particular point (e.g., through synchronization of apexes in different behavioral signals).

The pragmatic functions of nonverbal behavior entail the expression of social identity, personal traits, and psychological states on the one hand, and the signaling of reactions to acts of the interaction partner on the other hand. The fact that both vocal and nonvocal nonverbal behavior mark the social identity of an actor in terms of such factors as sex, age, social class, and geographical origin (Scherer & Giles, 1979), express personality dispositions (Scherer, 1979b), and can be used as valid indicators of psychological states such as emotions, psychopathology, or interpersonal attitudes (Scherer, 1979a, 1981a, 1981b) has been well documented. Furthermore, there can be little doubt that the course of a conversation is strongly influenced by the participants' inferences and attributions as to the social identity, personality disposition, and respective psychological states of their partners.

In addition, nonverbal signs often serve as indicators of the listener's reaction to the content of a speaker's utterance. This is the case, for example, in the well-known backchannel or listener responses that encourage the speaker to continue to hold the floor and assure him of the attention of the listener. In many cases, such signals serve to assert shared meaning or shared values or to indicate approval or negation of

what is being expressed by the speaker at the time, allowing the latter
to shorten, elaborate, justify, or otherwise adapt his utterance to the
perceived evaluation by the listener. Thus, in terms of conversation analysis,
the course and structure of a particular utterance is often uninterpretable
or is interpreted wrongly if nonverbal, often inaudible, listener responses
are not taken into account.

Finally, the dialogic functions of nonverbal signs concern the assertion
of an existing relationship between the participants in a conversation and
the regulation of the contributions of the participants to the conversation.
Nonverbal signs such as seating patterns, body posture, and voice quality
may reflect the relationship of the interactants in terms of both an attraction–
sympathy dimension and a power–dominance dimension (Mehrabian,
1969, 1972). The relative congruence of the sympathy and status cues
in the nonverbal behavior of the conversation partners reflects the degree
to which there is a shared definition of the situation in terms of the
underlying relationship. That relationship has a powerful impact on the
course of the conversation. One of the major and most visible phenomena
in the regulation of conversational behavior is the organization of turn
taking (Duncan, 1974; Duncan & Fiske, 1977; Kendon, 1970; Schegloff,
1972; Wiemann & Knapp, 1975).

Clearly, most nonverbal behaviors are multifunctional, that is, they
serve not just one of the functions outlined above but many at the same
time. Thus a change of body posture, for example, can serve both to
reemphasize the status differential between the interaction partners and
to indicate a topic change intended by the speaker, while at the same
time expressing an underlying personality trait or emotional state. Yet
a conceptual and theoretical distinction between the different functions
of nonverbal signals in conversation plays an important role in the generation of hypotheses for research and for the selection of appropriate
research techniques and paradigms. This is exemplified in the following
two sections of this chapter.

In order to illustrate the somewhat abstract methodological discussion,
we are interspersing examples from a long-term study of interviews between
civil servants in social welfare offices and their clients. The type of
conversation to be found in such 'focused interactions' (Goffman, 1961)
is highly suitable for systematic discourse analysis since the role relationships between the participants are conventionally established and
there is a clear task structure involving a goal to be attained in the
interaction, namely, the exchange of information and the reaching of a
decision. At the same time, the study of such civil servant–citizen interactions is highly relevant for applied social psychology since it is often

assumed that much of the popular discontent with modern bureaucracy stems from conflicts generated in the citizens' personal enounters with bureaucrats (Scherer, U., & Scherer, K. R., 1980). In the course of this long-term project, our research group at the University of Giessen has studied both naturally occurring civil servant–citizen interactions in municipal offices in several West German cities and experimental simulations using highly realistic case material.

These simulations were part of two-day social skills training courses for civil servants in the interaction laboratory at the University of Giessen. Thirty-nine male civil servants from municipal social welfare agencies, holding the same type of job (dispensing monetary assistance to people with a monthly income below a certain limit), role played two cases each (the same cases for each civil servant) with two amateur actors. The simulations took place in a room equipped with video cameras behind one-way mirrors and in the ceiling and were video- and audio-taped.

During the experimental simulations each civil servant had to deal with two realistic cases that could have occurred in his normal workload. They constituted two very different types and demanded different procedures and strategies. The first was an application for financial aid by an unemployed person. The payment of his unemployment compensation had been suspended for a month because he had refused to apply for a job in a city 150 km away from his hometown. The case itself was not completely clear-cut, and each civil servant had some discretion to grant or not to grant financial aid. The second case basically constituted a request. The civil servant had to demand a contribution from a person whose estranged elderly mother depended on financial assistance from the welfare agency. Again each civil servant had to decide within his discretion whether the reasons for the estrangement were valid enough for not requesting a contribution.

The clients were played by two amateur actors. Each actor showed either aggressive or submissive behavior and played a member of either the middle or lower-middle to lower class. Class membership was manipulated by dress and speech characteristics and behavioral differences by detailed instructions. The cases were varied slightly to allow for differences in social class. The arguments put forward in the interactions with the civil servants, however, were kept constant. The actors were requested to use all of these standard arguments and were not allowed to improvise new ones.

Various aspects of the nonverbal behavior of both the civil servants and the amateur actors simulating citizens were analyzed by using some of the techniques discussed above. In addition, the impressions generated by the behavior of the civil servants were assessed by using lay judges (secretaries and other university staff) to rate the behavior of the civil servants on the basis of the video-recorded interactions.

METHODS FOR THE ASSESSMENT OF NONVERBAL BEHAVIOR

Variables, Measurement, Data

As pointed out above, the choice of a particular research method and a particular variable to be measured depends on the nature of the question. If one is interested in the way nonverbal signs segment the conversation into macroscopic elements, choosing microscopic nonverbal behaviors, such as eye blinks, which are unlikely to have the structural properties required for that particular type of segmentation, is not appropriate. If one is interested in studying the way verbal and nonverbal behavior is synchronized in terms of production, it would be unwise to employ observer inferences concerning the synchronization since such inferences are too far removed from the process of production. The variables to be studied and the methods chosen for their measurement must be closely adapted to the problem being investigated.

In measuring nonverbal behavior we must distinguish between different types of variables, different types of measurement, and different types of data. Variables differ in terms of locus of description, that is, the points at which they are being assessed. For example, in studying a vocal emblem such as *oh,* one can assess motor variables (the particular phonatory and articulatory processes that precede the utterance of this sound), distal variables (the sound waves measured by electroacoustic apparatus, that emanate from the speaker's mouth), or proximal variables (the impressions of the listener via the auditory sense and the cognitive inference system). Clearly, the nature of the question determines the type of variable to be assessed. If one is interested in production, one must choose motor variables; in transmission, distal variables; in pragmatic effects, proximal variables. In some cases two sets of variables may be useful. For example, for diagnostic, medical, or psychological purposes, it may be appropriate to measure both motor and distal variables. Also, since there is a causal chain from motor over distal to proximal variables, there may be strong correlations between the respective variables. However, this is not necessarily the case, and serious errors may result if, for example, subjective proximal judgments of pitch are chosen to study objective fundamental frequency patterns.

It is also important to choose the proper type of measurement. This is a dimension ranging from objective instrument measurement on the one hand to observer judgment on the other hand. Since human operators are always involved, even when instruments are used, this is a continuum rather than a discrete scale in terms of the degree of inference permitted to the observer (Scherer & Ekman, 1982). Clearly, some types of measurement are more appropriate for particular types of variables. For example, observer judgment, involving a strong degree of inference, is more suitable for the measurement of proximal variables than for the study of motor variables.

Finally, there are two major types of data: physical parameters (exact time-and-space measurements of physical processes) and functional categories (human classifications of patterns or configurations of physical data in terms of the social or individual functions of behavior types). For a particular measurement system it is very important not to mix these different types of variables, measurements, and data.

Methods for the Assessment of Nonverbal Vocal Behavior

In line with the general typology of variables discussed above, we can distinguish between motor, distal, and proximal vocal measurement. The level of description that deals with motor processes encompasses the physiological phonatory and articulatory processes that are involved in the production of the speech sound. Most of the research projects in which vocal behavior is assessed at the motor level deal with voice and speech production or vocal pathology. Often these studies involve the use of sophisticated equipment such as high-speed motion picture cameras together with laryngeal mirrors or x-ray film equipment.

Motor Variables

Most of these techniques are not very relevant to the study of discourse processes. Moreover, many of the techniques could not be easily employed in studying ongoing conversation in real-life settings. However, the phonatory–articulatory measurement of voice quality may be an exception to this. Changes in voice quality play an important role both in terms of social marking and in the expression of emotions and attitudes. Since voice quality is mainly produced by different laryngeal, pharyngeal, and articulatory settings, measurement at the motor level is clearly the most objective approach. Most speech scientists are able to infer the nature of the production process on the basis of acoustic patterns, enabling them to assess voice-quality variables on the basis of auditory judgment. One of the most promising, theoretically consistent, and well-documented systems of categories for the assessment of voice quality on the phonatory–articulatory level has been proposed by Laver (1975, 1980).

Distal Variables

The next level of description, the distal assessment of vocal behavior, consists of the objective measurement of the speech sound once it has radiated from the lips of the speaker, that is, the study of acoustic waveforms. While this approach has been mainly used in acoustic phonetics and psychoacoustics, it is highly promising for the study of discourse patterns. Distal, acoustic measurement is usually based on tape-recorded utterances of speakers and thus does not require much of an intrusion into ongoing conversations. Recordings can often be made without disturbing the participants. Since the acoustic speech signal is quite stable and many of its characteristics are well known, it is well suited for the development of a number of different parameters of physical measurement. The main type of data to be generated by this measurement is that of physical parameters, rather than functional categories. In measuring various aspects of acoustic waveforms, three major domains have to be distinguished: time, amplitude, and frequency.

Time Domain.   In the time domain, the presence or absence of sound and the duration of intervals of sound and silence are the major variables of interest. The objective study of sound and silence patterns in conversation, often called "interaction chronography" (Chapple, 1956; Feldstein & Welkowitz, 1978), yields a large number of variables related to speaker and listener states and interaction patterns in the conversation. For example, utterance frequency and length, pause frequency and length, interruptions, latency times, and speech rate can all be measured with comparative ease. Therefore, there is quite a large literature on speech variables in the time domain showing relationships to cognitive and emotional processes, personality, and interaction processes such as convergence or accommodation (Feldstein & Welkowitz, 1978; Scherer, 1979b; Siegman, 1978; Siegman & Feldstein, 1978).

We have used the material from the civil servant study to examine possible convergence processes between civil servant and citizen–amateur actor for the variables 'length of utterance duration' and 'pause length'. Since at least some of the interactions were by design more antagonistic in nature, we wanted to check under which conditions convergence would occur. One of the major problems in this task was the appropriate operationalization of the concept of 'convergence'. In most earlier studies (see summary in Giles & Smith, 1979) the intraclass correlation coefficient has been used to study whether conversation partners behave more alike at the end (or the second half) of a conversation or after several earlier conversations than at the beginning of their relationship. Unfortunately, this measure has the disadvantage of correlating over many dyads of speakers. This allows the establishment of possible tendencies toward a greater similarity in conversational behavior, but it does not allow the plotting of convergence processes for individual dyads. Knowledge of individual-dyad convergence, however, seems necessary for a more adequate test of the convergence hypothesis, particularly in cases where one cannot assume that all of the dyads in the sample will conform to a pressure toward accommodation or convergence (because some encounters are likely to be more antagonistic than others, for example). Therefore, we attempted to develop a different approach to the measurement of convergence using a criterion concerned with the change in differences between a particular type of behavior of the two interactants over time.

In the civil servant study, we divided the total interaction into three parts, aggregating the measurement for length of pauses and length of utterance durations for each of these thirds. We then plotted these data points for both participants and measured the differences. After trying a large number of fairly complex decision rules, we finally decided to use the following fairly simple criterion, which seems to capture the major assumption involved in the concept of convergence: Difference in third interval $< \frac{1}{2}$ (difference at first interval + difference at second interval).

Using this criterion, we found that there was a tendency toward convergence in the first case and a tendency toward divergence in the second case. However, more specifically, we found that there were large individual differences and that it was more useful to investigate convergence or divergence on the basis of such individual differences and situational determinants (i.e., first and second case). Public servants, for instance, who seem to converge in the first case according to our criterion, were judged as being significantly less energetic, less stable, less reliable, but more aggressive and uncertain than public servants who diverged. In the second case, however, public servants who converged were judged as being more energetic, self-secure, but less uncertain than public servants who diverged (Höfer, Wallbott, & Scherer, in preparation).

In general, there is an unfortunate tendency in distal measurement of vocal behavior in the time domain to confuse levels of description and type of measurement. For example, the term "pause," which refers to a functional interpretation by the observer that the speaker intends to continue after a break in his speech flow, is sometimes used to denote the physical measurement of absence of energy in the vocal channel. Since the latter use of the term implies that the physical measurement of acoustic energy entails information about the intention of the speaker, which is not correct, it is preferable to use the term "silent period" for distal measurement of acoustic energy (Scherer, 1982a). In addition to objectively measuring sound energy, it is possible to have trained judges evaluate time-based speech phenomena on the basis of descriptive or functional categories such as 'juncture pauses' versus 'hesitation pauses' (Boomer & Dittmann, 1962) or 'respiration pauses' (Goldman-Eisler, 1968). Similarly, the distinction between silent pauses and filled pauses has to be made on the basis of auditory judgment, because such differences cannot be automatically distinguished.

Amplitude Domain.   It is also comparatively easy to objectively measure the amplitude or energy of the speech signal using sound-pressure recording devices. Unfortunately, the values obtained in such a manner are often difficult to interpret because of the large number of situational factors that affect the amplitude of a recorded signal, such as distance and angle to the microphone and ambient noise. In addition, it is necessary to pay attention to the physical relationships between amplitude, energy, and intensity (Small, 1973). Most importantly, these values cannot be interpreted as measuring loudness of the voice, as is often done, since loudness is a subjective proximal impression. Objectively measured energy of a speech signal is related to the vocal effort of the speaker rather than the listener's impression of loudness. While the two are obviously correlated in most cases, they are not equivalent (Glawe & Rietveld, 1975). Although there is little empirical work in this area so far, there is some evidence that relative energy of the speech signal is related to emotional states and personality of the speaker and that it may be subject to convergence or accommodation processes (Natale, 1975; Scherer, 1979b, 1982b).

Frequency Domain.   The major variable here is the fundamental frequency (F_o) of the voice and the changes of F_o over time as mapped by intonation curves or contours. A number of F_o extraction techniques have been developed for digital computer analysis (Licklider & Pollak, 1948; Sondhi, 1968), which allow reliable F_o measurement in many cases, although a number of technical problems still exist. Much of the work in psychology has shown interesting relationships between F_o (averaged across lengthy utterances) and emotion and personality (Scherer, 1979a, 1982a).

For example, using our Giessen Speech Analysis System (GISYS) we extracted F_o for random selections of the utterances of the speakers in the civil servant study. The data supported the assumption that this variable may be a very powerful indicator of arousal and emotion in discourse.

Figure 11.1 shows that the civil servants' average F_o is significantly higher when dealing with lower-class clients or aggressive clients and particularly high when the civil servant has to deal with an aggressive lower-class client. This tendency, which is probably due to increased nervousness, anger, or other emotions of this sort, seems to be particularly pronounced for civil servants with a negative attitude toward clients. These data show that F_o can be used as an important unobtrusive behavioral measure that enables the researcher to continuously monitor the affective state of speakers in the course of a conversation.

Of greater interest than average F_o, however, are changes in F_o over time, called F_o contours or intonation contours. (This is not to imply, of course, that the linguistic phenomenon of intonation may not also involve amplitude and timing variables as well.) An issue of major interest to discourse analysis, which so far has often been avoided by linguists because of its complexity and its closeness to psychological interpretation, is the way in which intonation is involved in communicating attitude or emotion. Our research group in Giessen has embarked on a long-term interdisciplinary study of this issue, trying to find a balance between a

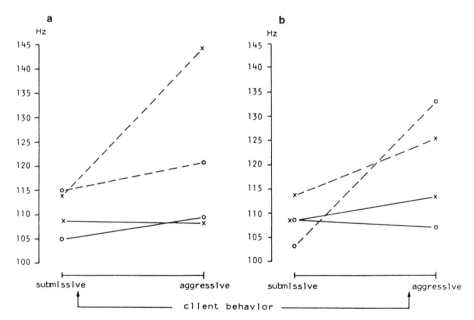

Figure 11.1 Voice pitch as indicator of arousal in simulated interactions ($N = 39$): a, unemployment case; b, support case; x, low client orientation; o, high client orientation; – – –, low social class; ———, high social class (from Scherer, U. & Scherer, K. R., 1980, p. 321).

more psychological research strategy, which assumes that there is a specifiable relationship between attitudinal or emotional meaning and measurable acoustical cues, and a more linguistic research strategy, which tends to deny the existence of such correlations and assumes that pragmatic meaning—including the expression of emotion and attitude—is established by using specific features in the language-based intonation system in certain contexts (Ladd, Silverman, & Scherer, 1985).

One of the major tools required to settle this issue is the ability to objectively and systematically describe intonation, since the graphic plotting of F_o contours does not in itself provide useful parameters or variables (Lieberman, 1965; Takefuta, 1975). Recent work in acoustic phonetic studies of intonation has suggested a number of descriptive features that can be fairly objectively determined on the basis of intonation contours. As part of our project, Ladd (1983) has developed a peak-feature model of intonation that is based on intonation peaks, the major change points in the contour, and their location in relation to the associated segmental units. This system builds to a great extent on earlier work by Bruce and Garding (1978) and Pierrehumbert (1981). It allows operationalization of a number of fine phonetic variables of intonation while at the same time preserving generalizations about the linguistic function of global intonational traits (e.g., falling intonation).

In our intonation project we have again been using material from the civil servant corpus. Figure 11.2 shows the F_o and amplitude contours for two selected utterances. Utterance A is judged by listeners as strongly indicative of impatience (*Ungeduld*). Utterance B, on the other hand, is judged as highly indicative of politeness and friendliness (*höflich* and *freundlich*). The semantic content of the utterances seems to have little to do with this judgment, as shown by ratings based on verbal transcript only (which were obtained by using a different group of judges). At the same time, it seems unlikely that the clearly communicated pragmatic meaning is carried exclusively by the intonation contour since there is very little difference between the two contours as assessed by the peak-feature model mentioned above. Furthermore, the pragmatic meaning is still recoverable for judges who are exposed to these utterances in a form where the speech signal has been strongly degraded in addition to masking the content: Judges still hear utterance A as impatient and utterance B as polite and friendly if the speech signal is played backwards, electronically low-pass filtered at 300–500 Hz, or random spliced (Scherer, 1971, 1982a). Since different aspects of the total acoustic pattern are destroyed by each of these methods, it is unlikely that attitudinal meaning is communicated exclusively by a single parameter, such as F_o contour,

Figure 11.2 F_0 and amplitude contours for two utterances. Utterance A: *Wie alt sind die Kinder?* 'How old are the children?' judged as *ungeduldig* 'impatient'. Utterance B: *Wie hoch ist ihre Mietbelastung?* 'How high is your monthly rent?' judged as *freundlich, höflich* 'friendly, polite'.

voice quality, or timing. In addition to a more intensive study of the role of various acoustic cues in mediating attitudinal meaning via signal degradation experiments and speech resynthesis experiments, our preliminary results thus show that linguistic context needs to be taken into account.

Frequency–Amplitude Domain. Modern electroacoustic equipment and digital speech processing allow us to determine a large number of variables in this domain, mostly parameters extracted from the power spectrum of speech (Scherer, 1982a). These include relative energy in octave bands of the spectrum, formant location, amplitude, and bandwidth. Since most of these variables are not particularly well suited to the type of suprasegmental analysis required for discourse analysis, these methods are not described in detail here. The available evidence shows, however, that spectral parameters of the voice may be important indicators of speaker state (Scherer, 1981a, 1982a).

Observer Measurement of Distal Variables. Since objective electroacoustic measurement or digital processing of speech is expensive and time-consuming, there have been a number of attempts to use human observers to assess various aspects of the acoustic speech waveform. Unfortunately, most of these attempts, including the paralinguistic transcription systems proposed (e.g., Poyatos, 1976; Trager & Smith, 1957), consist of rather messy mixtures of variables on different levels of description and of rather different status of data. For example, phonatory–articulatory, acoustic, and auditory impression variables are all used indiscriminately in the same system (Scherer, 1982a). This is problematic since what is to be measured remains unclear. In addition, the degree of observer inference that enters into the description of the vocal phenomena varies across different categories. In some cases, extensive inferences are required, such as in the judgment of the deviation of a particular speech characteristic from a correct or modal level, for example, in terms of loudness, pitch, or amplitude. Such judgments are required by a number of the available paralinguistic description systems (Duncan, Rice, & Butler, 1968; Markel, Meisels, & Houck, 1964; Trager & Smith, 1957). As one would expect in cases where observers are required to base judgments on inherent, poorly defined standards, the reliability of such systems is not well established (Crystal & Quirk, 1964, pp. 21–23; Dittmann & Wynne, 1961). While it may be possible to obtain a reasonable degree of observer agreement for very specific cases (Duncan, Rice, & Butler, 1968; Duncan & Rosenthal, 1968), the practicability of such systems remains doubtful.

Proximal Variables

As has been shown elsewhere, the difficulty of finding a scientifically satisfactory description of the subjective perception of speech variables has frequently resulted in the use of 'folk categories' to describe the impressions of listeners. There are some attempts to develop voice and speech attribute scales for use in measuring listeners' subjective impressions (Scherer, 1982a).

Measurement of Facial Behavior

The face is certainly one of the most important areas of nonverbal signal production systems. Because of its complex musculature, the face is not only the primary site for the expression of emotions (Izard, 1971) but is also important as a source of interactionally important cues that help the receiver infer the speaker's state or attitude.

Facial behavior consists of facial expression (mimic activities of the face), visual behavior (eye movements, direction of gaze, and eye contact), and physiological changes (sweating or blushing). As with vocal behavior, one can distinguish methods for measuring motor, distal, and proximal variables of facial behavior.

Motor Variables

Facial behavior, except the physiological changes mentioned, is in sum the combined movements of the complex and differentiated musculature of the face. Thus the techniques employed most often for measuring motor variables of facial behavior are EMG (electromyogram) measurements. These techniques, where electrodes or sensors are attached to the facial skin, or, for fine-grained measurements, even implanted into the relevant muscles, allow exact analyses of the tonic and phasic muscle tensions but are of course very obtrusive. In addition, it is possible that these measurement techniques can affect the data being gathered. For instance, facial expressions might be altered as a result of the sensory feedback subjects receive from attached electrodes. Such techniques are therefore rarely used to study facial expression in ongoing human interaction. They have, however, been successfully employed to study and detect very small and visually undetectable facial activities and expressions (Schwartz, Fair, Salt, Mandel, & Klerman, 1976).

Visual behavior can be studied in a similar way by placing electrodes (which can detect eye movements) around the eyes. Other techniques to assess the motor activity involved in eye movements include different types of eye cameras. These eye cameras usually consist of a helmet containing a small light that is projected into the eyes and a camera that records the light reflected from the eye differently depending on the direction the eye is moving. Another technical principle makes use of the darkest spot in the eye, the pupil. The camera detects and follows the pupil automatically. These techniques are also quite obtrusive. They have been used most often in industrial research, in advertisement testing, and in reading research. They are useful in studying how subjects scan texts or advertisements visually (Argyle & Cook, 1976). The measurement of the dilation of the pupil in response to emotional stimuli has been used to study emotional reactions (Hess, 1975).

Distal Variables

As with vocal variables, distal variables of visible behavior can be measured when a motor activity is visually detected by an observer, a film- or video camera, or by some other instrument. Two main approaches to the distal analysis of facial expression may be distinguished, physical measurement of facial movement and coding or category approaches.

Physical measurement involves all automatic or semiautomatic devices that measure coordinates of certain selected points representing a moving body part or facial part in time. These coordinates can also be measured by hand using frame-by-frame film or video monitoring. Wörner (1940) measured coordinates of the corners of the mouth and selected points on the forehead to study facial expressions of primates and to depict the movements of the muscles involved. Heimann and Lucacs (1966) took a similar approach in studying facial behavior of schizophrenics. They transformed their coordinate measurements of the corners of the mouth and the outer eyebrows in relation to a reference system. The reference system was defined by a straight line through the vertical middle of the face and an orthogonal straight line through the eyes' inner corners. This yielded parameters like the 'activation coefficient' (measuring total facial activity) or the 'symmetry coefficient' (measuring movement predominance of the left or right half of the face).

For visual behavior, measurement techniques using the interaction chronograph (see above) have been devised. These allow continuous recording of gaze direction for two interaction partners over a period of time (as judged by observers). This procedure results in on–off patterns of gaze direction, which can be processed like the vocal patterns of speech and silence (Ellgring, 1977; Exline & Fehr, 1982; Rutter & Stephenson, 1972). Vocal–interaction chronography and eye-contact chronography are often combined in order to study interaction as a two-channel system (Exline & Fehr, 1982; Kendon, 1967).

Category approaches to facial behavior first appear in the work of Darwin (1872), who described facial expressions in some detail. Frois-Whitmann (1930) was one of the first researchers to study the relation between categories of facial expression (defined on the basis of the underlying muscular movements, as far as these are visible) and the perception and attribution of emotions. The most sophisticated category system so far for the analysis of facial expressions based on such definitions is the Facial Action Coding System (FACS) by Ekman and Friesen (1978). Their system defines 46 categories or action units that are visually distinct and can be reliably detected by trained observers. Furthermore, FACS includes an intensity code for action units, which is used to indicate how strong the observed muscle activity is. Ekman (1982) has compiled a comprehensive survey of coding systems for facial expression and their respective advantages and disadvantages. FACS seems to be the optimal system currently available.

Proximal Variables

Proximal descriptions of facial behavior range from free or anecdotal descriptions, as, for instance, in the old German psychology of expression (Lersch, 1932; for an overview see Asendorpf, 1982; Asendorpf & Wallbott, 1982) to categorical approaches using functional categories. The functional categories used are defined on the basis of expressed emotions as units (Ekman & Friesen, 1975; Izard, 1971), ethological concepts (Grant, 1969), or other units like illustrators or emblems (Ekman, 1979; see below), depending on the theoretical orientation of the researcher.

Measurement of Body Movement

Body movements, both gross changes in posture and smaller gestures involving one body part, such as movements of the hands, the head, the torso, or the whole body, are important components of interaction and communication. Not only do body movements serve as one component of speaker-turn signals (Duncan & Fiske, 1977), they also can indicate status or sympathy relations to a discourse partner (Mehrabian, 1972).

Motor Variables

The primary focus in measuring motor variables of body movement must again be at the muscular level. Therefore EMG techniques have often been employed to determine tonic and phasic muscle innervation during movement or to record the synchronization of muscular innervations.

Furthermore, a whole range of different measurement devices is available to assess acceleration and velocity of body parts during movement (accelerometers), the force or energy of a moving body part (goniometers, etc.), and other physical movement characteristics (for an overview see Wallbott, 1980). The obtrusiveness of all these techniques (sensors and wires have to be attached to subjects) makes them largely unsuitable for discourse analysis or interaction research. On the other hand, they can be profitably employed in sports science, rehabilitation research, and other fields concerned with the objective physical measurement of human movement (Paul, 1975).

Distal Variables

Techniques for the automatic analysis of movement parameters belong somewhere between measurement techniques for motor and distal aspects of body movement. Small light-emitting or reflecting devices (LEDs or LRDs) are attached to the body parts being investigated. The movements of a subject are recorded with special cameras or sensors connected to computers. This allows the immediate measurement of parameters like velocity or acceleration, as the computer automatically determines the coordinates of the moving LEDs or LRDs in time. Examples of such techniques are the SELSPOT system (Gustafsson & Lanshammar, 1977) and the CODA system (Mitchelson, 1975). Though these techniques allow very high spatial and temporal resolution, thereby guaranteeing very exact measurements, the same problems of obtrusiveness and artificiality again arise. As a result, other techniques for the analysis of movement patterns recorded either on film or video have been developed. These range from semiautomatic techniques, which measure movement coordinates from the recorded video picture (Wallbott, 1982), to manual methods, early attempts of which involved projecting a film frame by frame and measuring coordinates by hand (Efron, 1941), to coding techniques where an observer is asked to judge physical characteristics of the movements observed. Frey and Pool (1976), for example, have developed a cross-hair device that can be inserted into a video recording. Observers then have to judge the relative location of body parts involved in a movement within certain spatial dimensions as defined by the cross hairs. Mehrabian (1972) has defined physical categories for the measurement of bodily displacement and body posture. In that system observers have to judge angles (for instance, the degree to which the upper body is inclined towards an interaction partner) and distances between interaction partners.

Proximal Variables

Aside from anecdotal descriptions of movement behavior (Wallbott, 1980), the more important approaches to the measurement of proximal variables of movements consist of categorical approaches with well-defined categories and high intercoder reliability. The best known of these is the coding system developed by Birdwhistell (1970), which attempts to note all visible movements by means of rather narrow, anatomically defined categories. Although the system aims at completeness, in practical terms it is cumbersome and problematic. Functional category systems have also been devised especially for hand movements. Ekman and Friesen (1969, 1972) distinguish between illustrators, adaptors or manipulators, and emblems. Illustrators are movements that closely accompany speech and are tightly associated with the flow, rhythm, and intonation of utterances. Adaptors or manipulators are movements largely independent of speech, for example, scratching oneself. Emblems are movements with specific meaning understood by all members of a culture, subculture, or group. These categories were used primarily to study hand movement but may also be applicable to head movements or torso movements (for instance, head movements accompanying speech as illustrators, rubbing one's ear against the shoulder as adaptor, head nods or head shakes as emblems, the shoulder shrug to mean helplessness or lack of knowledge). The distinctions made by Mahl (1968), Rosenfeld (1966) and Freedman (see Freedman, 1977; Freedman, Blass, Rifkin, & Quitkin, 1973) are quite similar to Ekman and Friesen's approach to the analysis of hand movements. Freedman distinguishes between object-focused hand movements (i.e., illustrators) and body-focused hand movements (i.e., adaptors) and introduces further subclassifications of these categories.

The use of these functional hand-movement categories in the analysis of a conversation in the civil servant study has produced a number of interesting results (Scherer, K. R. & Scherer, U., 1980; Scherer, U. & Scherer, K. R., 1980). It appears that the gestural behavior of the civil servant is strongly influenced both by his personality and by the conversational situation and type of client behavior. Similarly, the use of various hand movements has an impact on the impression that observers obtain from the conversational behavior of the civil servant.

Measurement of Distance

The measurement of interpersonal distance (between participants) has been an important topic in nonverbal behavior research since Hall (1963)

first raised the issue. Hall's distinctions were based on the type of conversation and the status–sympathy relations between the persons involved.
He divided distance between participants into four categories: intimate,
informal, social–consultative, and formal. Currently, distinctions are made
between territory, body buffer zone, and interpersonal distance. By 'territory' is meant a spatial region that a subject claims to be his or her
personal space. Territory differs from body buffer zone by being bound
to places and locations or possessions (e.g., a person's home or car).
'Body buffer zone' is the "invisible bubble" a person carries along and
does not like to have others enter. 'Interpersonal distance' is the distance
from another that a person selects according to sympathy and status
relations with the discourse partner, having taken into account the social
situation and surroundings.

Since all aspects of distance refer by definition to relationships between
self and another person or objects, motor variables of distance, in the
sense defined above, do not exist. Thus distance and body buffer zones
are usually assessed as distal variables either simply by measuring the
distance or distance changes between two or more discourse partners
(Boucher, 1972; Horowitz, 1968; Sommer, 1969), or by using the stop
technique, in which subjects are asked to approach an interaction partner
until they feel uncomfortably close (Horowitz, 1968).

Proximal variables of distance can be measured by presenting subjects
with videotapes or schematic representations of discourse settings to
evaluate and collecting their impressions and judgments. These techniques
can be used to show that equal distances between interactants are perceived
differently depending on the context (situational background) or on information the subjects have about sex or race of the interactants (Greenberg,
Strube, & Myers, 1980).

Multichannel Research

So far, different channels of nonverbal behavior (voice, face, body
movement, and distance) have been isolated and discussed separately.
Obviously, a person functions as a multichannel sender and receiver
(Birdwhistell, 1970) in an interaction, and discourse analysis has to take
this into account.

In order to do justice to the reality of multichannel communication,
several ways of integrating the data gathered in analyses of the different
nonverbal behavior channels have been suggested. Behavior plots or
behavior scores, which allow different channels of the behavioral stream
(Barker, 1963) to be depicted over time, are commonly proposed. These
plots or charts, with time on one axis and different behavior channels

on the other (Condon & Ogston, 1966), are one way of mapping behavioral data in a concise and organized way.

Behavior plots can be produced for either one or both interactants. In the first instance, this facilitates the study of behavioral synchrony between different channels, or the relationship between verbal and nonverbal behavior. In the second instance, interactional synchrony can be studied, relationships between the subject's respective behaviors established, and the succession of events observed over time.

Figure 11.3 shows a behavior plot for a civil servant in one of the conversations with a client played by an amateur actor. In this example, different parameters (such as voice-analysis data and movement data) were analyzed separately, stored on different files in a computer, and plotted automatically by the computer.

The predominant problem inherent in using behavior plots is that no suitable statistical techniques for further analysis (for example, the detection of interchannel behavior patterns) are currently available. Furthermore, the choice of time increment may cause problems depending on the resolution and velocity of changes of the variables in the different channels. F_0, for example, changes in a few milliseconds, while relatively gross functional body movements (e.g., illustrators) usually have durations of a few seconds. Thus, by choosing a time increment that is too large, it may not be possible to represent sufficiently detailed information about F_0. On the other hand, by choosing a time increment that is too small, F_0 changes can be accurately depicted, but slower variables consume many pages of printout before showing any change.

This problem leads directly to the problem of which of the variables can be combined in a multichannel behavior plot. As a rule of thumb, variables to be combined should be of a similar type, that is, motor, distal, or proximal parameters. Furthermore, distal parameters measured by physical devices (like F_0 and movement coordinates) should be combined, as should variables based on judgment approaches (since for the most part, physical variables are finer grained and vary faster in time then the broader and slower categorial variables).

An example of the combination of physical variables in all channels is shown in Figure 11.4, where coordinate measurements of movements of both hands are combined with the concomitant F_0 and voice energy changes as measured by a digital computer.

The multichannel behavior plots discussed above provide a useful approach to the study of the synchronization of nonverbal behavior in different channels over time. They cannot be used, however, to obtain aggregate data on nonverbal behavior in different channels, which is often required in psychological research. In order to derive more global,

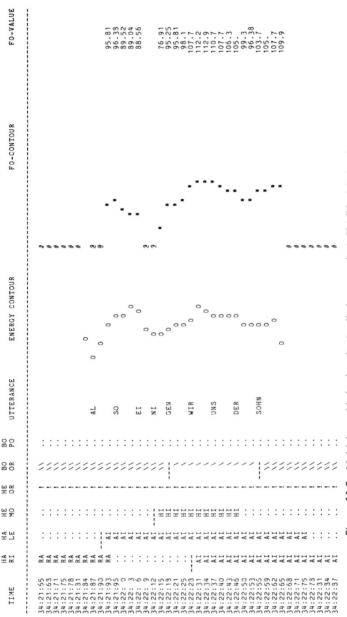

Figure 11.3 Multichannel behavior plot (preliminary version); HA RI, right hand movements; HA LE, left hand movements; HE MO, head movements; HE OR, head orientation; BO OR, body orientation; BO PO, body position; RA, repetitive adaptor; AI, speech accompanying illustrator; HI, head illustrator; !, head orientation downward; \, body orientation strongly toward interaction partner; \, body orientation toward interaction partner; – – –, start of behavioral event; . ., no event; #, silent period; @, voiceless speech segment.

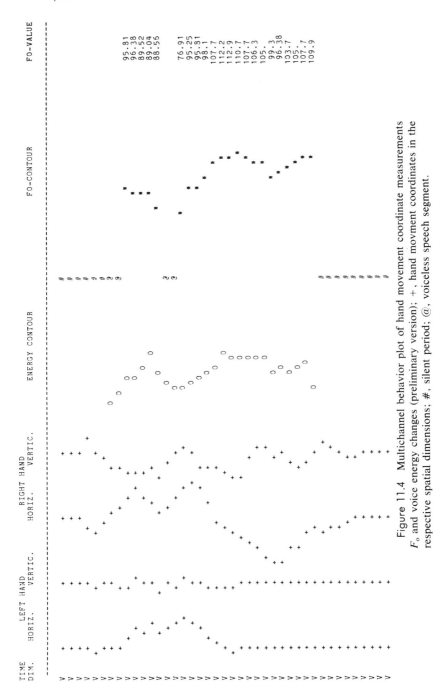

Figure 11.4 Multichannel behavior plot of hand movement coordinate measurements F_0 and voice energy changes (preliminary version); +, hand movment coordinates in the respective spatial dimensions; #, silent period; @, voiceless speech segment.

multichannel nonverbal behavior variables we developed behavior-style scales on the basis of empirical results using factor analyses and theoretical considerations. These behavior-style scales are computed by summing the standard scores (z scores) for molecular behavior measures. The behavior styles identified in the civil servant study are listed in the following. As shown by a number of highly significant results in this study, these behavior-style scales seem to provide a powerful indicator of personality, attitude, and emotional state, differences between conversational partners, and situational variables in discourse (Scherer, U. & Scherer, K. R., 1980; see below):

Verbosity
   total verbal output in seconds
Domineering speech behavior
   many interruptions of the client
   few interruptions by the client
Emotional manner of speaking
   high pitch variability
   many head illustrators
   many hand illustrators
   (rhythmic or underlining speech production)
Frequent listening responses
   many back channel head nods
   many verbal back channel signals
Immediacy
   head often oriented toward the client
   head rarely oriented toward the table
   body rarely upright or leaning backwards
Controlled expressive behavior
   many positions with hands touching each other
   few repetitive adaptors
   few pointing illustrators
   relatively deep voice with low pitch variability
Preoccupation with records
   long pauses
   frequent handling of papers

RESEARCH PARADIGMS AND STRATEGIES

Scherer and Ekman (1982) have pointed out that the study of nonverbal behavior is characterized by two major foci of interest: the study of the individual and the study of the interaction. Researchers focusing on the behavior of the individual in conversation have generally been interested in the externalization or expression of traits and states, in inferences from nonverbal cues, and in the intraindividual organization of behavior. Researchers focusing on interaction processes have studied the nature of cultural communication codes, the coordination of behavior in social interaction, and the development of interpersonal relationships. Clearly, the particular research orientation adopted strongly determines the kinds of paradigms and models used in studying nonverbal behavior in conversation.

One of the major choices lies in the gathering of the material to be analyzed. Are conversations recorded or observed in the field or in the laboratory? Do these conversations consist of naturally occurring or of arranged behavior? One of the major misconceptions is that there are particular approaches that are inherently superior to others. This is not the case. Often it depends on the nature of the questions whether one should observe conversation in a natural context or whether it is necessary to create a situation in which a particular type of conversation can be arranged or provoked. The assumption that behavior observed in natural situations is always natural and behavior occurring in an arranged manner is always artificial is quite erroneous (Scherer & Ekman, 1982). In many cases, it is possible to create experimental simulations that afford the experimenter a large degree of control over a number of variables without rendering the conversation artificial (Scherer, K. R. & Scherer, U., 1980).

Similarly, the use of a single case study, as opposed to several conversations of the same type, also depends on the nature of the question(s) being asked. Quite a number of phenomena can be well studied in the context of a single case. These include the microstructure of behavior, for example. Others, however, need replication over several conversations, particularly if individual differences are expected to play a significant role. A further misconception is that there is an inherent dichotomy between qualitative, structural, and interactional approaches on the one hand, and experimental, quantitative, and psychological studies on the other. This is not necessarily the case. A qualitative, hermeneutic approach to conversational phenomena is the basis for all hypothesis formation underlying a quantitative, experimental approach. Similarly, quantitative evidence can be well suited to strengthening qualitative observation. The differences between the various approaches described in the literature (Duncan, 1969) are mainly due to the particular predilections of researchers from differing traditions as far as research strategies are concerned. However, this gap has to be bridged if the empirical study of nonverbal behavior in conversation is to become scientifically respectable. The major prerequisite for a convergence of these separate research traditions is the development of techniques that allow a quantitative analysis of qualitatively important phenomena.

One of the dangers of quantitative approaches is that the bulk of fine-grained observation tends to obscure the important processes. For example, the use of the behavior-score plot illustrated above results in such a mass of data for lengthy periods of conversation that it is almost impossible to process. Therefore, one needs to develop some kind of critical incident technique that allows focusing on particularly important points or phases in the interaction. Once these were well defined and operationalized, it would be possible to use a number of such incidents to examine nonverbal behavior processes quantitatively. Again, it is possible to use relatively objective methods to determine such points or phases in the interaction, as, for example, with the behavior-playback technique, which requires actors to view their own behavior on videotape and identify major units of behavior (observers can also be asked to perform this task). In addition, there is some hope that the techniques of sequence and cluster analysis (van Hooff, 1982) will provide an important means for determining structure in large numbers of behavioral observations.

Just as the gap between qualitative and quantitative research needs to be bridged, so does the gap between expression and impression research. Most of these processes have long been examined independently in psychology. One promising conceptual tool is the Brunswikian lens model (Scherer, 1978, 1982b), which allows us to study both expression and impression within an integrated-process model of communication and can serve as the basis for a more dynamic approach to the study of conversation.

Figure 11.5 shows an example of a Brunswikian lens model from the data in the civil servant study. The figure shows how the personality trait of machiavellianism affects various aspects of nonverbal behavior of the civil servants and how this in turn affects the impression that observers gain from being exposed to the behavior of the civil servants (via video records). This is a somewhat simplified version of the complete lens model as described in Scherer (1978). Path-analytic procedures can be used to assess the adequacy of the model for expression and impression processes in conversation.

CONCLUSIONS

In this chapter we have attempted to provide a rough overview of the research paradigms, the variables, and the measurement procedures that are available for the analysis of nonverbal behavior in the study of discourse. In many cases, highly complex and little-understood processes

PERSONALITY   NONVERBAL   JUDGES'
(OF CIVIL SERVANT)   BEHAVIOR   IMPRESSION

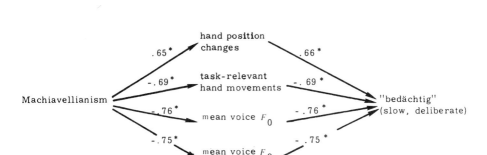

Figure 11.5 Example of a Brunswikian lens model showing some of the results from the civil servant study; $N = 10$; numbers on arrows are Pearson rs; $*p < .05$; civil servants videorecorded in the field study.

and relationships have had to be dealt with in a fairly superficial manner. Thus, we can hope for little more than acquainting the reader with some of the approaches to the use of nonverbal behavior in discourse analysis that seem fruitful at the present time. As mentioned in the introduction, one of the major problems with nonverbal behavior is that, although highly interwoven with language and speech (to the extent of being frequently called "paralinguistic"), it seems to consist of a signal system that is organized differently from the language system. Yet it is equally clear that a straightforward parametric approach, as often used in psychology, is not very promising because of the close interdependence between language and nonverbal behavior. One of the major requirements for future research in this area is clearly the ability to use objective, operationalized measurement in conjunction with a more structural, context-dependent approach as used in linguistics and anthropology. Hopefully, the increasing frequency of interdisciplinary contact between researchers will lead to a flexible, eclectic approach, which is more appropriate for the study of the nonverbal signal system in discourse.

ACKNOWLEDGMENT

This chapter is based on work conducted by the research group on Interaction and Communication at the University of Giessen, West Germany, which consists of Günter Bergmann, Rolf Gebauer, Ilse Höfer, Robert Ladd, Kim Silverman, Reiner Standke, Frank Tolkmitt, and the authors of this chapter. The work reported has been supported by the West German Ministry of Technology (BMFT) and the Deutsche Forschungsgemeinschaft (DFG). The authors gratefully acknowledge helpful comments and support by Ruta Noreika and Robert Ladd.

REFERENCES

Argyle, M., & Cook, M. (1976). *Gaze and mutual gaze*. Cambridge: Cambridge University Press.
Asendorpf, J. (1982). Contributions of the German expression psychology to nonverbal behavior research. Part 2: Facial expression. *Journal of Nonverbal Behavior, 6*, 199–219.
Asendorpf, J., & Wallbott, H. G. (1982). Contributions of the German expression psychology to nonverbal behavior research. Part 1: Theories and concepts. *Journal of Nonverbal Behavior, 6*, 137–147.
Barker, R. G. (Ed.) (1963). *The stream of behavior: Explorations of its structure and content*. New York: Appleton-Century-Crofts.
Birdwhistell, R. L. (1968). Kinesics. In D. L. Sills (Ed.), *International encyclopedia of social sciences* (Vol. 8) (pp. 379–385). New York: Macmillan and the Free Press.
Birdwhistell, R. L. (1970). *Kinesics and context*. Philadelphia: University of Pennsylvania Press.
Boomer, D. S., & Dittmann, A. T. (1962). Hesitation pauses and juncture pauses in speech. *Language and Speech, 5*, 215–220.
Boucher, M. L. (1972). Effect of seating distance on interpersonal attraction in an interview situation. *Journal of Consulting and Clinical Psychology, 38*, 15–19.
Bruce, G., & Garding, E. (1978). A prosodic typology for Swedish dialects. In E. Garding, G. Bruce, & R. Bannert (Eds.), *Nordic prosody* (pp. 219–228). Lund: Travaux de l'Institut de Linguistique de Lund.
Chapple, E. D. (1956). *The interaction chronograph manual*. Norton, CT: E. D. Chapple Co.
Cohen, J., & Cohen, P. (1975). *Applied multiple regression/correlation analysis for the behavioral sciences*. Hillsdale, NJ: Erlbaum.
Condon, W. S., & Ogston, W. D. (1966). Soundfilm analysis of normal and pathological behavior patterns. *Journal of Nervous and Mental Disease, 143*, 338–347.
Crystal, D., & Quirk, R. (1964). *Systems of prosodic and paralinguistic features in English*. The Hague: Mouton.
Darwin, C. (1872). *The expressions of the emotions in man and animals*. London: Murray. Reprinted 1965. Chicago: University of Chicago Press.
Dittmann, A. T., & Wynne, L. C. (1961). Linguistic techniques and the analysis of emotionality in interviews. *Journal of Abnormal and Social Psychology, 63*, 201–204.
Duncan, S. D. (1969). Nonverbal communication. *Psychological Bulletin, 72*, 118–137.
Duncan, S. D. (1974). On the structure of speaker–auditor interaction during speaking turns. *Language and Society, 3*, 161–180.
Duncan, S. D., & Fiske, D. W. (1977). Face-to-face interaction. Hillsdale, NJ: Erlbaum.
Duncan, S. D., Rice, L. N., & Butler, J. M. (1968). Therapists' paralanguage in peak and poor psychotherapy hours. *Journal of Abnormal Psychology, 73*, 566–570.
Duncan, S. D., & Rosenthal, R. (1968). Vocal emphasis in experimenters' instruction reading as unintended determinant of subjects' responses. *Language and Speech, 11*, 20–26.
Efron, D. (1941). *Gesture and environment*. New York: King's Crown.
Ekman, P. (1976). Movements with precise meanings. *Journal of Communication, 26*, 14–26.

Ekman, P. (1979). About brows: Emotional and conversational signals. In M. von Cranach, K. Foppa, W. Lepenies, & D. Ploog (Eds.), *Human ethology* (pp. 169–202). Cambridge: Cambridge University Press.

Ekman, P. (1982). Methods of measuring facial action. In K. R. Scherer & P. Ekman (Eds.), *Handbook of methods in nonverbal behavior research* (pp. 45–90). Cambridge: Cambridge University Press.

Ekman, P., & Friesen, W. V. (1969). The repertoire of nonverbal behavior: Categories, origins, usage, and coding. *Semiotica, 1,* 49–98.

Ekman, P., & Friesen, W. V. (1972). Hand movements. *Journal of Communication, 22,* 353–374.

Ekman, P., & Friesen, W. V. (1975). *Unmasking the face.* Englewood Cliffs, NJ: Prentice Hall.

Ekman, P., & Friesen, W. V. (1978). *The facial action code: A manual for the measurement of facial movement.* Palo Alto, CA: Consulting Psychologists' Press.

Ellgring, J. H. (1977). Kommunikatives Verhalten im Verlauf depressiver Erkrankungen. In H. W. Tack (Ed.), *Bericht über den 30. Kongress der Deutschen Gesellschaft für Psychologie, Regensburg, 1976* (pp. 190–192). Göttingen: Hogrefe.

Exline, R. V., & Fehr, B. J. (1982). The assessment of gaze and mutual gaze. In K. R. Scherer & P. Ekman (Eds.), *Handbook of methods in nonverbal behavior research* (pp. 91–135). Cambridge: Cambridge University Press.

Feldstein, S., & Welkowitz, J. (1978). A chronography of conversation: In defense of an objective approach. In A. W. Siegman & S. Feldstein (Eds.), *Nonverbal behavior and communication* (pp. 329–378). Hillsdale, NJ: Erlbaum.

Freedman, N. (1977). Hands, words, and mind: On the structuralization of body movement during discourse and the capacity for verbal representation. In N. Freedman & S. Grand (Eds.), *Communicative structures and psychic structures* (pp. 109–132). New York: Plenum Press.

Freedman, N., Blass, T., Rifkin, A., & Quitkin, F. (1973). Body movements and the verbal encoding of aggressive affect. *Journal of Personality and Social Psychology, 26,* 72–85.

Frey, S., & Pool, J. (1976). *A new approach to the analysis of visible behavior.* Bern: Research Reports from the Department of Psychology.

Frois-Wittmann, J. (1930). The judgment of facial expression. *Journal of Experimental Psychology, 13,* 113–151.

Giles, H., Scherer, K. R., & Taylor, D. M. (1979). Speech markers in social interaction. In K. R. Scherer & H. Giles (Eds.), *Social markers in speech* (pp. 343–381). Cambridge: Cambridge University Press.

Giles, H., & Smith, P. H. (1979). Accomodation theory: Optimal levels of convergence. In H. Giles & R. St. Clair (Eds.), *The social psychology of language* (pp. 45–65). London: Blackwell.

Glawe, R. D., & Rietveld, A. C. M. (1975). Is the effort dependence of speech loudness explicable on the basis of acoustical cues? *Journal of the Acoustical Society of America, 58,* 875–879.

Goffman, E. (1961). *Encounters: Two studies in the sociology of interaction.* Indianapolis: Bobbs-Merrill.

Goffman, E. Response cries. (1979). In M. von Cranach, K. Foppa, W. Lepenies, & D. Ploog (Eds.), *Human ethology. Claims and limits of a new discipline* (pp. 203–240). Cambridge: Cambridge University Press.

Goldman-Eisler, F. (1968). *Psycholinguistics: Experiments in spontaneous speech.* New York: Academic Press.

Grant, E. C. (1969). Human facial expression. *Man, 4,* 525–536.

Greenberg, C. I., Strube, M. J., & Myers, R. A. (1980). A multitrait–multimethod investigation of interpersonal distance. *Journal of Nonverbal Behavior, 5,* 104–114.

Gustafsson, L., & Lanshammar, H. (1977). *ENOCH—An integrated system for the measurement and analysis of human gait.* Unpublished doctoral dissertation, University of Upsala.

Hall, E. T. (1963). Proxemics: The study of man's spatial relations. In I. Galdston (Ed.), *Man's image in medicine and anthropology* (pp. 422–445). New York: International University Press.

Heimann, H., & Lukacs, G. (1966). Eine Methode zur quantitativen Analyse der mimischen Bewegungen. *Archiv für die Gesamte Psychologie, 118,* 1–17.

Hess, E. H. (1975). *The tell-tale eye: How your eyes reveal hidden thoughts and emotions.* New York: Van Nostrand Reinhold.

Höfer, I., Wallbott, H. G., & Scherer, K. R. *Interactional convergence reconsidered: New methods for measuring convergence and divergence.* (In preparation.)

Horowitz, M. J. (1968). Spatial behavior and psychopathology. *Journal of Nervous and Mental Disease, 146,* 24–35.

Izard, C. E. (1971). *The face of emotion.* New York: Appleton-Century-Crofts.

Kendon, A. (1967). Some functions of gaze-direction in social interaction. *Acta Psychologica, 26,* 22–63.

Kendon, A. (1970). Movement coordination in social interaction: Some examples described. *Acta Psychologica, 32,* 100–125.

Kendon, A. (1972). Some relationships between body motion and speech. In A. W. Siegman & B. Pope (Eds.), *Studies in dyadic communication* (pp. 177–210). New York: Pergamon Press.

Ladd, D. R. (1983). Phonological features of intonation peaks. *Language, 59,* 4.

Ladd, R., Silverman, K., & Scherer, K. R. (1985). An integrated approach to studying intonation and attitude. In C. Johns-Lewis (Ed.), *Intonation and discourse,* Beckenham, Kent: Croom Helms.

Laver, J. (1975). Individual features in voice quality. Unpublished doctoral dissertation, University of Edinburgh.

Laver, J. (1980). *The phonetic description of voice quality.* Cambridge: Cambridge University Press.

Lersch, P. (1932). *Gesicht und Seele. Grundlinien einer mimischen Diagnostik.* München: Reinhardt.

Licklider, J. C. R., & Pollak, I. (1948). Effects of differentiation, integration, and infinite peak clipping upon the intelligibility of speech. *Journal of the Acoustical Society of America, 20,* 42–50.

Lieberman, P. (1965). On the acoustic basis of the perception of intonation by linguists. *Word, 21,* 40–54.

Mahl, G. F. (1968). Gestures and body movements in interviews. In J. Shlien (Ed.), *Research in psychotherapy* (Vol. 3, pp. 295–346). Washington, D.C.: American Psychological Association.

Markel, N. N., Meisels, M., & Houck, J. E. (1964). Judging personality from voice quality. *Journal of Abnormal and Social Psychology, 69,* 458–463.

Mehrabian, A. (1969). Significance of posture and position in the communication of attitude and status relationships. *Psychological Bulletin, 71,* 359–372.

Mehrabian, A. (1972). *Nonverbal communication.* Atherton: Aldine.

Mitchelson, D. L. (1975). Recording movement without photography. In D. W. Grieve, D. I. Miller, D. L. Mitchelson, J. P. Paul, & A. J. Smith (Eds.), *Techniques for the analysis of human movement* (pp. 33–65). London: Lepus.

Natale, M. (1975). Convergence of mean vocal intensity in dyadic communication as a function of social desirability. *Journal of Personality and Social Psychology, 32,* 790–804.

Paul, J. P. (1975). Instruments for force measurement. In D. W. Grieve, D. I. Miller, D. L. Mitchelson, J. P. Paul, & A. J. Smith (Eds.), *Techniques for the analysis of human movement* (pp. 150–171). London: Lepus.

Pierrehumbert, J. (1981). Synthesizing intonation. *Journal of the Acoustical Society of America, 70,* 985–995.

Poyatos, F. (1976). *Man beyond words. Theory and methodology of nonverbal communication.* New York: The New York State English Council.

Rosenfeld, H. M. (1966). Instrumental affiliative functions of facial and gestural expressions. *Journal of Personality and Social Psychology, 4,* 65–72.

Rutter, D. R., & Stephenson, G. M. (1972). Visual interaction in a group of schizophrenic and depressive patients. *British Journal of Social and Clinical Psychology, 11,* 57–65.

Scheflen, A. E. (1964). The significance of posture in communicative systems. *Psychiatry, 27,* 316–331.

Schegloff, E. A. (1972). Notes on a conversational practice: Formulating place. In D. Sudnow (Ed.), *Studies in social interaction* (pp. 75–119). New York: Free Press.

Scherer, K. R. (1971). Randomized splicing: A note on a simple technique for masking speech content. *Journal of Experimental Research in Personality, 5,* 155–159.

Scherer, K. R., (1977a). *The effect of stress on the fundamental frequency of the voice.* Paper presented at the Acoustical Society of America Meeting, Miami, FL. (Abstract in *Journal of the Acoustical Society of America,* 1977, *62,* Supplement No. 1, 25–26)

Scherer, K. R. (1977b). Affektlaute und vokale Embleme. In R. Posner & H. P. Reinecke (Eds.), *Zeichenprozesse-Semiotische Forschung in den Einzelwissenschaften* (pp. 199–214). Wiesbaden: Athenaion.

Scherer, K. R. (1978). Personality inference from voice quality: The loud voice of extraversion. *European Journal of Social Psychology, 8,* 467–487.

Scherer, K. R. (1979a). Nonlinguistic vocal indicators of emotion and psychopathology. In C. E. Izard (Ed.), *Emotions in personality and psychopathology* (pp. 493–529). New York: Plenum.

Scherer, K. R. (1979b). Personality markers in speech. In K. R. Scherer & H. Giles (Eds.), *Social markers in speech* (pp. 147–209). Cambridge: Cambridge University Press.

Scherer, K. R. (1980). The functions of nonverbal signs in conversation. In R. St. Clair & H. Giles (Eds.), *The social and psychological contexts of language* (pp. 225–244). Hillsdale, NJ: Erlbaum.

Scherer, K. R. (1981a). Speech and emotional states. In J. Darby (Ed.), *The evaluation of speech in psychiatry* (pp. 189–220). New York: Grune & Stratton.

Scherer, K. R. (1981b). Vocal indicators of stress. In J. Darby (Ed.), *Speech evaluation in psychiatry* (pp. 171–187). New York: Grune & Stratton.

Scherer, K. R. (1982a). Methods of research on vocal communication. Paradigms and parameters. In K. R. Scherer & P. Ekman (Eds.), *Handbook of methods in nonverbal behavior research* (pp. 136–198). Cambridge: Cambridge University Press.

Scherer, K. R. (1982b). The nonverbal dimension: A fad, a field, or a behavioral modality. In H. Tajfel (Ed.), *The social dimension: European developments in social psychology.* Cambridge: Cambridge University press.

Scherer, K. R., & Ekman, P. (Eds.) (1982). *Handbook of methods in nonverbal behavior research.* Cambridge: Cambridge University Press.

Scherer, K. R., & Giles, H. (Eds.) (1979). *Social markers in speech.* Cambridge: Cambridge University Press.

Scherer, K. R., & Scherer, U. (1980). *Nonverbal behavior and impression formation in naturalistic situations*. Paper presented at the XXIInd. International Congress of Psychology in Leipzig, GDR.

Scherer, U., & Scherer, K. R. (1980). Psychological factors in bureaucratic encounters: Determinants and effects of interactions between officials and clients. In W. T. Singleton, P. Spurgeon, & R. B. Stammers (Eds.), *The analysis of social skill* (pp. 315–328). New York: Plenum.

Schwartz, G. E., Fair, P. L., Salt, P. S., Mandel, M. R., & Klerman, J. L. (1976). Facial muscle patterning to affective imagery in depressed and non-depressed subjects. *Science, 192,* 489–491.

Siegman, A. W. (1978). The telltale voice: Nonverbal messages of verbal communication. In A. W. Siegman & S. Feldstein (Eds.), *Nonverbal behavior and communication* (pp. 183–243). Hillsdale, NJ: Erlbaum.

Siegman, A. W., & Feldstein, S. (1978). *Nonverbal behavior and communication.* Hillsdale, NJ: Erlbaum.

Small, A. M. (1973). Psychoacoustics. In F. D. Minifie, T. J. Hixon, & F. Williams (Eds.), *Normal aspects of speech, hearing and language* (pp. 343–420). Englewood Cliffs, NJ: Prentice Hall.

Sommer, R. (1969). *Personal space.* Englewood Cliffs, NJ: Prentice-Hall.

Sondhi, M. U. (1968). New methods of pitch extraction. *IEEE Transactions on Audio and Electroacoustic., 16,* 262–266.

Takefuta, Y. (1975). Method of acoustic analysis of intonation. In S. Singh (Ed.), *Measurement procedures in speech, hearing and language* (pp. 368–378). Baltimore: University Park Press.

Trager, G. L., & Smith, H. L., Jr. (1957). *An outline of English structure.* Washington, DC: American Council of Learned Societies.

van Hooff, J. (1982). Categories and sequences of behavior: Methods of description and analysis. In K. R. Scherer & P. Ekman (Eds.), *Handbook of methods in nonverbal behavior research* (pp. 362–439). Cambridge: Cambridge University Press.

Wallbott, H. G. (1980). The measurement of human expression. In W. v. Raffler-Engel (Ed.), *Aspects of nonverbal communication* (pp. 203–228). Lisse: Swets & Zeitlinger.

Wallbott, H. G. (1982). *Bewegungsstil und Bewegungsqualität.* Weinheim: Beltz.

Wiemann, J. M., & Knapp, M. L. (1975). Turn-taking in conversations. *Journal of Communication, 25,* 75–92.

Wörner, R. (1940). Theoretische und experimentelle Beiträge zum Ausdrucksproblem. *Zeitschrift für angewandte Psychologie und Charakterkunde, 59,* 257–318.

CHAPTER 12

Text Processing: A Psychological Model

Walter Kintsch

INTRODUCTION

The research literature on psychological aspects of text processing has been discussed by Bower and Cirilo (this *Handbook,* Vol. 1). The purpose of this chapter is to illustrate how one psychological processing model works. The intent is to illustrate rather than to present the model in all its detail, which is not really possible within the constraints of a handbook chapter. Furthermore, no specific reasons can be given here for the particular properties of the model; the original sources must be consulted for a more detailed presentation and justification of the model.

The processing model considered here is that of van Dijk and Kintsch (1983). Brief descriptions of this model have also been given in Kintsch (1982a, 1982b). A computer simulation of the model has been described by Miller and Kintsch (1980).

The van Dijk and Kintsch (1983) model distinguishes several major components of text processing, not all of which are treated in equal detail. These components can be considered stages of processing: First comes the linguistic parsing of the text, followed by the construction of atomic propositions that represent its meaning elements; next, these meaning elements are organized into a coherent textbase, which represents the full meaning of the text; from this textbase, the macrostructure of the text is derived, representing its essence or gist. At all of these levels, we are dealing with representations of the text proper. In addition, however, text comprehension results in the construction of a situation model, which is not a representation of the text itself but of the situation referred to by the text. The model describes these various construction processes in real time, subject to known human processing limitations, mainly with respect to short-term memory.

HANDBOOK OF DISCOURSE ANALYSIS, Vol. 2
Dimensions of Discourse

Copyright © 1985 by Academic Press London.
All rights of reproduction in any form reserved.
ISBN 0-12-712002-5

One of the components that is not developed in the van Dijk and Kintsch model is linguistic parsing. The model bypasses this stage and starts out not with a text proper, but with a text-plus-annotations. These annotations provide the model with the kind of information it needs for its further processing, for example, the formation of propositions. There is, however, no explicit rule system that would compute these annotations from the textual input. The process of constructing propositions, on the other hand, is fully specified, given the annotated text as input. In essence, the model reads the text word by word (more precisely, in terms of small word groups called "text expressions", as is explained below), building propositional frames for each term as it is encountered, with dummy arguments in those cases where the required information has not yet been received. When the missing word is read, a second process fills in the corresponding argument, which now replaces the provisional dummy variable. The model knows what sorts of propositions to build, because along with the text it is also provided with the necessary knowledge about the meaning of the words in the text. What needs to be specified is the form of the propositional frame that is to be constructed, some semantic relations (such as subordination), and some meaning postulates specifying implications that are crucial for understanding the text. A formal theory of knowledge structures and inference from which the required knowledge sources could be derived for a text is, however, not a part of the model, and the knowledge sources, just as the syntactic annotations, must be constructed for each text ad hoc.

A central component of the model is the next stage, in which the atomic propositions just constructed are organized into a coherent textbase, called the microstructure of the text. In an earlier version of the model (Kintsch & van Dijk, 1978), this was done in an oversimplified way: The only coherence relation considered was the repetition of propositional arguments. Van Dijk and Kintsch (1983) describe a much richer set of strategies by means of which coherent textbases are constructed. Normally, the propositional organization closely mirrors the syntactic structure of the sentence from which the propositions have been derived. This is achieved by the use of a propositional schema, with the main verb of the sentence as the focal concept. The propositional schema consists of a predicate–argument structure, with optional modifiers, and a circumstance category (specifying time, place, modals, consequences, etc.).

The macrostructure of the text is formed from this propositional structure, again in a strategic way under the control of the reader's goals and plans. Some of the strategies involved are illustrated below. The form of the macrostructure may be based on some schematic superstructure, of which the narrative schema is the best-known example.

These processes are illustrated below with some simple texts. The first example serves to show how the model works and what it actually does, in a case where the text is extremely simple and brief. The example is described in great detail, and the reader should have no trouble following the model, from the initial input to the formation of the macrostructure. The second example deals with a slightly more complex text; it serves to illustrate some features of the model in more detail for those readers who want to know more about the model than can be conveyed by the altogether too-simple first example.

In both examples, the reader is invited to follow the processing of the model step by step: Tables 12.1–12.4 are processing traces, not of some computer simulation, but of a hand simulation of the model. Ideally, Tables 12.1 and 12.2 (as well as 12.3 and 12.4 should be read together, from top to bottom. Processing starts on the top line on the left side with the first text expression and then procedes both downward in the table (in time) and to the right (parallel processing at higher levels).

EXAMPLE 1

Since the model lacks a parsing mechanism, we have to annotate the text in such a way that it resembles the output of a parser. We break up the text into text expressions, as shown in Table 12.1, and annotate these expressions with the necessary syntactic and semantic information. Text expressions are words or small groups of words. Function words indicating semantic cases are combined with the appropriate content words into single text expressions. Articles are not separated from their nouns, and auxiliary verbs are grouped with adjacent words.

The annotations identify semantic cases (*buses* is the object of Text Expression E5, *crowd* its goal, etc.), or indicate modifiers (*pleasant* modifies E9), number (*eighty* quantifies E4), or connectives (*after* connects E2 and E5). These annotations are sufficient to derive semantic units from the text. In addition, there may be syntactic annotations when they are needed in organizing the textbase (e.g., the main verb of a sentence may be marked).

In addition to the annotated text expressions, we need knowledge about the words used in the text expressions. People know, of course, a great deal about football games, crowds, buses, municipal transport, and so on—and much of that knowledge might be involved in understanding even such a simple text as the one in Table 12.1. However, we supply the model only with minimal knowledge, which, of course, can support only the most rudimentary understanding. But we are interested in the

Table 12.1
A Sample Text and Its Representation: Proposition Formation

Annotated text expressions	Knowledge sources	Propositions	
		Build	Fill
E1 *After*$_{connective(E2,E5)}$	time: AFTER(X,X)	P1 AFTER(E2,E5)	P1 AFTER(P1,E5)
E2 *the football game*	(X)	P2 FOOTBALLGAME = x_1	
E3 *eighty*$_{number(E4)}$	number(X)	P3 EIGHTY(E4)	P3 EIGHTY(x_2)
E4 *buses*$_{object(E5)}$	(X)	P4 BUS = x_2	
E5 *were waiting*	WAIT(object:X,goal:X)	P5 E5(x_2)	P1 AFTER(P2,P5)
			P5 WAIT(x_2)
E6 *for the crowd*$_{goal(E5)}$	(X),synonym:MANY(PEOPLE)	P6 CROWD = x_3	P5 WAIT(x_2,x_3)
E7 *The people*$_{patient(E9)}$	(X),subordinate:PERSON	P7 PEOPLE = x_4	
		P8 E9(x_4)	
E8 *were pleasantly*$_{modifier(E9)}$	modifier(X)	P9 PLEASANT(P8)	
E9 *surprised.*	SURPRISE(patient: PEOPLE, source: UNUSUAL)		P8 SURPRISE(x_4)

Table 12.2
A Sample Text and Its Representation: The Micro- and Macrostructure

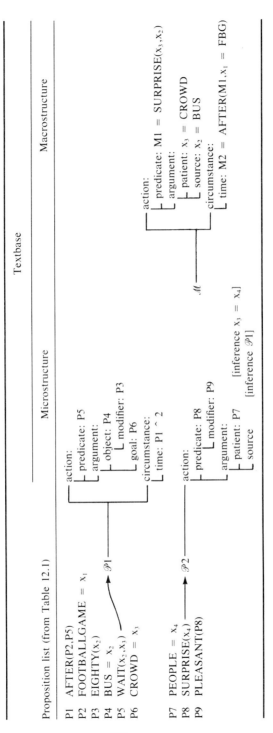

Textbase

Proposition list (from Table 12.1)   Microstructure   Macrostructure

P1 AFTER(P2,P5)
P2 FOOTBALLGAME = x_1
P3 EIGHTY(x_2)
P4 BUS = x_2
P5 WAIT(x_2,x_3)
P6 CROWD = x_3

P7 PEOPLE = x_4
P8 SURPRISE(x_4)
P9 PLEASANT(P8)

action:
┌ predicate: P5
└ argument:
    ┌ object: P4
    └ L modifier: P3
    └ goal: P6
circumstance:
└ time: P1 ^ 2

action:
┌ predicate: P8
│ └ L modifier: P9
└ argument:
    ┌ patient: P7   [inference x_3 = x_4]
    └ source   [inference $\mathscr{P}1$]

action:
┌ predicate: M1 = SURPRISE(x_3,x_2)
└ argument:
    ┌ patient: x_3 = CROWD
    └ source: x_2 = BUS
circumstance:
└ time: M2 = AFTER(M1,x_1 = FBG)

$\mathscr{P}1$

$\mathscr{P}2$

$\mathscr{M}$

235

principles by means of which this understanding is achieved, even if it is only rudimentary. The same principles could support a deeper understanding if we were to provide the model with more knowledge.

The knowledge base actually used in the illustration shown in Table 12.1 is quite primitive. It permits *pleasant* to modify anything, *after* to connect any two expressions, *eighty* to be the number of anything— none of which is strictly correct, but it is all we need to know for a first pass. About *football game* and *bus* the model is told nothing specific. *Wait* and *surprise* are identified by the frame they take, but in a very superficial way: We let anything wait for anything, and any PERSON be surprised by anything UNUSUAL. In addition, *people* is identified as a subordinate of PERSON and *crowd* as a synonym of MANY, (PEOPLE).

Provided with this minimal knowledge and the annotated text, the model first constructs a representation of the text in terms of semantic units or elementary propositions. It sets up a proposition for every content word it encounters, disregarding function words. The knowledge base tells it what the form of that unit should be, and the text with its annotations tells it what its content must be. Thus *after* is identified as a relational term with two arguments, which are to be based on E2 and E5. The Build process constructs a semantic unit P1 with AFTER as the relational term and dummy expressions E2 and E5, which are to be filled by the appropriate semantic units at a later time. When Build encounters *football game,* P2 is constructed. A second process called Fill now uses P2 to replace the provisional E2 in P1. *Eighty* leads to the construction of a new semantic unit P3 with a provisional argument E4. *Bus* triggers P4 and P5, the latter via the annotation that identifies *bus* as the object of E5; P3 can now be completed. On the next line, the input *wait* permits us to fill in the missing predicate in P5 and thereby in P1 as well. The Build and Fill operations on lines 6–9 follow the same pattern.

As each semantic unit is constructed from the annotated text, each unit is checked against the knowledge base to see whether it matches whatever knowledge constraints there are. Since we have kept the knowledge base extremely unconstrained in this example, nothing of interest happens here. In the one case where there was a constraint—SURPRISE requires a member of the class of PERSON as a patient—the match is positive.

The next step in the model is to organize the propositions just constructed into a coherent textbase. This involves two steps: A focus concept must be selected from the input, and the text must then be organized around that focus concept. The strategies for selecting a focus concept may take into account information from various sources. In the present case however, faced with a minitext out of context, we can do no more than fall back on some default strategies: Use the syntax as a guide, and select the main verb as a focus concept. In consequence, the knowledge source WAIT becomes the structure around which the text proposition is built. It is not a very rich structure, since all we know is that WAIT takes an object and a goal. Thus we have a schema—WAIT—with two slots, object and goal. The propositions P3–P6 fit into these slots. Since any proposition may also have a time slot, and P1 is a TIME unit, a third slot containing P1 and P2 can also be added to the proposition $\mathcal{P}1$, as shown in Table 12.2. A coherent structure has now been created to interrelate all semantic units derived from the first sentence.

A problem arises with P7–P9, which are not directly related to $\mathcal{P}1$. Furthermore, SURPRISE is missing a source. At this point, another strategy comes into play: The model assumes that it is receiving well-formed text, and since there is no other candidate for the source of SURPRISE, it assumes that $\mathcal{P}1$ is it and attempts to construct a connection between P8 and $\mathcal{P}1$, which succeeds via CROWD and PEOPLE. Hence $\mathcal{P}2$ is set up with $\mathcal{P}1$ embedded into it as one of its arguments.

Given the extreme simplicity of our example, not much can be said about the formation of the macrostructure. The only macrostrategies that apply are, once more, default cases. No interesting inference processes are triggered by this text and the macrostructure is formed mostly by deletion: $\mathcal{P}1$ is deleted as a separate unit because it is embedded in $\mathcal{P}2$; the modifier is deleted from $\mathcal{P}2$, and the source–inference $\mathcal{P}1$ is reduced to x_2 (BUS), first by reducing $\mathcal{P}1$ to its main propositon P5, then by stripping from P5 the redundant argument x_3 as well as the predicate. In addition, P1 and P2 may be retained in the macrostructure by a strategy that prevents the deletion of setting at the lower levels of the macrostructure (it may be an important element of coherence if the text continues). Thus we are left with the two macropropositions shown in Table 12.1. By means of production rules a verbal summary could be derived from these macropropositions, for example, "The crowd was surprised about the buses after the football game."

The model's understanding of the text consists of the structures as shown in Tables 12.1 and 12.2. Note that we have not given the model any knowledge to determine whether P1 is UNUSUAL, as required by the frame for SURPRISE. Hence, the model could not answer a simple question about why the people were surprised. One could, of course, construct a more sophisticated model with knowledge about municipal transport, but the principles upon which such a model would be based would remain unchanged.

Very little computation was necessary in this first example. The propositions as well as macropropositions were copied quite directly from the text. The following is a somewhat more complex example where this is no longer the case.

EXAMPLE 2

The second text is illustrated in Table 12.3. Note that this time we must have more knowledge for understanding than in Example 1. The conventions used are the same as those in Tables 12.1 and 12.2. Thus *bikers* is identified as a concept, (X), which triggers the formation of an existential proposition P1, BIKER = x_1; in addition, we need to know that BIKER is a PERSON. For *wear*, we supply the appropriate verb frame and note it as a subordinate of USE (which we need for later inferencing). *Helmet* is identified as an ARTICLE-OF-CLOTHING (to permit its being used as an argument of WEAR), with location ON-HEAD (we need that later to understand the second sentence), and we need to connect its use with not suffering injuries, which we do by means of the meaning postulate CONSEQUENCE (USE (PERSON, HELMET),NOT (SUFFER(PERSON,INJURY))). The knowledge sources for E5–E10 are similar in form and are motivated by similar considerations. For the concept ACCIDENT, an event schema needs to be specified with slots very much in the same way as for verb frames.

The construction of atomic propositions on the basis of the input is also shown in Table 12.3. There is nothing really new here, and we need not be concerned with this process in detail. The main problem is not to get confused, and not to lose track of the various expressions and units. It is the sort of thing a computer program does infinitely better than a person working with paper and pencil.

The real interest in Example 2 lies in the construction of the propositional organization for the semantic units (Table 12.4). As in the first example, we start reading a text out of context and hence must fall back on some general, all-purpose organizational strategy. As before, we use the syntax of the sentence as our cue, find the main verb of the sentence, and work around that. In order to do that, the processor has to look back at the textual input itself and cannot merely work with the proposition list. In our case, P2, ABLE(x_1P3), is identified as the proposition derived from the text expression marked as 'main verb'. However, a check of the knowledge sources shows that ABLE is marked as a MODAL, and one of the organizational strategies of the model is not to choose modals as the basis for organization; instead, the proposition embedded in the modal proposition is foregrounded. Hence, P3 becomes the focal proposition, leading to the structure $\mathscr{P}1$. The only unusual feature of this structure is the embedding of one propositional schema in another: The agent slot of the main schema (BIKER) is modified by another propositional schema containing propositions P4 and P5 in its slots. The cue for embeddding this schema into $\mathscr{P}1$ (instead of constructing a new unit, for instance) is the relative pronoun *who*, which was annotated as mod(E1). Thus the propositional structure of $\mathscr{P}1$ mirrors the syntactic structure of the sentence.

This is quite different from the other two sentences in the text. Sentence 2 (*"John collided with a car, fell, and is still paralyzed below the head."*) introduces all new concepts—there is no argument repetition to connect $\mathscr{P}1$ with the new material. Clearly, there can be no question of adding the propositions derived from Sentence 2 to $\mathscr{P}1$. A new structure must be built, but first we need to determine how it is to be connected with the old structure, $\mathscr{P}1$. The strategy of the model at this point is to examine the concepts of $\mathscr{P}1$ for possible connections to the newly formed propositions. Several connections are found: INJURY connects to PARALYZED, ACCIDENT connects to COLLIDE, FALL, and (indirectly) to PARALYZED; indeed, P11–P17 fit nicely into the slots of the ACCIDENT schema. Hence, an inference is made that the events described here are an ACCIDENT, and the ACCIDENT schema will be selected for organizing P11–P17. One more inference is needed: We know of JOHN only that he is a PERSON, but because the PERSON in the previous text-unit P1 was a BIKER, we jump to the conclusion that JOHN, too, is a BIKER, and that we have here an instance of the event described in the first sentence.

The third sentence (*"In contrast, George rammed head-first into a truck that stopped in front of him but was saved."*) is processed similarly. Once again, the model recognizes that it is dealing with an ACCIDENT and organizes the text accordingly.

The proposition P18 INCONTRAST (P14, P26) connects the two accidents and gives us an important clue for forming the macrostructure of the text.

For the macrostructure (or rather, one of the possible versions of a macrostructure that could be derived from this text by employment of appropriate macrostrategies), we first activate another, high-level knowledge schema: our knowledge about the rhetorical form of 'illustration', which consists of a general statement plus examples. The condition for activating this schema is the text itself, which says something about ACCIDENT in Sentence 1 and then provides two examples in the following sentences.

The first two macropropositions, M1 and M2, are formed from $\mathscr{P}1$. M1 is almost equal to the main proposition of the microstructure, P3, but one more argument is added to it: the instrument HELMET. The

Table 12.3
A Sample Text and Its Representation: Proposition Formation

Annotated text expressions	Knowledge sources	Propositions	
		Build	Fill
E1 Bikers_agt(E6,E7)	(X),sub:PERSON	P1 Biker = x_1 P2 E6(x_1) P3 E7(x_1)	
E2 who_agt(E3),refl(E1),mod(E1)			
E3 wear	sub:USE WEAR(agent:PERSON,object: ARTICLE-OF-CLOTHING)	P4 E3(x_1)	P4 WEAR(x_1)
E4 a helmet_obj(E3)	(X),sub:ARTICLE-OF-CLOTHING loc:ON-HEAD(HELMET) CONSEQUENCE(USE (PERSON, HELMET),NOT (SUFFER(PERSON, INJURY)))	P5 HELMET = x_2	P4 WEAR(x_1,x_2)
E5 are often_mod(E6)	mod(P)	P6 OFTEN(P2)	
E6 able_main verb	sub:MODAL ABLE(agt:PERSON,complement:P)		P2 ABLE(x_1)
E7 to avoid_complement(E6)	AVOID(agt:PERSON,obj:P, instrument:X,consequence: NOT(P))		P2 ABLE(x_1,P3) P3 AVOID(x_1)
E8 serious_mod(E9)	mod(X)	P7 SERIOUS(E9)	
E9 injury_obj(E7)	(X)	P8 INJURY = x_3	P3 AVOID(x_1,x_3) P7 SERIOUS(x_3)
E10 in an accident_time(E6)	ACCIDENT(participant:USE(PERSON, VEHICLE)event:ACCIDENT, consequence:SUFFER(PERSON, INJURY))	P9 ACCIDENT = x_4 P10 IN(P2,P9)	

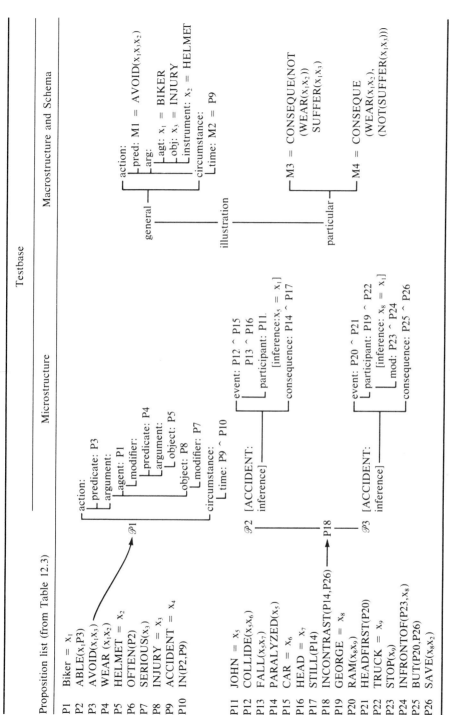

Testbase

model knows that AVOID may take an instrument, and it also knows that using a helmet may prevent injury. Some general rules (meaning postulates) can be stated (but are not given here) that permit the inference that the helmet was the instrument of avoiding injury.

The rest of the macropropositions we derive less from the text than from our knowledge about what helmets do. $\mathcal{P}2$ says nothing about a helmet and results in an injury; hence we assume M3—that not wearing a helmet caused this injury. $\mathcal{P}3$ specifies that a helmet saved someone from injury; hence we assume M4—that wearing a helmet prevented injury here.

Obviously, what we have done here is build a low-level macrostructure. A higher level could easily be obtained, for example, by using a strategy of example deletion when dealing with the illustration schema.

It is important to note that the macrostructure constructed here is merely one of a number of possibilities that could have been realized. Furthermore, by supposing that a rhetorical schema was activated, it is a version that requires a great deal of inferential activity. That this is within the possibilities of the model is, of course, the purpose of this example. It must be pointed out, however, that it is easy to state inference procedures when dealing with preselected, specially arranged knowledge sources, as in the present examples. To formulate general rules that would be efficient, or even workable, or to provide the model with a more realistic knowledge base, are problems beyond our present capabilities. But the limitations that we encounter here are limitations of the theory of knowledge representation and inference processes, not of text comprehension per se.

CONCLUSIONS

Certain aspects of the model have been neglected in these examples. For instance, we have not considered real-time processing aspects and the complications arising from limitations of short-term memory. A comprehender cannot hold in an active state arbitrarily large structures and hence information from the text that is needed for establishing coherence or for inferencing may be unavailable. These processing limitations have important consequences for how people deal with discourse, for example, with respect to readability (Kintsch & Vipond, 1979), or memory (Kintsch & van Dijk, 1978; Miller & Kintsch, 1980).

Another aspect neglected here concerns the situation model. With minitexts out of context, as in our sample analyses here, this aspect of text comprehension remains relatively insignificant. In general, however, it is important to distinguish text representations proper from representations of situations constructed (fully or partially) on the basis of that text.

When using the model presented here as a tool for studying some aspect of text processing, it is not always advisable to work with its most complex version. It may be more effective to simplify one or the other components of the model. Thus, if for instance we were concerned with memory for discourse at various age levels, comparing an adult group with younger or older people, we do not have to deal with all the complexities of the model concerning knowledge use, and it might be preferable to employ the simpler Kintsch and van Dijk (1978) version of the model. On the other hand, if we are specifically interested in questions of knowledge use, that version would be quite inadequate for our purposes.

Although the model discussed here has received some empirical support in several of the studies cited above, it would of course be premature to consider it a safely established theory. Much work remains in testing it against alternatives and in extending its scope to include some of the processing components that are neglected at present (often because they extend greatly beyond problems of text comprehension per se, such as the questions connected with knowledge representations and retrieval and those of inference). However, for all its tentativeness and incompleteness, the present model provides at least one explicit and comprehensive account of comprehension processes and a framework for research in this field.

REFERENCES

Kintsch, W. La comprehension des textes. (1982a). In J. F. LeNy & W. Kintsch (Eds.), *Langage et comprehension* (pp. 777–787). Paris: Bulletin de Psychologie, Special Annuel.

Kintsch, W. Aspects of text comprehension. (1982b). In J. F. LeNy & W. Kintsch (Eds.), *Language and comprehension* (pp. 301–312). Amsterdam: North-Holland.

Kintsch, W., & van Dijk, T. A. (1978). Toward a model of text comprehension and production. *Psychological Review, 85,* 363–394.

Kintsch, W., & Vipond, D. (1979). Reading comprehension and readability in educational practice and psychological theory. In L. G. Nilsson (Ed.), *Perspectives on memory research* (pp. 329–365). Hillsdale, NJ: Erlbaum.

Miller, J. R., & Kintsch, W. (1980). Readability and recall of short prose passages: A theoretical analysis. *Journal of Experimental Psychology: Human Learning and Memory, 6,* 335–354.

van Dijk, T. A., & Kintsch, W. (1983). *Strategies of discourse comprehension.* New York: Academic Press.

CHAPTER 13

Extracting the Proof from the Pudding: Coding and Analyzing Experimental Protocols

Nancy S. Johnson

The present chapter illustrates techniques used to compare the content and organization of a verbal protocol (e.g., a subject's recall of a story) with a standard of some kind (e.g., the presented text of the story). In psychological investigations, such comparisons are undertaken to determine how processes such as recall, summarization, and comprehension are influenced by differences among subject groups (e.g., differences in age or schooling), experimental conditions (e.g.,whether a text is presented once or twice before recall), and materials (e.g., whether the events in a story are presented in an expected or unusual order). For present purposes, I focus on protocols involving recall or summarization of traditional stories such as folktales and fables, but most of the issues considered here can be extended to other types of discourse and to other tasks (e.g., generating novel texts).

UNITS OF ANALYSIS IN CODING PROTOCOLS

One of the most basic decisions in developing a coding system for analyzing protocols involves dividing the original text into units. For example, to determine how accurately a subject has recalled the following story, one would typically divide the text of the story into units of some sort and then ask questions such as How many of the units are represented in the protocol?, Are they correctly sequenced?

Because subjects rarely reproduce the exact wording of a text, protocol

HANDBOOK OF DISCOURSE ANALYSIS, Vol. 2
Dimensions of Discourse
Copyright © 1985 by Academic Press London.
All rights of reproduction in any form reserved.
ISBN 0-12-712002-5

Story
    Setting-1: . . . .   *Once upon a time a hen and rooster lived together in the barnyard.*
  Episode
    Beginning-2: . . . .   *One day while they were eating their breakfast, the rooster began to choke on some corn.*
    Development
      Development
        Complex Reaction
          Simple Reaction-3:   *The hen felt sorry for him*
          Goal-4: . . . .   *and decided to get someone to take the corn out of his throat.*
      Goal Path
        Attempt-5: . . . .   *The hen ran to the farmer's wife and said, "Please come and help the rooster."*
        Outcome-6: . . . .   *The farmer's wife answered, "I'm too busy. You'll have to find someone else."*
    Development
      Complex Reaction
        Simple Reaction-7:   (Not expressed)
        Goal-8: . . . .   (Not expressed)
      Goal Path
        Attempt-9: . . . .   *The hen ran to the cow and said, "The rooster needs your help."*
        Outcome-10: . . . . . .   *The cow replied, "I can't come right now. I'm feeding my calf."*
    Development
      Complex Reaction
        Simple Reaction-11:   (Not expressed)
        Goal-12: . . . .   (Not expressed)
      Goal Path
        Attempt-13: . . . .   *The hen ran to the farmer and said, "Won't you please come and help the rooster?"*
        Outcome-14: . . . . . .   *The farmer ran to the rooster and took the piece of corn out of his throat.*
    Ending-15: . . . .   *The rooster thanked the farmer politely. Then the hen and the rooster finished eating their corn.*

analyses in psychology have rarely been based on syntactic units such as words or sentences. Instead, units have been specified by obtaining metalinguistic judgments from naive subjects or by using some sort of theoretically based rule system. When metalinguistic judgments are used, subjects other than those who are to recall or summarize the text are asked to divide the text into idea units; boundaries that are agreed upon by a majority of subjects determine the units to be used in coding (e.g., Brown & Smiley, 1977; Johnson, 1970).

At present, two types of rule-based systems are commonly used. In one, the text is divided into propositions, each of which includes a predicate (e.g., a verb or adjective) and its arguments (Frederiksen, 1975; Kintsch, 1974; Meyer, 1975). In the other, a system for characterizing the higher-order structure of a text is used to divide the text into labeled constituents, each of which may contain more or less than one proposition. This type of system, which is discussed further in the following section, is illustrated in the story display on p. 246 (See also Meyer, 1975; Rumelhart, 1975, 1977; Stein & Glenn, 1979; Thorndyke, 1977; van Dijk & Kintsch, 1977).

To some extent, the choice of units depends on the nature of one's investigation. However, rule-based systems that characterize the higher-order structure of a text often offer a more precise characterization than approaches based on either propositional or subject-determined units. (One can sometimes combine a characterization of higher-order units with either propositional or subject-determined units.) Also, use of the rule-based systems is generally less time-consuming than use of subject-determined units.

CODING PROTOCOLS: EXAMPLES OF "HOW TO DO IT"

The Model of Story Structure To Be Used

In this section of the chapter, I present a coding system based on the model of story structure developed by Johnson and Mandler (1980; Mandler & Johnson, 1977). The model characterizes the underlying structure of stories from the oral tradition in terms of rewrite rules that specify the required constituents of such stories and the causal or temporal relations between constituents. A simplified representation of the underlying structure of the Hen story, which is used to illustrate the coding system, is shown above. The terminal elements (Setting, Beginning, etc.) are the ones most frequently used as coding units; these elements are instantiated in a particular story by specific states and events, which are typically expressed as sentences or parts of sentences in the surface structure of a story.

The story begins with a Setting, which introduces the protagonist (the hen) and the location. The rest of the story consists of a single Episode. The Episode includes a Beginning, in which an initial event happens to the protagonist, a Development, which describes the protagonist's internal and external responses to the Beginning, and an Ending, which concludes the Episode by stating the final response of the protagonist or other characters or by emphasizing long-range consequences of the Development. The Development is the most complex constituent in a one-episode story; in the Hen story the highest-level Development subsumes three subordinate Developments, each of which consists of a Complex Reaction and a Goal Path. The Complex Reaction includes both a Simple Reaction, the protagonist's thoughts or feelings about the Beginning or preceding Development, and a Goal. The Goal Path includes both an Attempt to achieve the Goal and the Outcome of that Attempt. The Complex Reactions in the second and third Developments are not expressed in the surface structure of the story because their general nature can be inferred. A more complete presentation of this model of story structure can be found in papers by Johnson and Mandler (1980; Mandler & Johnson, 1977).

Coding Recall and Summary Protocols

To illustrate specific coding techniques that can be used to characterize similarities and differences among protocols, I have selected excerpts from four protocols based on the Hen story; these excerpts are presented in Tables 13.1–13.4. Subject A (a 12-year-old) recalled the story, and Subjects B (another 12-year-old) and C (an adult) produced two summaries that varied in length. (For Subject C, only the longer summary is presented.)

Table 13.1

Coding of Recall of a 12-Year-Old Child (Subject A)

Setting-1: QS = 1. RT = None.
  (1) Once upon a time there was a hen and a rooster (2) who lived together in a barnyard.
Beginning-2: QS = 1. RT = None.
  (3) And they were eating their breakfast one morning. (4) And a piece of corn got caught in the rooster's throat. (5) And he started to choke.
Simple Reaction-3: QS = 1. RT = None.
  (6) And then the hen felt sorry for the rooster.
Attempt-5: QS = 3. RT = None.
  (7) And she ran to the farmer's wife.
Goal-4: QS = 2. RT = Generalization.
  (8) to get help.
Outcome-6: QS = 1. RT = None.
  (9) And the farmer's wife said, "I'm too busy. (10) You'll have to find someone else."

Remaining nodes represented in protocol (In order of output):
  Attempt-9, Outcome-10, Attempt-13, Outcome-14, Ending-15.

Length of excerpt = 74 words; total length of protocol = 156 words.

Table 13.2

Coding of Longer Summary of a 12-Year-Old Child (Subject B)

Beginning-2: $QS = 1$. RT = None.
   (1) This one time a hen and a rooster was eating breakfast. (2) And
      the rooster got a piece of corn caught in his throat.
Attempt-5: $QS = 1$. RT = None.
   (3) So the hen went to the farmer's wife (4) and asked if she could
      come out (5) and help.
Outcome-6: $QS = 2$. RT = Generalization, Anaphoric textual reference.
   (6) But she said she couldn't.
Remaining nodes represented in protocol (In order of output):
   Attempt-9, Outcome-10, Attempt-13, Outcome-14, Ending-15.
Length of Excerpt = 45 words; total length of protocol = 100 words.

Each excerpt includes the statements (numbered from 1 to 10, 6, 4, and 8 in Tables 13.1, 13.2, 13.3, and 13.4, respectively) from the beginning of the protocol through the first Attempt and Outcome; in two of the summaries, these statements also represent subsequent nodes, because the subjects have combined nodes from different parts of the story. A statement was defined as a surface-structure phrase or clause that contained one main verb and its arguments. For a small subclass of verbs (e.g., *want, decide, say, ask, start, try*) that take sentential arguments, both the matrix statement and its argument were considered to be a single statement. The tables show the assignment of statements to terminal nodes and the quality score and relevant transformations for each node (see below).

Table 13.3

Coding of Shorter Summary of a 12-Year-Old Child (Subject B)

Beginning-2: $QS = 1$. RT = None.
   (1) The hen and the rooster were eating their breakfast. (2) And the rooster got a
      piece of corn caught in his throat.
Attempt-5, + Attempt-9: $QS = 3$ (both nodes). RT = Combination (both nodes).
   (3) So she went to the farmer's wife, the cow.
Outcome-6 + Outcome-10: $QS = 3$ (both nodes). RT = Combination (both
nodes),   Generalization (Outcome-6), Anaphoric textual reference (both nodes).
   (4) But they both said they couldn't.
Remaining nodes represented in protocol (In order of output):
   Attempt-13, Outcome-14.
Length of excerpt = 36 words; total length of protocol = 63 words.

Table 13.4

Coding of Longer Summary of an Adult (Subject C)

Setting-1: *QS* = 1. RT = None.

(1) There were a hen and a rooster (2) that lived together in a barnyard.

Beginning-2: *QS* = 2. RT = None.

(3) One day the rooster ate some corn. (4) And he got choked on it.

*a*Attempt-5 + Attempt-9 + Attempt-13: *QS* = 3 (all nodes). RT = Combination (all nodes), Generalization (all nodes).

(5) And the hen was running around to all the people on the farm

*a*Goal-4 + Attempt-5 + Goal-8 + Attempt-9 + Goal-12 + Attempt-13: *QS* = 2 (all nodes). RT = Combination (all nodes), Generalization (all nodes).

(6) trying to get help and cooperation.

*a*Goal-4 + Goal-8 + Goal-12: *QS* = 2 (all nodes). RT = Combination (all nodes), Generalization (all nodes).

(7) to help this rooster.

Outcome-6 + Outcome-10 + Outcome-14: *QS* = 2. RT = Combination (all nodes), Generalization (all nodes).

(8) But only one person would help the rooster.

Remaining nodes represented in protocol (In order of output):

Outcome-14 (repeated), Ending-15.

Length of excerpt = 57 words; Total length of protocol = 83 words.

---

*a*A node represented in two or more nonadjacent statements or in statements involving different transformations is assigned an individual quality score for each representation and an overall quality score. Attempts-5, -9, and -13 and Goals-4, -8, and -12 would be assigned an overall quality score of 2.

Presence of Nodes and Quality of Representation

One of the most commonly used measures in studies of recall or summarization is the total number of adequately represented units ('terminal nodes' in the present case) in each protocol, that is, the number of units from the original text whose main idea is represented. It is, however, often informative to differentiate between adequately represented, inadequately represented, and absent units (Mandler, 1978); we have made an additional distinction within the set of adequately represented units, based on whether or not subjects include detailed information (see Mandel & Johnson, 1984; Johnson, 1983). Thus for each terminal node in the original text, we decide before coding the protocols what information has to be present to assign a quality score (*QS*) of 1 (main point plus details), 2 (main point without details), 3 (inadequate representation of main point), or "absent." For example, Attempt-5 is assigned a *QS* of 1 in Table 13.2 because both the preaction (going to the farmer's wife) and the main action (asking for help) are represented; it is assigned a 2 in Table 13.4 because detailed information about where the hen went and the specific nature of the main action have been omitted; and it is assigned a 3 in Tables 13.1 and 13.3 because only the preaction has been stated. Outcome-6 is represented adequately with detail in Table 13.1, adequately without detail in Tables 13.2 and 13.4, and inadequately in Table 13.3 (because the elliptical statement *But they both said they couldn't* has no referent and hence is incoherent).

Reasonable Additions and Distortions

In addition to paraphrasing, deleting, and condensing information from the presented text, subjects sometimes add new statements or change the meaning of presented propositions. Following earlier work by Mandler (1978), we have divided such changes into two broad classes, reasonable additions and distortions. Reasonable additions include new material that is consistent with the presented text (e.g., presuppositions and plausible inferences). For example, the statement *The farmer didn't want the rooster to die* (added after Attempt-13) would be coded as a reasonable addition. Distortions are changes (including additions) that are irrelevant to or inconsistent with the presented material (e.g., replacing Ending-15 with the statements *But it was too late. The rooster had choked to death.*) More complete discussions of these types of changes and their relation to the organization of a story can be found in papers by Mandler (1978) and Mandel and Johnson (1984).

Condensing Information:
Transformations that Occur in Summaries

Subjects who are explicitly asked to summarize stories are more likely both to delete presented information and to condense the information that they do represent than subjects who are asked to recall stories (Johnson, 1983). Representative differences in methods used to condense information in recall and summary protocols can be seen by comparing Table 13.1 with Tables 13.2–13.4; for each node, the presence or absence of three types of relevant transformations (*RT*)—generalizations, anaphoric textual references, and combinations—is indicated.

Generalizations. Generalizations are transformations in which references to specific objects, states, or events are replaced with a more general statement (e.g., compare the original text of the story with the representation of Goal-4 in Table 13.1, Outcome-6 in Table 13.2, and the Goals, Attempts, and Outcomes in Table 13.4). Although deleting information from a statement often makes it more general, we have credited subjects with a generalization only when their statement substitutes a new, more general item for the information in the original text; thus, *they both said they couldn't* (statement 4 in Table 13.3) is coded as a generalization of Outcome-6 but not of Outcome-10.

Anaphoric Textual References. Anaphoric textual references take three forms: conventional grammatical ellipsis (compare Outcome-6 in Table 13.2 and Outcomes-6 and -10 in Table 13.3), "same" references, and pro form substitutions. In the latter two cases, subjects fill in the blank left by grammatical ellipsis, either with the phrase *the same thing* or with a pronoun or pro verb.

Subject B used grammatical ellipsis extensively in his longer summary (Table 13.2); Outcome-6, Attempt-9, Outcome-10, and Attempt-13 were represented by saying: *But she said she couldn't. So she ran to the cow and asked if she could. But she couldn't. So then she ran to the farmer and asked if he could.* Attempts-9 and -13 could have been represented by same references (e.g., *The hen asked the cow the same thing.*). The use of textual pro forms in summaries of this particular story was infrequent; an example would be representing Outcome-14 by saying *And so the farmer did that.*

Combinations of Separate Units. Subjects also condense by combining information from separate nodes into a single statement. Examples of such combinations can be seen in Tables 13.3 (statements 3 and 4) and 13.4 (statements 5–8). In coding combinations, one has to decide on the type of unit to be considered and the criterion to be used in deciding whether or not two originally distinct units have, in fact, been combined. In our work (Johnson, 1983) we have focused on combinations of information from separate nodes and have required that the information be expressed within a single statement (as defined above). A less stringent criterion would be to examine the nodes represented within a single matrix sentence, excluding sentences conjoined by *and, so, but,* and so on. Using the latter criterion, statements 7 and 8 of Table 13.1 would be coded as a combination of Attempt-5 and Goal-4; and statements 5–7 of Table 13.4 would be coded as a combination of Goals-4, -8, and -12 and Attempts-5, -9, and -13. (The other combinations in Tables 13.3 and 13.4 would be coded as before.)

Order of Output

Once statements in a protocol are identified as representations of particular units, the order of units in the protocol and in the presented text can be compared. Two general techniques have been used in the existing literature. One is simply to count the number of units in a protocol that are displaced (i.e., out of order) relative to their order in the original text (Mandel & Johnson, 1984; Johnson, 1983; Mandler, 1978; Mandler & Johnson, 1977). In using this technique, we have determined the minimum number of terminal nodes in the protocol that would have to be moved to reestablish the input order; by this criterion, Tables 13.1, 13.2, 13.3, and 13.4 contain one, zero, one, and eight displacements, respectively. Because the number of displacements depends, in part, on the number of units represented, displacement scores are usually expressed as a percentage of the total number of units represented.

The other technique involves computing the rank-order correlation (e.g., Kendall's *tau*—see Siegel, 1956) between the order of nodes in the text and their order in the protocol. The correlational measure, however, depends on both the magnitude and number of displacements. For example, the sequence Setting–Beginning–Attempt–Ending–Outcome would be more closely correlated with the input order Setting–Beginning–Attempt–Out-come–Ending (*tau* = .80) than would the sequence Setting–Ending–Beginning–Attempt–Outcome (*tau* = .40), even though the input order can be restored in both cases by moving the Ending.

Coding Generation Protocols

The preceding section dealt with protocols in which subjects have recalled or summarized a previously presented story. Similar approaches can be used when subjects generate novel stories. For example, one can code the presence or absence of terminal nodes, the extent to which the order of nodes matches the order predicted by a given model of story structure, and at least some methods of representation (e.g., anaphoric textual referents and the use of combinations). If, however, subjects either have difficulty generating their own stories or have a definition of a "story" that differs from the one underlying the model used to develop the coding system, some protocols may be difficult to characterize. In such cases, one can often modify the coding system to describe what the subjects are doing, rather than simply reporting that some percentage of all protocols or statements could not be accounted for. Examples of such alternative characterizations and more detailed discussions of techniques used to describe generated stories can be found in papers by Stein and Glen (1982) and Whaley (1981).

Analyses Based on Coded Protocols

Verbal protocols are amenable to a variety of types of analysis. Perhaps the most frequent is a comparison of the average number of occurrences of a given type of response as a function of differences among subject

groups, experimental conditions, or materials. Representative examples
of analyses based on the measures discussed above (presence of nodes,
displacements, etc.) can be found in papers by Mandel and Johnson
(1984), Johnson (1983), Mandler (1978), Mandler and Johnson (1977), and
Stein and Glenn (1979). These papers also illustrate analyses that assess
similarity in patterns of recall, comprehension, and summarization, for
example, whether different subjects tend to recall the same type of information from a story.

MISCELLANEOUS PRACTICAL ISSUES

Deciding What To Code in a Given Study

Although a number of different types of coding were discussed above,
the problem remains of deciding how to set up a coding system for any
particular study. To some extent, this set of decisions has to be made
each time one conducts a study, because the response measures that are
likely to be interesting or appropriate depend on the subjects, procedures,
and materials to be used. There are, however, some general factors that
can be considered. One is whether or not guidelines about what to code
can be derived on the basis of existing work. If such guidelines exist,
many decisions about coding can be made before the data are collected.
In the absence of guidelines or in cases where the subjects' responses
fall outside the a priori classifications, coding categories must be developed
on a post hoc basis.

A second general consideration is the amount of information to be
preserved in the coding. There are two aspects of "informativeness" to
consider. One is whether to attempt to account for each statement in a
protocol versus coding only selected portions or aspects of the protocols.
The other is the degree of detail to be represented within the coding
categories, given a decision about what to code.

Information, like virtue, is its own reward. In general, it is probably
better to code each protocol as completely as possible, maintaining whatever
distinctions seem likely to be interesting. Comprehensive, detailed coding
is particularly important during the initial phase of a research program,
because it is sometimes difficult to predict where a given effect will
appear (e.g., in the number of units recalled versus the number correctly
sequenced) and to estimate its magnitude (if the coding is too crude, one
may not detect differences that exist). On the other hand, the more
aspects of a protocol one codes and the finer the categorizations, the
more difficult and time-consuming the coding itself becomes. Also, if
too many categories are used relative to the number of statements to be

coded, the number of occurrences of each category may be too small to permit trends in the data to be observed.

Determining the Reliability of Coding

Many coding decisions depend on subjective judgments, for example, deciding that a given statement in a recall protocol represents a given node from a story. The degree to which such coding decisions are free from errors attributable to idiosyncratic judgments can be estimated by obtaining a measure of inter-rater reliability. The general process involves having more than one rater (usually two) code a set of protocols and then determining the extent to which they agree.

Although a complete discussion of reliability is beyond the scope of this chapter (for more information see Kerlinger, 1973; Mitchell, 1979; and Nunnally, 1967), the following points should be noted.

1. Low inter-rater reliability may reflect inadequate definition of the coding categories, inadequate training of one or both coders, or too small a number of occurrences of the category to be coded (in which case the reliability estimate itself may be inaccurate).
2. Before coding an entire set of protocols, one should determine the reliability of coding for a subset to insure that the categories are adequately defined and the coders adequately trained. Subsequently, one rater can code the entire set, two raters can each code half of the set, or both raters can independently code the entire set. The third option is unnecessarily time-consuming if the initial estimate of reliability is high. In all three cases, reliability should be assessed again when the coding is completed (on a randomly chosen but representative subset of protocols) to be sure that it is still adequate.
3. If a set of related categories is unreliably coded because the raters have difficulty making distinctions within the set, the categories can be combined.

Improving the Accuracy of Coding

To increase the accuracy of coding, one should minimize both unsystematic errors in use of the coding system and systematic errors attributable to experimenter expectations and changes over time in the experience of the coders (Christensen, 1980). The following suggestions are intended to reduce one or both sources of error:

1. The coding categories should be defined as clearly as possible, given the nature of the decision to be made. (But see Kerlinger, 1973, for a discussion of the hazards of excess operationalism.)

2. The coders should be thoroughly familiar with the definitions of the categories and should be aware of the range of responses that are acceptable exemplars of a given category.
3. Coding errors that result from a failure to notice a given type of response (e.g., an anaphoric textual reference) can be reduced by using standardized coding sheets, which indicate the decisions to be made about the correspondence between each unit in a text and its representation in a protocol. Also, if there are many coding decisions to be made, it is helpful to go through the protocols more than once, for example, to code the presence and quality of nodes before coding temporal displacements.
4. The influence of experimenter expectations (e.g., expecting children to recall less than adults) can be minimized by using naive raters who are unaware of the purpose and nature of the study and by concealing information about the condition or subject group a given protocol represents. Using naive raters is often difficult, both because it can be hard to find people who are willing to code protocols without knowing why they are doing so and because truly naive raters may not be sophisticated enough to make some types of coding decisions. It is, however, almost always possible to remove explicit identifying information before protocols are coded. When the differences between groups are extreme, as is the case when six-year-olds' summaries are compared with those of adults, removing explicit identifiers is unlikely to make much difference; but it is should reduce the influence of experimenter expectations when the groups are similar.
5. To minimize the possibility that changes over time in coding criteria (e.g., becoming stricter) will influence one group of protocols more than another, protocols should be coded in a random or counter-balanced order.
6. It is helpful to keep track of when each protocol is coded and to maintain a list of problematic coding decisions. If enough instances of a problem occur, it sometimes becomes apparent that the coding system should be modified. When such changes are made, one can note that protocols coded before the date of the change need to be reviewed.

REFERENCES

Brown, A. L., & Smiley, S. S. (1977). Rating the importance of structural units of prose passages: A problem of metacognitive development. *Child Development, 48,* 1–8.
Christensen, L. B. (1980). *Experimental methodology* (2nd ed.). Boston: Allyn & Bacon.

Frederiksen, C. H. (1975). Representing logical and semantic structure of knowledge acquired from discourse. *Cognitive Psychology, 7,* 371–458.

Johnson, N. S. (1983). What do you do if you can't tell the whole story? The development of summarization skills. In K. E. Nelson (Ed.), *Children's language* (Vol. 4) (pp. 315–383). Hillsdale, NJ: Erlbaum.

Johnson, N. S., & Mandler, J. M. (1980). A tale of two structures: Underlying and surface forms in stories. *Poetics, 9,* 51–86.

Johnson, R. E. (1970). Recall of prose as a function of the structural importance of the linguistic units. *Journal of Verbal Learning & Verbal Behavior, 9,* 12–20.

Kerlinger, F. N. (1973). *Foundations of behavioral research* (2nd ed.). New York: Holt, Rinehart, & Winston.

Kintsch, W. (1974). *The representation of meaning in memory.* Hillsdale, NJ: Erlbaum.

Mandel, R. G., & Johnson, N. S. (1984). A developmental analysis of story recall and comprehension in adulthood. *Journal of Verbal Learning & Verbal Behavior, 23,* 643–659.

Mandler, J. M. (1978). A code in the node: The use of a story schema in retrieval. *Discourse Processes, 1,* 14–35.

Mandler, J. M., & Johnson, N. S. (1977). Remembrance of things parsed: Story structure and recall. *Cognitive Psychology, 9,* 111–151.

Meyer, B. J. F. (1975). Identification of the structure of prose and its implications for the study of reading and memory. *Journal of Reading Behavior, 7,* 7–47.

Mitchell, S. K. (1979). Interobserver agreement, reliability, and generalizability of data collected in observational studies. *Psychological Bulletin, 86,* 376–390.

Nunnally, J. C. (1967). *Psychometric theory.* New York: McGraw-Hill.

Rumelhart, D. E. (1975). Notes on a schema for stories. In D. G. Bobrow & A. Collins (Eds.), *Representation and understanding: Studies in cognitive science* (pp. 211–236). New York: Academic Press.

Rumelhart, D. E. (1977). Understanding and summarizing brief stories. In D. LaBerge & S. J. Samuels (Eds.), *Basic processes in reading: Perception and comprehension* (pp. 265–303). Hillsdale, NJ: Erlbaum.

Siegel, S. (1956). *Nonparametric statistics for the behavioral sciences.* New York: McGraw-Hill.

Stein, N. L., & Glenn, C. G. (1979). An analysis of story comprehension in elementary school children. In R. O. Freedle (Ed.), *New directions in discourse processing* (Vol. 2) (pp. 53–120). Norwood, NJ: Ablex.

Stein, N. L., & Glenn, C. G. (1982). Children's concept of time: The development of a story schema. In W. J. Friedman (Ed.), *The developmental psychology of time* (pp. 255–282). New York: Academic Press.

Thorndyke, P. W. (1977). Cognitive structures in human story comprehension and memory. *Cognitive Psychology, 9,* 77–110.

van Dijk, T. A., & Kintsch, W. (1977). Cognitive psychology and discourse: Recalling and summarizing stories. In W. U. Dressler (Ed.), *Current trends in textlinguistics* (pp. 61–80). Berlin/New York: de Gruyter.

Whaley, J. F. (1981). Readers' expectations for story structures. *Reading Research Quarterly, 17,* 90–114.

CHAPTER **14**

Protocol Analysis

K. Anders Ericsson and Herbert A. Simon

INTRODUCTION

The terms 'verbal reports' and 'verbal protocols' are used almost interchangeably to refer to human subjects' verbalizations of their thoughts and successive behaviors while they are performing cognitive tasks. The protocols may be taken concurrently with the task performance or retrospectively. After an early period in which psychologists made heavy use of verbal protocols, they fell into disrepute during the era of behaviorism; but they have been revived since the 1970s as a major source of data for cognitive research.

In the course of this history, protocols have been used for widely varying purposes and have been gathered and interpreted according to quite different methodologies. In the earlier period, they were a mainstay of classical introspection (Titchener, 1912), the analysis of problem solving by Wuerzburg and Gestalt psychologists (Duncker, 1945; Selz, 1913, 1922; Wertheimer, 1945), clinical analyses of thought (Freud, 1914), and analyses of the development of children's thinking (Inhelder & Piaget, 1958). In the recent resurgence of their use (Newell, Shaw, & Simon, 1958; Newell & Simon, 1972), they have been employed within an information-processing framework, chiefly in the study of problem solving.

With the growing use of protocol data in psychology, it has become important to improve the methodology for collecting and interpreting protocols and to provide protocol analysis with a firm theoretical foundation. The early investigators uncritically regarded the verbal reports by trained subjects of their cognitive processes as direct observations of those processes, veridical and uncontroversial. There was lacking a theory of the cognitive processes generating such reports, as well as a theory of the

HANDBOOK OF DISCOURSE ANALYSIS, Vol. 2
Dimensions of Discourse

Copyright © 1985 by Academic Press London.
All rights of reproduction in any form reserved.
ISBN 0-12-712002-5

interpretive processes of the experimenter. When, as a result of these
deficiencies, verbal reports collected in different laboratories were found
to be mutually inconsistent, opponents of the introspective method, like
Watson, argued that the method was unscientific and should be discarded.
Only a sound empirically based theory of verbalization processes can
meet such objections.

To see what is involved in interpreting protocols, let us look at two
examples of verbal reports about the use of subgoals in solving a problem.

(1)   a.   Experimenter: Did you use X as a subgoal in solving this
                           problem?
           Subject: Yes

      b.   Experimenter: Tell me everything you can remember
                           thinking about while solving this problem.
           Subject: . . . I was first trying to get X and I . . .
                           when I attained X . . .

In (1a), we must trust the subject, because the report could have been
generated by guessing, making use of the demand characteristics of the
question. However in (1b), we must account for the fact that the subject
reported using a subgoal, and that this subgoal was X.

In many instances, an analysis of the task (Newell & Simon, 1972)
provides independent evidence that the verbalized information is or is
not relevant to the ongoing solution process, especially when the subject
makes a specific statement, like the mention of a subgoal, where there
are a large number of alternative logically possible responses. Veridicality
of protocol data can sometimes be demonstrated by showing that the
cognitive processes relevant to the verbal reports are the same as those
inferred from other kinds of data, like latencies, eye movements, and
so on. Further confidence can be placed in the verbal reports if they do
not violate memory limitations or known limitations on the information
available to the subject.

A MODEL FOR THE GENERATION
OF VERBAL REPORTS

With the help of information-processing theories of cognition, a model
can be constructed of the verbal reporting process that is consistent with
the data and that allows both the verbal protocol and the thought processes
that generate it to be viewed within the same framework of theory. In
its most general and abstract form, information-processing theory (Anderson
& Bower, 1973; Newell & Simon, 1972; Simon, 1979) postulates that

a cognitive process can be seen as a sequence of internal states successively transformed by a series of information processes. Moreover, each of these successive states can be described, in large part, in terms of the small number of information structures, or chunks, that are attended to or are available in the limited-capacity short-term-memory store (STM). Although information processes may also access information from the vast permanent memory (LTM) and sensory memories with brief duration, the result of such access processes is to make the information available in STM.

Within this theoretical framework, the basic assumption that underlies the interpretation of verbal protocols is that only information that is heeded, as the result of being brought into STM by the ongoing cognitive processes, can be processed further and verbalized directly. This assumption has some important implications for (1) the kinds of instructions to subjects that produce verbalizations revelatory of their cognitive processes, and (2) the kinds of methods that are effective for analyzing and interpreting the recorded verbalizations.

INSTRUCTIONS FOR VERBAL REPORTS

If we accept the model that has just been sketched, the ideal instruction for gaining information about subjects' information processes is to ask them to "think aloud" while they are working on a task. Under this instruction, subjects verbalize their thoughts as these enter consciousness, that is, when they are first heeded. Hence, the subjects are able to follow their normal sequences of thoughts and concurrently verbalize them. If the thoughts are already encoded in verbal form, they can be vocalized directly (e.g., thoughts during mental multiplication or rote rehearsal of words). If they are encoded in nonverbal form, they must be recoded verbally before they are reported aloud.

In a review of studies comparing subjects thinking aloud with subjects performing the same tasks silently, we found no differences in such measures of cognitive processes as success rate, methods employed, or speed of performance, except that in tasks where subjects used nonverbal codes in their thinking (e.g., tasks with a large visual perceptual component), performance was slowed down somewhat in the verbalizing condition (Ericsson & Simon, 1979, 1980, 1984).

The information-processing model also predicts that subjects will be able to report their thought sequences verbally just after a task has been completed. To generate such retrospective verbal reports, subjects use cues in STM to retrieve from LTM memory traces of the previously heeded thoughts. From our review of the literature, we conclude that subjects are able to recall accurately their retrospective thoughts for cognitive processes of relatively short duration if the report is generated immediately ater the task has been completed.

In both of these kinds of verbal reporting, subjects are instructed to verbalize their thoughts as they emerge, without trying to explain, analyze, or interpret those thoughts. The experimenter, not the subject, is the theoretician who seeks to explain the sequential process of thought. In our recent review, we studied a wide range of different instructions that have been used to elicit verbal reports, seeking to identify what cognitive processes would be needed for a subject to generate reports of reasons and motives for actions or reports of general strategies.

Often, when such information is requested from subjects, their verbal reports are inconsistent with other observed behavior. For example, some cognitive processes, like those used to recognize familiar words or objects, do not use STM for intermediate steps of recognition, but only for the final recognized object. If forced to give reasons for their recognition of a particular stimulus, subjects, lacking direct knowledge of the actual retrieval cues simply speculate and make the same kinds of inferences about the cues that observers would make (Nisbett & Wilson, 1977).

Subjects are sometimes asked to describe what they are doing in experiments extending over hundreds of trials. Since they cannot recall, under these circumstances, their thought processes in each trial, they often generalize from individual instances that they do recall. From simple analysis of the relation between the instructions for verbalization and the circumstances of the task behavior, strong inferences can often be drawn from the theory as to the veridicality of the reports. In particular, we find substantial empirical evidence for the validity of the contents of "thinking aloud" reports and immediate retrospective reports and no empirical evidence that these kinds of reports fail to reflect what the subject is actually heeding or has just heeded.

CONTENTS OF VERBAL REPORTS

According to the information-processing model, subjects, when they give concurrent verbal reports, generate overt verbalizations that correspond to the familiar information units (chunks) held in STM. From a careful analysis of the task given to subjects (Newell & Simon, 1972), it is usually possible to determine what kinds of information naive subjects must attend to in order to generate correct responses or solutions. This is the same information that a computer simulation model must access in order to find the solutions. The particular manner in which this information is organized and represented by subjects in a given task environment is to be determined by analyzing their thinking-aloud or retrospective protocols. Task analyses, and corresponding analyses of human protocols, have already been carried out for a considerable number of tasks, explicating the representations used by subjects in performing those tasks (see Ericsson & Simon, 1984 for references).

In the tasks that have been studied, most, but not all, naive subjects use essentially the same problem representations. This means that even before any protocols have been collected from subjects doing the task, the possible information units that subjects will attend to can be described. For purposes of protocol analysis, this description needs to be complete, in the sense of permitting all alternative hypotheses about the content and structure of subjects' thought processes to be described equally well.

There are two important reasons for prefacing protocol analysis with such an explicit description of possible encodings. First, it facilitates evaluating encoding reliability by making certain the different encoders will encode the same information from each protocol. Second, a great deal of contextual information about the task can be incorporated in the encoding categories. The encoder is only required to make a choice between well-defined categories and need not identify afresh the structures the subject is using. For example, in a concept-formation task, if a subject verbalizes the hypothesis 'big round things,' this hypothesis can be encoded immediately and unequivocally if it has already been determined by task analysis that the relevant variables are size (large, small) and shape (triangle, rectangle, square, circle).

For concurrent reports, the model assumes that as soon as some chunk is heeded it will be verbalized. On this interpretation, the verbalizations identify the inputs to information processes and the outputs produced by those processes—both heeded and held temporarily in STM. The smallest units of overt verbalizations, speech bursts corresponding to words or phrases consisting of a few chunks, are readily identified from tape recordings and can be encoded as the basic protocol segments for analysis. When information can be assumed to be held in STM in a verbal encoding, the speech bursts can be inferred to correspond directly with these STM structures. Examples might be the segments *6 times 4 is / 24,* two chunks uttered by a subject while performing a mental multiplication task and corresponding to the inputs and output, respectively, of an information process, or *6 2 4 / 9 4 5 7,* two chunks uttered during rehearsal of a digit string presented in a digit-span task.

On the other hand, when heeded information is not encoded verbally but must be transformed before it can be verbalized aloud, a heeded structure may correspond to several speech bursts, like *I want to protect the rook on / C4,* uttered by a subject while analyzing a chess position. Here converting an internal spatial reference into the verbal code "C4" very likely requires separate processing.

Verbalization of heeded thoughts appears to be a highly developed skill in adult subjects and to make small demands upon attention. Subjects often verbalize mental structures in very systematic and consistent ways. For example, subgoals are mostly verbalized with the future tense or a modal verb, as in *I must have the largest disk on the goal peg.* Actions that are being considered and plans are mostly reported in conditional form: *If I moved the eight then* . . . In Ericsson and Simon (1984), we discuss such regularities further and also review empirical evidence for the (apparently correct) hypothesis that verbalizations are sequential, produced in the same order as that in which the information must have been heeded.

EXAMPLES OF PROTOCOL ANALYSIS

We describe here briefly the analysis of two sets of protocols, selected from two rather different tasks: mental multiplication and anagrams. Since these tasks are familiar to most readers, they require little introduction. Furthermore, there is general consensus as to how the cognitive processes used in these tasks are to be described and what coding categories are appropriate.

There are some interesting differences in subject behaviors on the two tasks. Almost all subjects solve the mental multiplication problems in the same way, that is, they heed and verbalize the same sequences of information. In contrast, different subjects solving anagrams often heed and verbalize different information or the same information in different order. However, the kinds of information they heed and report are very similar and predictable.

Mental Multiplication

Subjects verbalize their thoughts readily while performing mental multiplications. They have received so much training and practice in arithmetic that the numbers and operations have uniform and readily accessible verbal labels. In multiplication, all the heeded inputs to processes beyond the first are also the outputs of previous processes. We can expect the verbal reports to include mainly mentions of numbers (*720*), and operations on numbers (*carry the 2,* or *144 plus 720*). In the encoding displayed below, we use standard mathematical notation except for the carry operation, which we code as C:. We show, side by side, a transcription of a segmented protocol and the corresponding encoding of each segment. Notice that in this example each segment can be encoded independently of its context and hence without the coder having access to the other parts of the protocol. Of course this is not true of protocols in all tasks.

Protocol	Encoding
36 times 24	36×24
um	
4 times 6 is 24	$4 \times 6 = 24$
4	4
carry the 2	C:2
4 times 3 is 12	$4 \times 3 = 12$
14	14
144	144
0	0
2 times 6 is 12	$2 \times 6 = 12$
2	2
carry the 1	C:1
2 times 3 is 6	$2 \times 3 = 6$
7	7
720	720
720	720
144 plus 720	$144 + 720$
so it would be 4	4
6	6
864	864

The encoding of this verbal protocol into data is simple and straightforward. With the encoding in hand, we can now account for the data by constructing a cognitive model of mental multiplication in the form of a computer program. The program, given the same task of multiplying 36 by 24, will then heed and verbalize exactly the same sequence of intermediate results and operations as the subject did. Of course, the construction of such a formal model and the comparison between its trace and the verbal protocol of the human subject is not always as simple as it is in this example.

Anagrams

In the anagram task, subjects are presented with a scrambled sequence of letters and asked to generate an English word using all the letters.

From previous published work reporting thinking-aloud protocols collected
for the anagram-solving task (Mayzner, Tresselt, & Helbock, 1964; Sargent,
1940), we know that subjects heed several different kinds of information
while solving these problems. Two types of information are especially
prominent in protocols.

First, subjects select likely combinations of letters (sequences that
occur frequently in English and use these as constraints for generating
longer strings or as probes to LTM to evoke words that contain those
combinations. We encode mentions of such combinations in the protocols
as C: L1–L2–. . .–L3 (Position), where C signifies Constraint, L1, L2,
L3 are letters, and Position refers to the beginning, middle, or end part
of the word.

Second, subjects generate alternative possible solution words. These
can derive from attempts to sound out letter combinations or can be
related words evoked from LTM. These possible solutions are encoded
as A: (spelling of word or combination of syllables), where A signifies
Alternative. Below, we give several short protocols of subjects solving
the anagram "npehpa." (The first two of these protocols are reproduced
from Sargent, 1940.)

Protocol 1	Encoding
N P, neph, neph	
Probably PH goes together	C:PH
Phan	A:phan
Phanny	A:phanny
I get phan-ep	A:phan-ep
No. Nap-	A:nap
Phep-an, no	A:phep-an
E is at the end	C:E(end)
Phap-en	A:phap-en
People, I think of	A:people
Try PH after the other letters	C:PH(end)
Naph, no	A:naph
I thought of paper again	A:paper
E and A sound alike	
couldn't go together without a consonant	
Try double P	C:PP
happy	A:happy
Happen	A:happen
Protocol 2	
Start with P	C:P(beginning)
No, it doesn't	
The two P's go together	C:PP
Happen	A:happen

Protocol 3	Encoding
All right	
Let's see	
NPEHPA	
Let's try what letters go together	
Do you want to tell me when I miss, okay	
PH go together	C:PH
but they're not very likely	
so how about APP	C:APP
got it	A:happen

Since these protocols depend heavily upon recognition processes and evocation of information from LTM, they are less informative than the mental-multiplication protocol about the intervening processes. A computer model could be programmed to produce qualitatively similar protocols, but it is impossible, in the absence of detailed knowledge of how subjects have information stored and indexed in LTM, to predict the sequence of events in any particular subject's thinking-aloud protocol. In spite of the use of common processes, different subjects arrive at the anagram solution along different routes.

SUMMARY

Verbal reports, especially concurrent thinking-aloud protocols, provide a valuable source of data about the sequence of events that occur while a human subject is solving a problem or performing some other cognitive task. By applying information-processing theory to the generation of such protocols, we are coming to understand just what information a subject will report in any given task situation and how that information can be encoded objectively and interpreted to throw light upon the subject's thought processes.

In general, protocols give relatively full information about the familiar chunks that a subject has heeded and stored temporarily in STM. Concurrent protocols and retrospective protocols obtained immediately after a task has been performed provide the most reliable information about processes. In general, instructions to think aloud do not interfere with subjects' thought processes, although they may slow them down somewhat if the subject is using a nonverbal code in his thinking.

In encoding data from protocols, a task analysis is usually performed first, to establish coding categories. It is frequently possible to infer models of the cognitive processes from the encoded data and to compare the predictions of these models with the behavior revealed in the protocols by using the techniques of computer simulation.

To build an adequate theory of a dynamic system like the human brain solving problems, observations must be made on that system at a temporal density commensurate with the speed of its processes. Although they are not fully adequate for catching the fine grain of thought processes, verbal protocols and recordings of eye movements have provided data at the highest densities we have as yet attained. For this reason, they have been and remain indispensable experimental tools in contemporary cognitive science.

REFERENCES

Anderson, J. R., & Bower, G. H. (1973). *Human associative memory.* Washington, DC: Winston.

Duncker, K. (1945). On problem solving [Entire issue]. *Psychological Monographs, 58*(5).

Ericsson, K. A., & Simon, H. A. (1979). *Thinking-aloud protocols as data: Effects of verbalization* (CIP Working Paper No. 397). Unpublished manuscript, Carnegie–Mellon University, Pittsburgh, PA.

Ericsson, K. A., & Simon, H. A. (1980). Verbal reports as data. *Psychological Review, 87,* 215–251.

Ericsson, K. A., & Simon, H. A. (1984). *Verbal reports as data.* Cambridge, MA: Bradford/ MIT Press.

Freud, S. (1914). *Psychopathology of everyday life.* New York: Macmillan.

Inhelder, B., & Piaget, J. (1958). *The growth of logical thinking from childhood to adolescense.* New York: Basic Books.

Mayzner, M. S., Tresselt, M. E., & Helbock, H. (1964). An exploratory study of mediational responses in anagram problem solving. *Journal of General Psychology, 57,* 263–274.

Newell, A., Shaw, J. C., & Simon, H. A. (1958). Elements of a theory of human problem solving. *Psychological Review, 65,* 151–166.

Newell, A., & Simon, H. A. (1972). *Human problem solving.* Englewood Cliffs, NJ: Prentice-Hall.

Nisbett, R. E., & Wilson, T. D. (1977). Telling more than we can know: Verbal reports on mental processes. *Psychological Review, 84,* 231–259.

Sargent, S. S. (1940). Thinking processes at various levels of difficulty. *Archives of Psychology, 249,* 5–58.

Selz, O. (1913). *Uber die Gesetze des geordneten Denkverlaufs.* Stuttgart: Spemann.

Selz, O. (1922). *Zur psychologie des productiven Denkens und des Irrtums.* Bonn: Friedrich Cohen.

Simon, H. A. (1979). *Models of thought.* New Haven: Yale University Press.

Titchener, E. B. (1912). The schema of introspection. *American Journal of Psychology, 23,* 485–508.

Wertheimer, M. (1945). *Productive thinking.* New York: Harper & Row.

Biographical Notes

DAVID BRAZIL is a Fellow of the Institute for Advanced Research in the Humanities and Birmingham University, where he has taught modern English language for the past ten years. Before that, he had extensive experience of other kinds of teaching, including a substantial period in teacher education. For three years at Birmingham he was engaged, as Senior Research Fellow, in a full-scale investigation of the significance of intonation on the structure of interactive discourse. Some of the results of this research have been published in his contributions to Birmingham ELR Monograph Series, of which the latest, *The Communicative Value of Intonation,* appeared in Autumn, 1984. In addition, he is coauthor of Brazil, Coulthard, and Johns, *Discourse Intonation and Language Teaching* and Sinclair and Brazil, *Teacher Talk,* and he has contributed substantially to Coulthard and Montgomery, *Studies in Discourse Analysis* and a number of international periodicals. He has lectured on intonation and other aspects of discourse analysis in many places in the United Kingdom and abroad.

WOLFGANG U. DRESSLER studied linguistics and classical philology in Vienna, Rome, and Paris. He has been a professor of linguistics at the University of Vienna since 1971 and has taught at various American universities. He was President of the Twelfth International Congress of Linguists, Vienna 1977; Vice-President of the Italian Linguistic Society, 1977–1979; Vice-President of the International Permanent Committee of Linguists, 1977–1982; corresponding member of the Austrian Academy of Sciences, since 1979; and President of the European Linguistic Society, 1980–1981. He is editor of *Folia Linguistica, Wiener linguistische Gazette, Wege der Textlinguistik,* and *Current Trends in Textlinguistics* and is author of over 150 publications, including *Studien zur verbalen Pluralität, Einführung in die Textlinguistik, Introduction to Text Linguistics,* with R. de Beaugrande, and *Études phonologiques sur le breton sudbigouden,* with J. Hufgrad.

ANDERS ERICSSON is an assistant professor in the Department of Psychology at the University of Colorado at Boulder, where he has worked since 1980. He obtained his Ph.D. from the University of Stockholm in Sweden and in 1977–1980 was a research associate in the Department of Psychology at Carnegie-Mellon University. His primary research interests are models of memory and thought, and in particular how verbal reports can provide data for such models.

ALESSANDRO FERRARA studied philosophy and philosophy of language at the University of Palermo (Italy), discourse studies at the University of Amsterdam, and pragmatics and sociology at the University of California at Berkeley. After a volume on text grammar, he published mainly work on pragmatics and the sociology of language. He edited a special issue of *Versus,* "Speech Act Theory: Ten Years Later" (1980), and has completed a Ph.D. dissertation in social theory at Berkeley. His present interests include the foundations of a critical sociology of language and the contribution of everyday conversation to the reproduction of the social order. He teaches in the Department of Sociology of the University of Rome.

ELISABETH GÜLICH received her Ph.D. (1969) from the University of Köln and her *Habilitation* (1976) from the University of Bielefeld. She presently is professor of French and general linguistics at the University of Bielefeld. She has published in the fields of syntax, text linguistics, discourse analysis, and pragmatics, with special emphasis on French and German. Among the topics she has dealt with are spoken French, narrative analysis, models of discourse analysis, text typology, discourse markers, stereotypes, reported speech, and communication in institutional settings. She is presently working on the interrelation between syntactic and interactive phenomena in conversational French.

MICHAEL HALLIDAY took his B.A. at London University in Chinese language and literature, then studied linguistics in China (Peking and Canton) and at Cambridge, where he received his Ph.D. He has had appointments in several universities, such as Cambridge, Edinburgh, and London, where he was director of the Communication Research Centre and a professor of linguistics. After an appointment at the University of Illinois at Chicago Circle, he became head of the new linguistics department of the University of Sydney. He had held many positions as visiting professor and received a honorary doctorate from the University of Nancy, France. Among his publications are *The Language of the Chinese "Secret History of the Mongols,"* with Angus McIntosh and Peter Strevens; *The Linguistic Sciences and Language Teaching; Intonation and Grammar in British English; A Course in Spoken English: Intonation; Explorations in the Functions of Language; Learning How to Mean: Explorations in the Development of Language; Cohesion in English,* with Ruqaiya Hasan; *System and Function in Language; Language as Social Semiotic; The Social Interpretation of Language and Meaning;* and *Readings in Systemic Linguistics,* edited with J. R. Martin.

NANCY S. JOHNSON received her Ph.D. from the University of California at San Diego and is currently an assistant professor of psychology at Bowdoin College, Brunswick, Maine. Her research focuses on the development of language and cognition, with an emphasis on the development of abilities involved in discourse processing.

WALTER KINTSCH is professor of psychology at the University of Colorado in Boulder, Colorado. He studied at the University of Vienna and the University of Kansas, where he received his Ph.D. in 1960, and taught at several universities in the United States before coming to Colorado. In 1982 he was a Fellow at the Center for Advanced Study in the Behavioral Sciences at Stanford. His research interests center on problems of memory, ranging from traditional list-learning experiments and mathematical models to discourse understanding and memory for discourse. His publications include *The Representation of Meaning in Memory* and, with T. A. van Dijk, *Strategies of Discourse Comprehension.*

JOSEF KOPPERSCHMIDT studied philology, philosophy, and rhetoric at the University of Tübingen and did his doctoral work there with Walter Jens. From 1966 to 1969 he was a member of the Department of Rhetoric of the University of Tübingen and from 1969 to 1973 taught in the field of verbal communication at the University of Stuttgart. Since 1973, he has been professor of language at the Fachhochschule Niederrhein in Krefeld. His main areas of research are historical and modern rhetoric, Christian reviews of rhetoric, and the theory of argumentation. Major publications include *Allgemeine Rhetorik, Das Prinzip vernünftiger Rede,* and *Argumentation.*

JÁNOS SÁNDOR PETÖFI received state diplomas in both mathematics and physics and German language and literature from the University of Debrecen. He received a Ph.D. and *Habilitation* in general linguistics from the University of Umeå. Since 1972 he has been a full professor of general linguistics at the Faculty of Linguistics and Literary Studies of the University of Bielefeld. His main research fields are semiotics, lexical and text semantics, and text theory. He is editor of the series *Research in Text Theory* and coeditor of the series *Papers in Text Linguistics.* He has published numerous journal articles and has authored and edited several books. A selection of recent publications includes *Transformationsgrammatiken und eine ko-textuelle Texttheorie; Grammars and Descriptions,* edited with T. A. van Dijk; *Text vs Sentence* (3 vols., ed.); *Vers une théorie partielle du texte; Probleme der modeltheoretischen Interpretation von Texten,* with H. Rieser; and *Studies in Text Grammar,* edited with H. Rieser.

UTA M. QUASTHOFF received her Ph.D. (1972) and her *Habilitation* (1979) from the Freie Universität Berlin. She presently is a Heisenberg Fellow of the German National Science Foundation, teaching at the University of Bielefeld. She has published books and articles in semantics, psycholinguistics, discourse analysis, and developmental linguistics. Among the topics she has investigated are stereotypes, conversational narratives, formation of language theories, definite article, discourse markers, doctor–patient interaction, and reference forms. She is presently working on the development of narrative skills in children and the possible contributions of text- and psycholinguistics and discourse analysis to cognitive science and artificial intelligence.

KLAUS R. SCHERER has been professor of psychology at the University of Giessen since 1972, after having held assistant professorships at the University of Pennsylvania (1970–1972) and the University of Kiel (1972–1973). He has published monographs on nonverbal communication and on aggression research and has edited several books on nonverbal communication and social-psychological aspects of language and speech, including *Handbook of Methods in Nonverbal Behavior Research,* with P. Ekman. He has contributed to numerous journals and readers in psychology, linguistics, and psychiatry. His major research interests are interpersonal perception and communication, emotion and coping, psycholinguistics, psychoacoustics, and applied social psychology.

HERBERT A. SIMON took degrees in political science at the University of Chicago and has held positions at the University of California at Berkeley, Illinois Institute of Technology, and Carnegie–Mellon University, where he is now Richard King Mellon Professor of Computer Science and Psychology. His research ranges from computer science to psychology, administration and economics, and his interests are especially focused on human problem solving and decision making. His work on computer simulation of these processes has contributed to the development of the field of artificial intelligence. His publications include *Administrative Behavior; Human Problem Solving,* with Allen Newell; *Models of Thought; Models of Discovery; Models of Bounded Rationality;* and *The Sciences of the Artificial.* He has received many awards and honorary positions and in 1978 received the Alfred B. Nobel Memorial Prize in Economics for his pioneering work on decision-making processes within economic organizations.

JOHN McH. SINCLAIR is professor of Modern English language at the University of Birmingham, England. His main field of interest is language education, in particular English. He has held teaching and advisory positions on the English language in over 20 countries and directs several projects in language research. His books include *A Course in Spoken English: Grammar; Towards an Analysis of Discourse,* with Malcolm Coulthard; and *Teacher Talk,* with David Brazil. He has published articles about language teaching, stylistics, project design, computation, lexis, and discourse.

TEUN A. VAN DIJK is professor of discourse studies at the University of Amsterdam, from which he received a doctorate in linguistics. After earlier work on linguistic poetics, text grammar, and discourse pragmatics, he did research (with Walter Kintsch) on the psychology of discourse processing. This work is currently extended toward the field of social cognition, with applications in the analysis of ethnic prejudice in discourse (media, textbooks, conversations) and of news in the press. His books in English include *Some Aspects of Text Grammars; Text and Context; Macrostructures; Studies in the Pragmatics of Discourse; Strategies of Discourse Comprehension,* with Walter Kintsch; *Prejudice in Discourse;* and *News as Discourse* (in preparation). He has edited several books and special journal issues and founded and edited *Poetics* and *Text.*

HARALD G. WALLBOTT has a doctorate in psychology and since 1975 has been lecturer and research associate at the University of Giessen. He has published a monograph on gestures and psychopathology, is coeditor of a reader on nonverbal communication with K. R. Sherer, and has contributed to a variety of books and journals of social psychology, nonverbal communication, and linguistics. His major research interests are nonverbal communication, methods of nonverbal behavior research, emotional expression and coping, and interpersonal perception and attribution.

Index

ARTS, MEDIA & DESIGN LIBRARY